MASS
INFORMATION
UTILITIES
AND
SOCIAL
EXCELLENCE

Harold Sackman has held research positions
with various companies including the RAND
Corporation, where he was a research as-
sociate, and System Development Corporation, where he was senior research leader.
He is a lecturer in the Department of Computer Science at U.C.L.A. and a contributor
to many professional journals. A member
of almost every important computer-related
professional society, he is currently chairman of the Committee on Social Implications of Computers for AFIPS.

Dr. Sackman is author of **MAN-COMPUTER
PROBLEM SOLVING** (AUERBACH Publishers
Inc., 1970), the first book devoted solely to
an evaluation of human effectiveness in
man-computer problem solving. He holds a
B.S. degree in psychology from City College
of New York; M.S. in psychology from Columbia University; and Ph.D. in psychology
from Fordham University.

$15.00

In **MASS INFORMATION UTILITIES AND SOCIAL EXCELLENCE,** a book devoted to mass communications systems and their political and social implications, author Harold Sackman—a Ph.D. psychologist and data processing research consultant—hitches a humanistic vision to his comprehensive discussion of computer technology. While providing the general reader with a provocative and intelligent discussion of the issues affecting mass information utilities, Dr. Sackman does not neglect the technocrats and data processing purists. For them, he describes many of the latest developments in information technology as they are related to mass communication systems, including an important evaluation of possible flaws, shortcomings, and obstacles which the first mass information utility is certain to encounter.

Throughout, however, the author casts a gentle eye toward "mass man" whose interest he champions in a fervent plea for proper use of information utilities. Dr. Sackman subscribes to the philosophy that "in a democracy, information power ultimately resides in the public," and that every individual possesses "the right to free access to open knowledge."

The mass information system under discussion would hook up the general consumer—whether a housewife searching for a cake recipe, a corporate accountant checking a credit reference, or a student acquiring research studies—with a central computer and its assorted information files. By pooling certain independent sources of information to form a national data bank and by transmitting over the CATV coaxial cable, a mass information utility could become reality even before some very tough questions are answered:

- What constitutes "open knowledge"?
- Who will dispense it?
- Which information should be free and which should be allowed to produce revenue?
- Who will regulate the seller and buyer?
- Will privacy, as we know it, become obsolete?

And what are the cultural implications of a mass information utility? It is evident that information technology is capable of reshaping not only the physical world but also the mores and folkways of cultures everywhere; it is also likely that global application of the information utility will launch man into a universal tribal experience. The chance to accomplish so much good—such as educational, social, political, and individual improvements on a worldwide scale—is close at hand. That is why Dr. Sackman urges computer scientists, who ultimately share a common destiny with the rest of humanity, to apply a public-spirited philosophy to their information systems and weld human values into their technological hardware.

MASS INFORMATION UTILITIES AND SOCIAL EXCELLENCE

by HAROLD SACKMAN

AUERBACH ®
Publishers
Princeton   New York
Philadelphia   London

*To the loving memory and inspiration
of my father, Louis Sackman*

Library of Congress Catalog Card Number: LC 72-145585
International Standard Book Number: 0-87769-065-0

First Printing

Printed in the United States of America

CONTENTS

PART I: COMPUTERS AND THE PUBLIC INTEREST

PART II: PROTOTYPE CASE HISTORIES

PART III: EXPERIMENTAL INVESTIGATION OF HUMAN PROBLEMS IN INFORMATION UTILITIES

PART IV: OPTIONS FOR SOCIAL RECONSTRUCTION

LIST OF FIGURES

LIST OF TABLES

PART I

COMPUTERS
AND THE
PUBLIC INTEREST

1

PROLEGOMENA:
THE INFORMATION UTILITY
AND
SOCIAL EFFECTIVENESS

A MAJOR STRUGGLE over what may become the richest prize imaginable is now gathering momentum among large industries in the United States and abroad. The prize is the concentration of information power embodied in mass information utilities. This is a new mode of power, and it has a vast potential for both good and evil which we can only dimly discern at present. The struggle is now being conducted almost exclusively along plutocratic lines by large industries that have a sizable stake in computer communications.

The stake of the general public, which overshadows the economic struggle, is either generally neglected or only grudgingly acknowledged by the major contenders. Worst of all, it isn't even vaguely recognized by the public. The public stake over the long run—as I shall demonstrate throughout this book—is nothing less than the quality of human intelligence and the effectiveness of social endeavor. At a time when the computer hardware industry, software firms, and communications carriers are well represented in the current inquiry of the Federal Communications Commission into the regulation and control of computer utilities, the public interest is the last to be considered, and the computer user is still the forgotten man. Narrow technical considerations, usually directed toward the interests of the few, should not be allowed to dictate broad humanistic consequences, yet this is the pattern that has characterized most technological innovation and resulting social change.

This indictment can and will be contested by those critics who choose to ignore or dismiss the problem. For example, are distributed computer communication services really public computer utilities or are they non-monopolistic, and highly competitive information services? Doesn't the Federal Communications Commission, as a large federal agency with broad powers in the communications field, look after and defend the public interest? Is the potential of the relatively small number of public and semipublic time-shared computing facilities now in operation of such importance to warrant sweeping generalizations concerning the quality of social intelligence and the level of social effectiveness? Has the development of computer science and technology been dominated more by immediate gain for narrow technical and economic considerations and less by humanistic concerns? Hasn't the public been repeatedly exposed to the potential evils of "giant brains," "Big Brother," and computerized "invasion of privacy," enough to be alert to the problems attending the extension of computers to social affairs? Shouldn't we allow the interested industries to work out suitable regulation and control of so-called computer utilities with the federal government in much the same way that regulation for all other utilities has evolved? And if information utilities become public utilities, why should they be any different from electricity, water, gas, transportation, and communications?

It is a leading task of this book to consider the various opposing viewpoints and to present the case for the unique, unprecedented, and vital status of mass information utilities in our future. This chapter is devoted to an introductory formulation of the problem of mass computer utilities and the public interest, their scope, some of the leading controversies they have engendered, and the key facets of this problem—aspects that are explored and analyzed in greater detail in other chapters.

1.1 FORMULATION OF THE PROBLEM

What are mass information utilities? In this book, the term refers to mass communications systems in which the consumer interacts directly with a central computer or a network of computers and associated information files in a manner such that he receives information at his terminal almost immediately after requesting it. The remote terminal is located in the user's natural environment—at his home, office, or school. Information utilities are also referred to in the broader sense of the various elements contributing to the total system, such as input keyboards, television displays, hard-copy printouts, communications lines, central and satellite computers, data stores, and support facilities. Finally, mass information utilities refer to large-scale use of open-end varieties of interactive computer services either by specialized publics (such as students) or the general public.

To many, the central problem of mass information utilities and the public interest is the immediate economic problem. The Federal Communications Commission currently regulates the communications carriers; the Commission does not regulate the computer hardware industry or the software bureaus that sell computer services. The computer hardware and software interests are concerned that the communications carriers enjoy a privileged position to invoke discriminatory price rates that could lead to monopolistic collusion among the carriers or between the carriers and selected computer firms. All vested economic interests are trying to minimize governmental regulation over their sector but are urging increased governmental control over the competing industrial sectors to ward off the threat of real or potentially unfair competition.

There are many economic, legal, and technological questions that have little or no precedent to provide useful guidance. What will the public demand be and how much will it be willing to pay for information services? Where does information processing end and where does communications begin in the sequence of events that starts in the consumer's living room, proceeds to the central computer, and culminates in useful information at the consumer's terminal? What kind of information is in the public domain, freely accessible to all, and what kind is restricted, and how are such restrictions to be legally enforced?

The vast social ramifications of these and related questions immediately reveal the shallow thinking behind any simplistic economic interpretation of the problem of the information utility and the public interest. Even so, the fact of the matter is that virtually no one, outside of vested economic interests, seems to be doing anything about the problem. The FCC has long been overworked and understaffed with the stupendous task of keeping up with telephone, radio, and television communications; that agency is hardly prepared to play an aggressive leadership role in the potentially larger field of computer communications. And so, by default, the problem continues to be treated as an economic contest between industrial giants (such as American Telephone and Telegraph and International Business Machines) and many would-be industrial giants.

We must look to a broader context for an effective formulation of the problem of the information utility and the public interest. Many think in terms of the generalized impact of computers on society. This may be an opprobrious banner loaded with Big Brother control, invasion of privacy, technological unemployment, and the rich getting richer while the poor get poorer, or alternatively a utopian state signifying the extinction of the Protestant Ethic—the end of work, unlimited leisure, and the rise of self-serviced robots. These are largely emotional responses that conveniently bypass the problem of the information utility and the public interest by leapfrogging over the present into an indefinitely projected future.

The problem of the information utility is kaleidoscopically complex. It raises serious questions that challenge our traditional concepts of public utilities—just what kind of a service is an information service? It raises large economic issues—there is virtually no limit to real and conceivable information services that can now or eventually be supported by mass computer utilities. Who will reap the material benefits of such services? The problem exerts a profound influence on the direction and development of computer science and technology. Will new computer science be oriented toward humanized man-computer communication, or will it continue to be directed toward hardware and software, but not toward people?

Scan the national scene and consider how mass information utilities could change democratic procedures and forms. The democracy that is exercised through information utilities can remain narrowly confined within restricted political confines, or can witness a dramatic extension into other spheres of society. Turn to the individual citizens, to Everyman—consider what information utilities can do to effective human intelligence and the structure of human values. The problem of mass information utilities emerges as a profound cultural problem with potentially revolutionary consequences for radical transformation of the individual and society.

Granted that the information utility is a widespread cultural problem, the question still remains—how is this problem to be tackled? We could settle for futuristic and utopian philosophizing; we could take sides on hard-headed economic factors; or we could deliberately grab hold of the information utility and mold it in the image of desirable social objectives, in the image of a beneficent public interest. From the viewpoint of deliberate social planning, mass information utilities represent an unprecedented problem that requires concerted solution at all social levels to extend the potentially revolutionary benefits of computerized information services to the entire public.

1.2 LEADING CONTROVERSIES

At this early point, controversies over mass information utilities can only be raised in gross outline. Definitions of terms, a systems framework, and the application of scientific method to tractable controversies are the task of other chapters. Table 1.1 lists 17 such controversies under five general headings which are briefly discussed in turn.

Few people are aware of the stormy history of public utilities both in this country and abroad. Although a massive legal tradition has been accumulated over many test cases for many types of utilities, there is still great diversity of opinion over the nature and extent of the public interest, the construction of cost standards and "fair" rates, regulatory techniques for assessing the quality of service, and the familiar tug-of-war between business and government over the extent of obligatory regulation. Mass information utilities may share some precedent from regulation over communications utilities, but many believe that such precedent is inadequate and unfair (e.g., a rate structure based on elapsed time of use of a communication line as opposed to rate of information transmitted). Entirely new problems will have to be faced for which there is no precedent, such as pooling the resources of many distributed computing centers and data stores and making their facilities equally available to each user. We can expect legal and economic conflicts between public and private information services sharing the same communication lines and perhaps the same computers.

Turning to the second grouping of controversies listed as Bounds of Information in Table 1.1, we encounter problems that will continually vex computer utilities over the indefinite future. A vast legal structure exists to protect and perpetuate restricted access to certain kinds of information. Military security is the most obvious area, proprietary industrial and institutional information is less well defined but is often fiercely safeguarded and locally enforced, and individual "privacy" is the most ambiguous and contentious area of all. With the advent of national data banks and cheaper electronic storage, kaleidoscopic combinations and permutations of public and restricted information defies comprehension. Many argue that present safeguards are more of a hindrance than a help in setting up adequate measures for the needed levels of protection, and that entirely new approaches will have to be worked out. Few are prepared to recognize, let alone pay the costs for, the kinds of information security they have in mind. There are those who take the position that restrictions placed on information should be minimum and that the maximum amount of information should be made available to the general public, not merely as a convenience, but as a basic right. Others argue that a man's personal information is his own castle, the last fortress for the privacy and sanctity of the individual against the ubiquitous inroads of a corporate, computerized society.

The next category in Table 1.1 is concerned with the distinction be-

Table 1.1. KEY CONTROVERSIES ON COMPUTER UTILITIES

Public Utilities

1. Is the concept of the public utility, as currently defined by legal and operational standards, applicable to mass distribution of information services?
2. What constitutes the public interest in other utilities and what is the public interest for information utilities?
3. Assuming that public information services are public utilities, should their growth and development be guided by laissez-faire competition or by government control?

Bounds on Information

4. What are the guidelines for distinguishing between public and private information, between free and restricted information in the computer utility?
5. Is the invasion of privacy with the information utility a real or an imagined threat to society?
6. Is information in the public domain a shared good that should ultimately be made freely available to all, or should information services always be paid by individuals in accordance with metered use?

Mass Information Utilities vs. Other Computerized Services

7. What is the dividing line between mass information utilities and other forms of computer services?
8. Given a particular information problem, which mode of data processing is more cost-effective—time-sharing or batch processing? Local or remote computer services? The large computer or the minicomputer?

Test and Evaluation of Information Utilities

9. Should advanced experimental prototypes be set up as test beds for mass information utilities prior to their installation for the general public?
10. Who tests and evaluates information utilities and what procedures are followed in defining standards, conducting tests, analyzing results and making them known?
11. Should experimental investigation of man-computer communication be subsidized or institutionalized to enhance human effectiveness with mass information utilities?
12. What is the status of real-time systems embedded in or linked with information utilities with respect to shared computer communications facilities and competing priorities?

Philosophical Problems

13. Will mass information utilities revolutionize the democratic process?
14. Will the information utility accelerate the extension of experimental method to social affairs to meet the increasing tempo of contemporary change?
15. Will the information utility radically transform individual intelligence and social effectiveness?

16. What new types of individuals will be shaped by mass information utilities and what value systems will they have?
17. What kind of philosophy is needed to meet the challenge of mass information utilities?

tween mass information utilities and other types of computerized services. Time-shared centers may be dedicated facilities, owned and operated independently from information utilities. Most computing today is still done by batch methods, one job at a time on a waiting line, and certain types of data processing tasks will continue to be more economical under batch procedures. Small computers are getting cheaper all the time and the new generation of minicomputers may capture a mass market. Organizations and individuals will seek computer services where they can get the most for their money, and that "most" may turn out to be a mixture of public and private information services. The private sector of this market will defend its interests against "unfair" encroachment from public information utilities.

Perhaps least understood of all is the next category on test and evaluation of information utilities. Will consumers get the service they expect and pay for? Will such service be prompt and accurate? What kinds of technical quality control and what sort of legal safeguards are required to protect users from their own errors and from central system errors? How will the problem of individual differences in user skill and experience be handled to train new users, and, at the same time, expedite the tasks of experienced users? Will self-tutoring at user terminals be required to introduce new information services, and what standards should be set up for certifying such computer-assisted instruction? More fundamentally, have we learned enough in the field of man-computer communication to warrant mass distribution of information services to the general public? If a growing scientific lag exists between our knowledge of man-computer communication and its application to the public, should we subsidize such study and set up experimental prototypes to test and certify proposed information utilities before they are allowed to be used by the public? And who evaluates the evaluators?

The last category in Table 1.1 covers broad social implications of the information utility under the generic title of philosophical problems. Many conceivable political, economic, individual, and other general cultural problems could have been placed in this area. Democracy, the extension of experimental method, human intelligence, and personal values were singled out as deserving special consideration. But why these particular categories? Because, if the information utility does eventually lead to an increased level of effective citizen intelligence, and if democracy does spread to all walks of life, then society as we know it would be radically transformed and individuals would have value structures and a mode of life virtually inconceivable to us today. The intent, plain and simple, is not to point to a "surprise-free" future, to a mere extrapolation of present trends, but to raise the possibility of a qualitative leap, a cultural mutation toward a new type of man and a new society.

The questions in Table 1.1 have obviously not led to answers but only to more questions. They underscore the complex interdisciplinary nature of mass information utilities and the diverse problems that follow in their wake at legal, economic, technological, scientific, philosophical, and generalized cultural levels. The rest of this book is an attempt to partition these multifarious and controversial problems into more manageable pieces.

1.3 KEY FACETS OF THE PROBLEM

The plan of this book unfolds in four stages: Part I, a description of the origins, status, and direction of mass information utilities and the public interest; Part II, case histories of early computer utilities from organizational and individual points of view; Part III, an exposition of the preferred method to be used in dealing with this problem—experimental method in a systems science context; and Part IV, a review of the leading social implications of mass information utilities. In essence, the four main parts of this book progress from a formulation and description of the problem to potential approaches and options for social solutions. The aim of this sequence is to encourage new thinking on mass information utilities where it counts most—in terms of social effectiveness. People, all the people, are the overriding concern, not the narrow technological-economic considerations that have dominated the development and extension of computer utilities since their introduction in the early 1960's.

Chapter 2 sets the broad social tone of the book by casting information utilities into the perspective of generalized public utilities and the changing, conflicting interpretations of the public interest. Thus, Chapter 2 highlights the unique properties of information as a new object of the public interest in contrast to historical precedent for such diverse public utilities as electrical power, gas, water, transportation, and communications.

Chapter 3 describes the trend toward computer-serviced societies, and presents the case for the manifest destiny of advanced industrialized nations to evolve toward computer-serviced cultures. As social computerization takes a giant leap forward with the extension of mass information utilities, the relation between information power and the public interest assumes major proportions for every citizen. This chapter surveys the broad evolution of the computer applications and distinguishes public information utilities from other competing and noncompeting computer services.

Chapter 4 focuses on the remarkable recent development of time-shared computing systems, the technological basis for information utilities. The origin and nature of such systems, their growth and diversification, their recent marriage to the communications industry, and the subsequent emergence of information utilities are critically reviewed from the viewpoint of the user and the public interest. The paucity of verified knowledge on time-sharing users is highlighted and described as a growing humanistic lag in the application of information utilites.

Chapter 5, the first chapter in Part II, enables the reader to take a close look at a concrete time-sharing system—a pioneering, general purpose facility that has been in existence for almost a decade. The design, development, and changing services of this system are reviewed, the lessons in working with this system are critically evaluated, and tentative extrapolations are made from this system to leading problems that are likely to arise in the operation of public information utilities.

In Chapter 6, the reader has an opportunity to see interactive computer services from the viewpoint of the individual user. A case-history of self-tutoring serves as the vehicle for describing some of the nuts and bolts of time-sharing terminal usage and individual reactions to success and frustration. The account is cast in a research framework to illustrate some of the techniques and problems encountered in research toward more effective man-computer communication.

Part III starts off with an introduction to scientific work in man-computer communication. The value, advantages, limitations, and prospects of an applied, scientific approach to man-computer communication are described in Chapter 7. Special emphasis is given to the method and findings of user studies in time-shared systems. The experimental lag in user studies and its intimate relation to the growing humanistic lag for information utilities provides the setting for Part III.

The multibillion dollar confrontation between time-sharing and batch processing systems is also stressed in Chapter 7. The competition between these online and offline modes of information services has generated great controversy in the computer world and has provoked strong partisan positions. After many years of armchair polemics, the first controlled experimental studies comparing these two types of systems have only recently appeared. These studies are summarized and critically evaluated in this chapter, with significant implications for man-machine effectiveness in mass information utilities.

In Chapter 8 a conceptual framework is constructed for user studies in man-computer communication to anticipate and meet user problems in mass information utilities. The proposed framework is offered as an initial step to reduce the experimental lag and to instill a stronger sense of humanism in man-computer communication. An evolutionary systems approach is adopted and a broad classification of user problems is offered to anticipate and meet the requirements of swift technological changes in mass information utilities and the changing needs of the public interest.

Chapter 8 treats the difficult problem of objective testing and evaluation of information utilities. Inquiry into system effectiveness has different meanings at different stages of system evolution, such as early design, initial installation, ongoing operations, and phaseover to a successor system. Flaws, obstacles, and shortcomings in established testing techniques for computer-aided systems are pointed out, and the case is presented for corrective grass-roots feedback from individual users in mass information utilities.

Part IV, which concludes the book, starts off with a review of social options in Chapter 9. The results of a recent conference on "The Information Utility and Social Choice" are reviewed for national and international implications, for regulatory and political options. The possibilities of self-supporting economics for mass information utilities are raised. Further possibilities of dedicating mass information utilities to democratic process and lifelong education are suggested for long-range social planning. Counterarguments and special problems sprout from all sides in this difficult area.

For example, the technological potential of public computer utilities makes it obvious that democratic inquiry, voting, and expression of opinion will be possible at electronic speed and could lead to real-time command and control of social change. New democratic forms will appear and be challenged and modified in the light of changing social experience. The concept of democracy as cooperative real-time social experimentation in the public interest could emerge from mass information utilities.

Chapter 10 reviews traditional notions and attitudes toward intelligence and contrasts these against the prospects for qualitative modification of individual and group intelligence with the advent of mass information utilities. The prospects for a radical transformation of society when cultural knowledge is electromagnetically pooled and made available to all is put forth as perhaps the greatest of human adventures—a plunge into the uncharted domain of concentrated global intelligence and universal creativity.

In Chapter 10, the related problems of individualism and privacy are treated in the context of mass information utilities. Traditional forms of individualism, such as laissez-faire, rugged, and corporate individualism are reviewed, and a pattern is sketched for new and more freely diversified forms of individual personality and group syntality. The institutionalization of evolutionary experimental techniques is offered as the preferred method of vigilance to secure the changing needs of individual privacy in public information utilities.

In contrast to time-encrusted precedent, the case is presented for legal systems that are more responsive to rapid changes in the human condition, for real-time legal adaptation in the era of the information utility. The implications of experimental legal systems are outlined in relation to new forms of individual responsibility for democratic conduct and guidance of social affairs.

In Chapter 11, the focus is on the potential impact of mass information utilities on social planning—the possibilities of online social planning. For the democratic order, citizens will probably insist upon increasng responsibility for charting and directing their future. This chapter reviews planning theory and techniques and finds them wanting. Suggestions are offered toward more scientific approaches to planning. Possibilities for participatory online planning are described, with special emphasis on adversary systems leading toward working consensus among dispersed participants for advanced mass information utilities.

The last chapter is a philosophical synthesis of the material in the book. The author's philosophical debt to American Pragmatism is acknowledged, and new departures from these taproots are pointed out in response to possible futures for public information utilities. The successful cultural internalization of experimental method and democratic process is a leading value in the development of this philosophy. The challenge of worldwide information utilities is set forth, and the problem of an acceptable international philosophy to link national facilities into global information networks is formulated. A humanistic philosophy is proposed for a fundamental human right: the right of free access of all individuals to open knowledge, including cross-cultural knowledge; the right, perhaps even the sacred right, of each generation to freely enjoy the common cultural legacy of all who precede them. "If a man is fortunate he will, before he dies, gather up as much as he can of his civilized heritage and transmit it to his children. And to his final breath he will be grateful for this inexhaustible legacy, knowing that it is our nourishing mother and our lasting life" (Will and Ariel Durant, 1968).

2

PUBLIC UTILITIES,

INFORMATION SERVICES,

AND

THE PUBLIC INTEREST

COMPUTERIZED INFORMATION SERVICES cover a vast spectrum of applications which eventually may become coextensive with social endeavor. Some believe that such information services are fundamentally a private affair, a transaction between buyer and seller, as with any other commercial commodity. Others hold that the growing union of public communication utilities with computerized information services will lead to distributed computer utilities on a national scale. Still others are convinced that, ultimately, with national networks, man-to-man communication will be inseparably linked with man-computer communications in principle and in practice.

A serious inquiry into the potential status of information services as a public utility needs to take into account the broad concept of the public utility, the history of different types of public utilities, the similarities and differences between information services and those services dispensed by public utilities, and leading problems in defining and developing the public interest in the domain of information services. It is rarely appreciated that the historical context for the computer utility includes not only the technical development of computer science and technology, but also the evolution of public utilities and the impact that each may have exerted on the other. The history of public utilities, which is considerably longer and more complex than the history of computers, is briefly treated in this chapter to provide a preparatory social framework for the public interest in computer communications. The history of computers and associated public information services is covered in subsequent chapters.

2.1 COMPARATIVE HISTORY OF PUBLIC UTILITIES

The terms public utility and its correlative, public interest, have always been highly controversial. These concepts have been defined and operationally used in many different ways for different services, by different social groups, at different times in different countries. Advocates take opposite sides on numerous issues: more vs. fewer industries under the rubric of public utility; more vs. less governmental regulation of existing utilities; private vs. cooperative vs. quasi-governmental vs. direct government ownership of utilities; federal vs. state vs. municipal regulation; more vs. less direct and indirect competition with established utility services; incentive vs. fixed regulation of profits of utility companies; endless disputations and changes in utility pricing, cost, and accounting systems; continual litigation between utilities, consumers, regulatory agencies and other governmental agencies; chronic inability to objectively measure quality and social effectiveness of services; and many others. Certain concepts and practices have become fairly well established only to be rudely jarred by the intrusion of new technology—most recently, in the field of computers and communications. The history of public utilities shows no grand evolutionary plan, in which the advent of new technologies unfolds logical extensions of old and new utilities for an enlightened public interest. Rather, we see a patchwork pattern of a series of conflicts between parties with vested interests marked by erratic victories and defeats for various camps—all after climactic struggles rather than rational planning. Will this sorry picture be the blueprint for computer utilities?

Before proceeding with an interpretative history of public utilities and the current situation for computer communications, the literature base for this account should be briefly mentioned. Hunt (1965) has systematically listed the recent and historical literature in leading public utilities. The Americana and Britannica encyclopedias provide useful contrasting overviews of public utility developments. Troxel (1947) and Shepard and Gies (1966) offer critical appraisals on earlier and current economics of public utilities. In the field of government regulation, Minow (1964) and Metcalf and Reinemer (1967) offer valuable inside views on communications and electric power utilities, respectively. The report of the Senate Subcommittee on Intergovernmental Operations (1967) puts forth an empirical survey of the status of state utility commissions, their strengths and weaknesses, as determined by an extensive questionnaire. Finally, developments in the current FCC probe into the computer communications industry have been followed by consulting various trade magazines and professional publications (e.g., the joint computer conferences of the American Federation of Information Processing Societies). The literature on public utilities is large and highly controversial—the subsequent account has been selected, condensed, and organized for its potential bearing on information utilities.

The concept of public utilities is as old as urban civilization itself. Four major classes of public utilities may be distinguished: transportation, water and sanitation, communications, and power. The remarkable irrigation works in ancient Egypt and Mesopotamia, and the renowned highways and aquaducts of the Roman Empire are examples of the antiquity of public utilities. The main difference between modern and ancient utilities stems from the appearance of two new social forces—western democracy and the industrial revolution—both spurred by advances in science and technology. These two forces are focal because technology supplied the means and democracy justified the ends for subsequent development of public utilities as we know them today and as we would like to shape them for the future. The accelerating advance of science meant that technical means must continually be reconstructed in the light of new technology, that public utilities constitute responsively changing commodities and services. And, in a democratic context, the social configuration of public utilities had to be consistent with a democratic interpretation of the public interest.

The leading philosophical concept in western democracies in the early growth of public utilities was "laissez-faire," which was developed in theory —exemplified by Adam Smith in his *Wealth of Nations,* published in 1776 —and put into practice in England at the time of the Industrial Revolution. The general aim of this philosophy was to encourage individual opportunity and initiative, curtail the scope of government restrictions, and, in this way, allow the openly competitive market to maintain higher standards at minimal costs.

By the nineteenth century, the rapidly spreading factory system of the Industrial Revolution increased the need for public utilities in fast-growing urban centers in the western world. Extensive public utilities appeared for transportation, communication, water supply, sanitation, and power and light. At first the various utilities were privately owned. The great need for adequate service, the widespread abuses encouraged by unrestricted monopolies of private owners, and the cutthroat competition to gain exclusive monopolies led, about 1840, to a concerted revolt against complete adherence to laissez-faire doctrine in England and America. From this revolt the modern public utility emerged—conceived as a public service managed by private enterprise, under explicit public regulation by duly constituted governmental authority. Thus, the older, privately owned utilities became publicly regulated activities operating under a franchise, as an authorized monopoly for the given service.

The problem of a lag in public regulation of private enterprise has always existed, up to this day. New technology exploited by private enterprise has easily raced ahead of public regulation. The invention of the steam engine and the construction of canals and turnpikes in the eighteenth century, the commercialization of the steamboat and the steam railroad in the early nineteenth century, the introduction of the telegraph and the telephone and the beginnings of electric power in the late nineteenth century, and the spread of radiotelephony, electronics, television, and computer communications in the twentieth century, have all been marked by a fundamental pattern—rapid commercial exploitation of the new technology, followed by a collision course with the public. The advantage of the few had been promoted at the expense of the many, and after a pitched battle between private and public interests, lagging regulation of the new utilities was eventually instituted to deal with excesses of monopolistic practice.

Initial regulation occurred in the courts. But litigation alone could not handle the numerous and difficult cases that arose in different parts of the country. The need for continual surveillance, response, and adjustment to changing conditions by a regulatory body was recognized; the duty was discharged by municipal and state regulatory commissions, with the right of litigation remaining for controversial areas. This, in turn, was supplanted by federal regulatory bodies for jurisdiction involving interstate public utilities. In addition to the Interstate Commerce Commission previously mentioned, there appeared the Federal Power Commission (1920), the Federal Communications Commission (1934), the United States Maritime Commission (1936), and the Civil Aeronautics Authority (1938), more recently reorganized in 1958 as the Federal Aviation Authority.

The regulatory lag in state and federal public utility commissions has been well documented. The recent report of the Senate Subcommittee on Intergovernmental Operations (1967), based on a survey of state commissions, was instigated, in part, by widespread evidence of the inadequacies of state commissions to perform their tasks. The findings generally confirmed the original expectations. As reported by the majority of state commissions, staffs were inadequate, salaries were too low, electronic data processing was not applied to most commission records, and, in most cases, no research staff or facilities were available.

Table 2.1.   GROWTH OF STATE COMMISSIONS FOR PUBLIC UTILITIES
(from the Senate Subcommittee on Intergovernmental Relations, 1967.)

Period	No. of State Commissions
Before 1870	1
1870–1879	5
1880–1889	5
1890–1899	5
1900–1909	6
1910–1919	23
1920–1929	1
1930–1939	4
1940–1949	3
1950 to present	2
Total	55

Senator Metcalf and his coauthor Reinemer have critically analyzed the regulation of electric power. Their conclusion is the title of their book —*Overcharge*. They argue, in essence, that continual improvements in power technology, the steady growth of the general population, and the captive mass market, have led to enormous increases in technical efficiency that have not been passed along to the public in an equitable manner. They charge that such gains have been absorbed as protected profits by investor-owned utilities. The electric utilities have defended their position by pointing to continually improving service, in war and peace, and to the maintenance of relatively constant price rates at a time when most commodities have risen steadily in cost under inflationary trends. Metcalf and Reinemer contend that state and federal regulatory agencies cannot keep up the necessary surveillance and detailed accounting to exert effective control on behalf of the public with the meager resources that are available to them. Computerization of regulatory techniques is one of the key recommendations made by the authors for more effective regulation. They portray regulatory commissions as understaffed, underbudgeted, hands-tied, and a very poor second in aggressive dissemination of their facts and findings to the public. Here is a situation that contrasts starkly with the multimillion dollar blandishments that fill the advertising campaigns of investor-owned utilities.

Newton Minow paints a similar picture of the status of the Federal Communications Commission from his vantage point as chairman of that commission. He points out that the agency staff is chronically overworked, with an inadequate budget, that it can only handle selected top priority controversies, that the notion of the "public interest" is highly ambiguous, that the leading communications utilities exert virtually overwhelming power at many social levels to defend their interests, and that the swiftly growing responsibilities of the FCC are incommensurate with its capabilities and its available resources. As indicated later in this chapter, these problems of the FCC have since been exacerbated by increased regulatory responsibilities for communications satellites, community antenna television, and computer communications.

The history of judicial disputes winds through the tortuous road that public utilities have had to traverse to arrive at their present uneasy status. Most of the litigation has been an endless wrangle over the establishment of fair rates of return and, more fundamentally, standardized accounting procedures to authenticate such rates. Field accounting procedures are often held to be essential for valid regulation, but they are beyond the budget of most regulatory agencies.

With the early utilities, malpractice was common on both sides. The government saw to it that investments in public utilities were a highly risky affair: the franchise was issued for limited time periods only; tenure was not secure; other forms of competition were allowed, and no arrangements were made for public purchase of utility properties at the end of the franchise. Under the continual threat of major loss of their investment, owners were easily induced to make a quick killing to recoup their capital out of earnings—rate discrimination, watered stock, pyramiding of holding companies, and other unsavory practices were cultivated and pursued for profit. These abuses led to current state and federal regulatory agencies with the judiciary functioning as an appeal agency.

The "public interest" doctrine was first promulgated in the United States by Chief Justice Morrison Waite in *Munn* v. *Illinois* (94 U.S. 113 [1877]). In upholding the validity of the Illinois statute, Waite quoted English precedent some 200 years earlier stating that business "affected with a public interest" ceased to be a private concern. Waite further asserted: "When, therefore, one devotes his property to a use in which the public has an interest, he, in effect, grants to the public an interest in that use, and must submit to be controlled by the public for the common good, to the extent of the interest that he has thus created."

In a later case, *Wolff Packing Company* v. *Kansas* (262 U.S. 522

[1923]), Chief Justice William Howard Taft added a further qualification to the "public interest" doctrine by stating that "The circumstances which clothe a particular kind of business with a public interest, in the sense of *Munn* v. *Illinois* and other cases, must be such as to create a peculiarly close relation between the public and those engaged in it, and raise implications of an affirmative obligation on their part to be reasonable in dealing with the public." This qualification adds a more explicit note of obligatory service for public utilities, as compared to the more neutral statement of public regulation in *Munn* v. *Illinois*.

The legal relation between public utilities and the public interest has been elaborated into a system of rights and responsibilities known as the law of public service undertakings. Nine features of this doctrine summarize its current status:

1. Public utilities are required to provide adequate service to all who apply.
2. Service is provided without discrimination within a prescribed geographical area.
3. The service should be continuous and available when needed by users.
4. The service should be safe and convenient.
5. As legal monopolies, public utilities must set their rates in accordance with regulatory procedures.
6. Service should be provided up to the limits of the effective capacity of the object utility with due regard to authorized rates of return.
7. Service is dispensed within the framework of reasonable rules and regulations for consumers.
8. Service can be discontinued only under prescribed conditions after giving due notice to customers.
9. The utility cannot go out of business unless it follows procedures specified by the regulatory agency.

Despite the continuing litigation and legislation on public utilities, the scope of such services and the precise nature or test of the public interest remains ambiguous. Attempts were made, particularly during the depression of the 1930's, to subject diverse businesses to regulatory control —theater ticket agencies, grocery stores, private employment agencies, ice production plants, and gasoline stations. These efforts to extend the domain of public utilities were declared unconstitutional by the United States Supreme Court and were rejected by various State courts.

In 1932, in the midst of legal contests to extend the jurisdiction of public utilities, Justice Brandeis peered far ahead into the future with a remarkable plea to fuse legal progress with scientific method. In *New State Ice Company* v. *Liebmann* (285 U.S. 262), he recommended the concept of the experimental public utility in a minority opinion. Troxel cites his astute recommendations (pp. 20-21). "To stay experimentation in things social and economic," he warns his fellow justices as he argues for a flexible concept of public utility regulation, "is a grave responsibility." He is willing to use a single state, such as Oklahoma, as a laboratory to ". . . try novel social and economic experiments without risk to the rest of the country. . . . We must forever be on our guard, lest we erect our prejudices into legal principles. If we would guide by the light of reason, we must let our minds be bold."

Brandeis's bold thoughts—the marriage of law and science in the concept of an experimental public utility, and the radical notion of an entire state serving as a laboratory—were too far ahead of his own time and for that matter, well ahead of our time. We still do not have large-scale experimental prototypes to systematically test changes in existing public utilities, or to develop initial procedures for new public utilities. One of the key positions adopted in this book is that the time for experimental public utilities is long overdue and is urgently needed if we are to gain the technique and the knowledge to design and implement socially effective information utilities.

This quick historical survey has shown that public utilities were an integral part of ancient civilizations, that they grew with the rise of cities, that their most rapid growth has been associated with the industrial revolution and the concomitant advance of science and technology. We have also seen that in the United States the original pattern of the wholly public-owned or wholly private-owned utility has been superseded, in large part, by the current notion of the investor-owned public utility regulated by an authorized government agency. This transition was triggered and sustained by an era of suspicion in which abuses of monopolistic power were curbed by the regulators, an era lasting through the depression of the 1930's. What are the characteristics of public utility regulations in the post World War II period?

The regulators (more than 12,000 for all utilities) and the regulated (a significant segment of the national population) no longer view each other as mortal enemies. One of the hard-won lessons of the Great Depression is that a free flow of capital investment is required for public utilities to keep up with technological advance and improved services. Profits should not merely be minimal, they should be sufficient to encourage research and development to enhance progress. Current rates of return vary from 5 percent to 9 percent with an average near 6 percent (contingent upon the accounting method employed).

Public utilities provide returns comprising some 5 percent of the gross national product with an annual outlay of some 10 billion dollars in new equipment and services. There is increasing interest in incentive regulation and in flexible pricing, increasing emphasis on continual feedback from changing performance to reduce regulatory lag, on regulation to promote progress, on frequent, informal exchanges between commissions and utilities rather than lengthy public hearings, on experimental pricing schemes, and, in public pronouncements, on social effectiveness.

Research on the cost-benefit effects of regulation has been minimal. There was a marked decline of interest in public utilities as an object of research in the 1950's and this has only begun to change relatively recently in response to rapid technological progress, particularly in communications. Although the regulatory concept is widely accepted, there is no evidence as to how effective regulation has been.

For example, Stigler and Friedland (1966) have shown that regulated electrical power rates are not statistically different from unregulated rates, and further, that length of regulatory activity is also unrelated to rates. These results were demonstrated in regression analyses comparing regulated against unregulated states over an extensive time period. Their analyses revealed that other factors, such as population trends, cost of fuel, per capita income, and competing sources of energy were apparently more influential in affecting price levels. Although these findings are controversial, they are not countermanded by other research. An objective assessment of the effectiveness of regulation remains a moot point as long as polemics and armchair discussion prevail over scientific method.

Until quite recently, no radical changes in the structure and functions of public utility regulation have been proposed either inside or outside government. Most suggestions have been confined to evolutionary extensions that could be handled by the current configuration of public utilities, such as the previously mentioned incentive regulation, experimental pricing, continual surveillance, and after-dinner lip service to innovations for social effectiveness. The outlook on both sides of the fence is apparently for more of the same. But the unrelenting pressures of new science and technology are bringing together strange bedfellows whose proximity was undreamed of when the foundations of public utilities were constructed. The next logical development is the computer utility.

2.2   THE DILEMMA OF COMPUTER UTILITIES

The transition of computer communications into the world of public utilities has not benefitted from historical precedent. Computer utilities are following the chaotic birth pangs of other public utilities—regulatory agencies are following events rather than leading them, patching up conflicting interests after the fact, rather than anticipating problems and planning orderly growth. Although it should be the other way around, this young giant is dragging the FCC, which held off as long as it could, into the era of public computer utilities.

Predisposing and precipitating factors do exist that lead toward public computer utilities, and they are primarily economic. Among these predisposing factors consider the following: General Electric and Informatics, among others, have predicted that most computing will be done online (rather than with batch techniques) during the 1970's; Western Union has predicted that more than half of all computers will be integrated into the nation's communications networks; and the Bell System believes that at least half of all information transmitted over telephone lines will eventually be computer data.

The precipitating factors that culminated in the FCC inquiry into computer communications have been documented by Irwin (1967). These factors include four events: 1) the Bell Telephone System and Bunker-Ramo disagreed over the regulatory status of the Bunker-Ramo stock quotation service; 2) an IBM letter to the FCC attempted to clarify the operational distinction between data processing and the transmission of data over communication lines; 3) the diversification and extension of Western Union services in computer communications raised questions as to where regulation begins and where it ends; and 4) two international communications carriers, a subsidiary of International Telephone and Telegraph and a subsidiary of the Radio Corporation of America, who are in direct competition with each other, clashed over the issue of obligatory announcements of tariffs for similar computer communications services. The details of these cases need not concern us. The main point should be clear—controversial issues arose on all sides from computer hardware and software firms and from regulated communication carriers on the nature and extent of regulated public utilities in computer communications. The din became too great for the FCC to ignore any longer.

On November 25, 1966 the Federal Communications Commission issued Docket 6979 announcing its intention to conduct an inquiry into the "interdependence of computer and communication services and facilities." The Federal Communications Commission has since collected opinions from the computer industry, related professional associations, regulated communication carriers, and other agencies in government such as the Justice Department. The responses are currently being studied in preparation for a position to be taken by the FCC specifying its role in the runaway computer communications industry.

The basic questions are the hardest to answer. First, is the computer utility a true public utility falling under the jurisdiction of the law of public service undertakings? If so, what is the public interest—not merely the interest of the computer industry, nor that of the communications carriers, nor that of governmental agencies, but the interest of all the people? Granted that major alternative public interests are known, what are or should be the leading social objectives of pending regulation? Within the framework of such social objectives, what kinds of regulation should be imposed on utilities? Can the FCC provide such regulation in a competent manner commensurate with the specified public interest? More generally, is the current framework for the principles and practice of public utilities adequate to serve new forms of the public interest or are other alternatives, perhaps radically new approaches, required to serve the long-range public need for information services? Brief answers to these questions, based on initial responses to the FCC inquiry, are presented from four points of view—computer hardware and software firms, regulated communication carriers, the Justice Department, and the "public."

The responses tend to favor vested economic interests. In regard to the first question, whether the computer utility is a true utility, no one argues the point concerning regulation of message transmission from one location to another over public communication facilities. This portion of computer communications has been and is expected to continue as a public utility, with the exception of currently authorized provisions for private or leased lines. The controversy arises over data processing services and the attachment of terminals and computers ("foreign devices") to communication lines.

The public communication carriers argue that communications is the dominating factor and that all utilities for computer communications should be regulated. The computer industry insists (as in the aforementioned IBM letter to the FCC) that data processing is logically distinct and different from the transmission of data from one location to another. They point out that data processing is a highly competitive industry that would only be inhibited by premature regulation. They further insist that the restrictions on the attachment of devices to communication lines should be liberalized to encourage the growth and proliferation of information services.

The Justice Department supports the computing industry on all three counts in its recommendations to the FCC (Hirsch, 1968). Data processing is a young and extremely competitive industry that should be allowed to follow its own course of technological progress with greater cooperation from the common carriers and minimum governmental regulation. The Antitrust Division in the Department of Justice further recommends that if the common carriers desire to compete for the data processing market, they should be allowed to do so only through affiliated corporations which maintain separate accounts and separate facilities, and only after communication tariff restrictions have been removed which may give them an unfair competitive advantage in remote data processing.

The second question is the most vital of all, the most difficult and the least understood—what is the public interest? The common carriers, the computing industry, and Justice Department are all agreed on one point, minimum cost to users consistent with quality service. They disagree over the means to achieve this goal. But this response is narrowly economic. Psychological, political, educational, and other broad sociological considerations bearing on social effectiveness are embarrassingly conspicuous by their absence, although there is universal breast-beating over the ill-defined issue of privacy. A binary logic appears to exist when it comes to the public interest; the economic issue is apparently the real thing, and privacy somehow takes care of all the other social issues. But "privacy" is merely a sop to the public interest, a smoke screen that hides a Pandora's box of insistent human needs that will burst out sooner or later, making today's narrow economic viewpoint a sorry spectacle for future historians.

Suppose now that we adopt a humanistic view of the public interest, and suppose that we link the equitable extension of computer utilities over the long term with the destiny of democracy. Suppose further, that the glaring inequalities of our society—as reflected, for example, in the Black Revolution—are fundamentally due to the inequitable distribution of available social information and public intelligence among different strata of our society. It might then be argued that dedication of computer utilities to free and open access to knowledge in the public domain could lead to a wiser, more enlightened citizenry, and to a higher standard of living for all through the release of latent effective intelligence. It might further be argued that such dedication of information services could bring about greater individual fulfillment in a more humane democracy that prizes human intelligence above material gain.

If these kinds of propositions, or similar propositions, represent the public interest, then the entire configuration of legislative, executive, and judicial action requires radical change, and the public utility ceases to be a privileged *economic* utility, and becomes a true public utility, or, better yet, a *social* utility.

The public objectives of the information utility and the kinds of regulation required challenge the adequacy of the current concept of the public utility when they are approached from the proposed social viewpoint, as compared to the traditional concept. The traditional economic interpretation would urge free competition and unfettered technological advance in data processing and in communications as the fundamental objectives of the public interest. What is good for industry is good for Everyman. It follows from this line of reasoning that the least regulation is the best regulation. Since the FCC is scarcely capable of providing more than minimum regulation, and this only when prodded into it, the current concept of the public utility is optimal for the public interest. Here is where the ostensibly large differences between the common carriers and the computing industry turn out to be small differences. From the viewpoint of industry, we live in the best of all possible worlds in our current public utility situation for computer communications; the only problem for the individual vested economic interest is to maneuver into an optimally favorable position in the regulatory picture for future growth and profits.

If social objectives are selected as the goal of information utilities, such as the objective to increase the level of effective intelligence of all the citizenry, then the nature of regulation has to be redefined and reconstructed. Since we have no precedent in public utilities for broad-band social effectiveness, it would become necessary to attack the problem in an experimental manner to gain the knowledge and experience to approach this social objective. Here is where the suggestion of Justice Brandeis comes to our aid—the concept of an experimental public utility under legal sanction. Under this notion, the concept of the public utility is changed from regulation of established services to evaluation of alternative experimental design, test, and development of public services in the public interest.

The proposed change goes deep because it is a fundamental change in philosophy, not only in the philosophy of the objectives of regulation, but also in the philosophy of the method of public regulation. The methodological change is a switch from ex post facto regulation to experimental regulation in which problems are anticipated well in advance and are resolved by institutionalized and open experimentation on leading alternative solutions. The methodological switch is from the spectator role of passive laissez-faire to directed experimentalism. The change in philosophical objectives is the main battleground—the change from narrow economic interests to broader social values where these values themselves are continually subject to social experiment under evolving democratic forms.

Note that no brief is made for particular social experiments nor for a particular type of regulatory agency to oversee such experiments. This has to be worked out through available democratic process, through executive agencies, legislation, and the courts. It is apparent that the FCC as presently constituted is inadequate to discharge experimental studies into the social benefits of information services. It is also apparent that the current concept of the public utility, from the viewpoint of both the law and the various regulatory commissions, is not commensurate with cooperative experimental development of public services. For that matter, there is no tradition in industry for cooperative participation in alternative experimental prototypes for public services.

2.3 ALTERNATIVE SOLUTIONS

The final solution for the dilemma of computer utilities is that there is no such thing as a fixed, final solution. Recognizing this is the first step toward workable methods that could lead to *evolving* solutions for changing computer utilities. Regrettable though it may be, there is no place for absolutistic logic in the kaleidoscopic world of scientific and technological advance. What is needed is a transformation of the current institution of the public utility from a relatively fixed and static legal entity, to a dynamically responsive social force that can anticipate, lead, and adapt to scientific, technological, and social change. A reconstruction of public utilities is needed to allow them to perform as evolutionary pace-setters and as social catalysts rather than as technological laggards.

These transformations are not entirely without precedent in the history of public utilities. It was mentioned earlier that regulatory commissions superseded the courts in response to the need for continual social surveillance over public utilities; that lengthy and cumbersome formal legal hearings are giving way to informal dialogue and faster agreements resulting in quicker response time to new conditions; that experimental and flexible pricing techniques are increasingly being tried out. If the original judicial procedures have given way to improved techniques of continual surveillance in the evolution of the public utility, why not move from continual surveillance to early warning and advanced planning?

The prospects in the computer communications area are for an increasing tempo of social and technological change with mounting pressure from a great diversity of unsolved problems. The technical problems are more easily discernible and they seem to be converging from all sides. For example, it is often claimed that telephone service is more reliable than data-processing services. The telephone companies use the argument of long tenure in public service to support their position toward a fully regulated computer communications utility. In any case, public involvement in mass computer utilities will require a higher level of error-free service than has been characteristic of computer facilities in the past. Emergency backup and duplex service facilities as used in real-time military command and control systems may have to be implemented more widely for computer utilities.

A leading cost problem lies in the inefficient use of voice-grade telephone circuits for the transmission of digital data. For example, a computer utility user often has to pay the full charge for the exclusive use of a telephone line when he is transmitting data over the line only 1 percent of the elapsed time that he is using it. Gold and Selwyn (1968) have found this 1 percent estimate based on empirical studies of remote users in time-sharing systems. They argue that the use of message concentrators, or other forms of time-sharing of communication circuits, could cut such communications costs down to almost 1 percent of current line costs for a large number of users. Pugh (1968) has gone through a similar analysis and has arrived at similar results. He estimates that the use of message concentrators will reduce the monthly communications costs for a 64 remote terminal system from $28,500 to $6000. These analysts argue that communications costs for remote data processing are quite high, often well in excess of data-processing costs, and that public information services can be strangled in the crib if relief from runaway communications costs is not forthcoming from technological advances in the collection, storage, forwarding, and transmission of computer data. The common carriers are well aware of this situation and have plans under way to provide such relief, but to date it has been too little and too late, as far as the data-processing industry is concerned.

As mentioned in the historical review of public utilities, these utilities have never been absolute monopolies free from significant competition. All have faced waxing and waning competition from other industries in varying forms; economic research has indicated that competitive industries may have exerted a greater impact in regulating the cost of utilities than have the regulatory commissions. Increasing competition is the prospect for the communications carriers from such sources as communications satellites and community antenna television cables (CATV).

Communication satellites have proved less costly in initial operations than competitive submarine cable for international communications (Early, 1968). Many believe that the comsats are also less expensive for the national market. Irwin (1968) has described the stormy and uneasy compromise that has been reached between the regulated communications carriers and the Communications Satellite Corporation. In essence, the FCC ruled that COMSAT be franchised as a wholesaler to the overseas carriers to remove COMSAT as a competitive threat to the common carriers, and it further ruled that a compromise price be placed into effect between higher cable costs and lower COMSAT costs. As a result of this ruling, some critics have argued that the international carriers are enjoying nothing less than a direct subsidy.

CATV incorporates a coaxial cable capable of carrying signals from 12 to 30 video channels directly into the consumer's home. Recent developments show considerable increase in CATV channel capacity. The competitive threat posed by CATV applies not only to telephone carriers but also to television broadcasting. The high data-rate transmission of CATV makes possible the consideration of a host of broad-band information services that are not possible with voice-grade lines; for example, the transmission of visual displays and the possibility of interactive graphics on terminals with cathode ray tubes. CATV is in competition with the much-heralded Picturephone or visual telephone service. Many claims and counterclaims have been made regarding the relative cost-effectiveness of these various approaches to computer communications, and even while the controversy rages, new discoveries are being unveiled which alter the ground rules.

On the data-processing side, current time-sharing services are not only under intense competition with each other, but are also under increasing competition from the growth of small and inexpensive computers. Many look ahead to specialized local computer services in large buildings and to the possibility of cheap computers for family use. If computer power continues to rise as it has in the past, and if computer costs continue to decline, mass distribution and popular use of portable computers is not far off.

In surveying the technology of the computer utility, Baran (1967) drives home the central point that the burgeoning and bewildering profusion of information services requires a fundamental reorientation of regulatory theory and practice. He concludes (p. 27):

> We are moving headlong into an era where information processing will be available the same way one buys his electricity. ˙But the attributes that distinguish heterogeneous information from the homogeneous products distributed by the earlier utilities are so different that a fresh regulatory approach is needed for technological progress, safety, and the public interest.

It should be apparent that technical problems are mounting rapidly on both sides of the house, for computers and communications, and it should also be apparent that a high degree of technical expertise is required for intelligent selection of alternatives and judicious regulation of new information service. But keeping up with technical changes is only one side of the coin. Major social innovations will spring from the computer utility.

To take a current example, consider on-the-spot credit transactions. Many banks have online computer systems that keep a running account of deposits and withdrawals at the time they occur. With computer utilities in the home, buying and selling can be transacted from home terminals. Checks and cash can be largely eliminated for many services through central real-time accounting. But just stop to consider the legal safeguards necessary to protect the buyer and the seller, the banks, and the computer utilities, and ponder the new forms of record-keeping required to verify transactions and settle potential legal disputes. Here the advantage of experimental prototypes over inadequately tested social services makes itself felt.

Continuing education, or lifelong education, has already become a commonplace notion in our world of accelerating change. It is not difficult to see that much of the educational burden will fall on the shoulders of the computer utility through the use of computer-assisted instruction and the easy availability of the libraries of the world through home terminals. Testing for the acquisition of skills and knowledge can also be done via the home console. This testing can be a great technical improvement over our current and controversial paper-and-pencil techniques, because the performance of individuals can be automatically and comprehensively scored while they learn, as a by-product of the learning process itself. It takes no great stretch of the imagination to see that the accreditation of degrees, the certification of skills, the recording of educational performance, and the establishment of new standards are fraught with technical and social problems for individuals and institutions that have hardly been enumerated, let alone explored. Shall we wait until these problems surround us or shall we conduct needed experiments on alternative solutions in the public forum?

In a comprehensive review of commercial information-processing networks conducted for the National Commission on Technology, Automation, and Economic Progress in 1966, Flood (1966) recommended the institution of federally supported experimental prototypes of computer utilities. He urges (p. I-252) that:

> The Federal Government bring into being, as rapidly as technology permits, at least one limited but major information-processing network that is planned, developed, and operated to:
> (a) Accelerate technological advance and gain experience in appraising economic and social benefits and costs of information networks; and,
> (b) Help meet a recognized unmet national need, such as for better information transfer through a national network of libraries and specialized information centers.

The third and last example is the exercise of political power via the computer utility. Consider the information utility as a real-time polling booth, with the expression of public opinion and formal voting occurring far more frequently than lack of expression or public indifference. Here, plain and simple, is the technological potential for participant or direct democracy. Such polling could be supported by instantaneous access to Congressional. records and public documents for more intensive study of the issues and more informed voting. Major transformations of democratic procedures like this surely require comprehensive and long-range exploration of feasible alternatives in competitive experimental prototypes. Should we continue to procrastinate? Should we, in a computer-age rerun of Voltaire's *Candide,* proclaim loudly to the whole world that we live in the best of all possible democracies? Is it not time to begin finding out just how the computer utility can enhance the democratic process?

3

THE EMERGENCE OF
COMPUTER-SERVICED SOCIETIES

THE FIRST TWO CHAPTERS have concentrated on computer utilities viewed as mass information services for the general public; they have not been concerned with the total spectrum of computer services in society. The extension of computerized information services to the public, while perhaps the most dramatic development on the contemporary computer scene, needs to be cast in the broader perspective of overall computer evolution and related technological trends.

The integration of computer technology into the contemporary social pattern is depicted in this chapter, and we see the emergence of computer-serviced societies. But in the process we also see recurring confrontations between human and machine needs, between social as opposed to technical information services, and between the immediate economic interests of the few and the long-range welfare of all.

3.1 HISTORICAL ROOTS

Computers sprang from the need to count and measure, from mathematics. This union of computers and mathematics has extended down through the ages and its accounts for the impersonal spirit of the computer world today. The first analog and digital aids, used centuries ago, included observation of the position of the sun in the sky and the relative length of shadows, counting with fingers and pebbles, and the use of the abacus in the antiquity of China and Egypt. Mechanical aids for measurement have always been incorporated as indifferent technical means to achieve social ends, whether such aids were for humane or inhumane purposes.

The supreme feat of early civilization, according to Mumford (1967) was the invention of the megamachine (p. 188):

> This was an invisible structure composed of living, but rigid, human parts, each assigned to his special office, role, and task, to make possible the immense work-output and grand designs of this great collective organization . . . a technological exploit which served as a model for all later forms of mechanical organization.

The prevailing social ethic of antiquity was authoritarianism, sanctioned by timeless precedent over the span of human recall, the domination of the many by the few, the rule of the family, the tribe, and society by various hierarchies of privileged human beings over lesser human beings, subhumans, and slaves. The highly organized systems approach that went into the Egyptian pyramids—religious dedication, planning, specification, design, production, tests for operational readiness, the pomp and ritual of installation, and virtually trouble-free maintenance—was an engineering marvel of system development for all ages. These massive edifices still remain as mute but imperishable testimony to the power of the megamachine.

The technology of the ancients could not make radically new breakthroughs without the driving force of science, innovative experimental science, which came into its own with the Western Renaissance. Francis Bacon (1561-1626) foresaw the vast potential of science and urged its cooperative development for social aims—to deaf ears. Leonardo da Vinci (1452-1519), combined inspired craftsmanship with wide-ranging theory, and was one of the most versatile practitioners of experimental method in his or any age. He was poignantly aware of the awesome potential of science for good or evil and dreaded the social abuse of science. While inventing compulsively, he kept some of his most remarkable inventions, such as the submarine, away from princes who would use such weapons to further rather than limit man's inhumanity to man.

It was the monumental work in dynamics of Galileo (1564-1642) that established physics on a scientific basis through the successful marriage of empirical testing with a hypothetico-deductive framework formulated in mathematical terms. This work, for which he was relentlessly persecuted throughout his lifetime, paved the way for Newton's great synthesis. The extension of experimental method to a growing array of scientific disciplines, such as physics, chemistry, and astronomy, triggered technological changes that fueled the industrial revolution.

As science and technology rapidly became the driving engine of social change, a compromise was worked out with the dominant authoritarian ethic. In essence, the price that the fragile fraternity of early scientists had to pay for survival was that science belongs to the material world and not to the human and spiritual world. This fitted neatly into the scholastic version of Aristotelian hylomorphism, as it was reinforced by the mind-and-matter dualism of the day, articulated and rationalized by Cartesian philosophy. It was consonant also with the materialistic orientation of the physical sciences, which were the first to emerge.

This severance of the human condition from science was a priceless sacrifice for scientific survival, more precious than the small coterie of pliant Renaissance scientists could ever conceive. It was a misanthropic compromise that still haunts us. In this apocalyptic confrontation, Isaac was indeed sacrificed by Abraham to placate the jealousy of the reigning gods; and the scientific ancestors of the fathers of science continue to sacrifice their true seed down to this day, in the name of pure and holy science divorced from the human condition.

Concurrent with the scientific awakening that began with the Renaissance, the progress of analog and digital devices was steady, but not spectacular. Timekeepers, compasses, and slide rules were various forms of analog developments. Pascal (1623-1662) invented the first digital adder, and Leibnitz (1646-1717) improved on Pascal's device with a digital machine that could also subtract, multiply, divide, and extract roots. The motivation behind these devices, as with the abacus of antiquity, was to relieve the tedium of repetitive computation.

Babbage (1792-1872), an English mathematician who was appalled at the vast expenditure of human time and effort that went into the preparation of mathematical tables, is the outstanding figure in the development of computers prior to the twentieth century. In a remarkable anticipation of things to come, his "analytical engine," conceived in 1834, was a complex digital computer which operated on punched (Jacquard) card inputs, with arithmetic and storage units, and with automatic printout of results up to 20-place accuracy. Although Babbage's machine was never completed, he anticipated the key concepts of computer programing by sequential control as practiced today on high-speed electronic computers.

Desk calculators were designed, produced, and marketed in the nineteenth century and they went through successive improvements. Electrical sensing techniques were linked to punched cards and were first applied in mass use during the 1890 census on a data base representing some 62 million Americans. Statistical chores have since been among the most cost-effective applications of automatic computation. But the appearance of the general-purpose high-speed computer had to await the electronic technology of the twentieth century.

Thus, at the end of the nineteenth century, many analog and digital devices were being applied to a steadily increasing variety of measurement tasks. The motivation behind these developments continued to be greater ease, speed, and efficiency in counting, measuring, and calculation. The concept of computers as a medium for communication and control of human information and social action was only dimly perceived. But the template for future growth was well outlined. Computers were developed and nurtured by mathematicians and scientists who projected their value systems into their work.

In the meantime, nationalistic democracy had appeared and had scored major triumphs in the western world. In his *Democracy in America,* Alexis de Tocqueville (1805-1859) saw the end of the aristocratic principle and the irrepressible wave of democratic equality in the future. The democratic concept spread to science and helped stimulate the development of the biological and social sciences amid great expectations. On the philosophical scene, the grip of supernatural beliefs was weakened and a bewildering brood of new philosophies were beginning to hatch, based on material, national, class, and individualistic considerations.

By the end of the nineteenth century, the industrial revolution had taken firm hold of the western world. The military-industrial complex, forged in European power politics at that time, rapidly became a highly cultivated form of national policy. The megamachine was more efficiently organized along the new nationalistic lines as machine parts replaced human parts and as machine energy replaced human energy. Scientists, living in a well-tempered moral void, were the unwitting artisans of the new megamachines which could lead to the next step—the displacement of human intelligence by machine intelligence.

Karl Marx (1818-1883) saw what many scientists did not want to recognize—that scientific and technological change is fundamentally human and social change. Marx wanted to harness scientific method to social change. But when he embraced Hegel's dialectic as the paradigm for social science, he parted company with empirical, experimental science. The extension of experimental method to social affairs had to await the twentieth century, where it is still a hope rather than a realization.

The development of computers ran along lines essentially independent of the development of experimental method. Social scientists might have had use for them, for they entertained visions of illuminating social phenomena with the penetrating light of experimental method, but the large number of relevant variables, the open-ended nature of the embedding environment, and the shifting stream of experience in the transactions between living subjects and their environment conspired to frustrate the most ambitious attempts to define social science in a rigorous way. Thwarted in their abortive attempts to experiment with the real social world, social scientists substituted scientific aberrations. Some abandoned experimental method and speculated dogmatically from fixed ideas and fragmentary empirical evidence. Dialectical method, disembodied from the acid test of controlled empirical verification, became a widely practiced perversion of science. Others, following the irresistible example of the physical sciences, went to the opposite extreme and experimented more and more rigorously on less and less, leading to a culmination of their efforts in highly esoteric, antiseptic human behavior in artificial laboratory settings. Experimental method? Yes! Real world human behavior? No! Both approaches missed the mark.

John Dewey (1858-1952), perhaps the most eminent philosopher America has produced, believed that the most powerful of all techniques developed by man to understand and deal with himself and his environment is the method of science—the experimental method. Although he acknowledged that experimental method was not sufficiently developed in his time to deal effectively with human affairs, he never lost faith in his belief that it would ultimately triumph over competing methods and would eventually become the dominant approach in understanding and regulating social affairs. He constructed and reconstructed his philosophy of experimentalism on this basic belief over a span of half a century, building a remarkable conceptual edifice that was incompletely understood in his time and remains as a major challenge for our time.

The extension of experimental method to social affairs required two missing ingredients that emerged shortly after Dewey's death. The first is the systems approach to applied science, and the second is the high-speed electronic computer. The systems approach provides the equivalent of the operationally defined and physically specified man-machine environment for social reconstruction and control. The computer permits unprecedented communication and control of internal and external system information to achieve system goals. The physical embodiment of these two ingredients is the real-time information system in which events are shaped and controlled at the time they occur. The real-time information system is the technological prelude to real-world experimentation—to the extension of experimental method to social affairs. Herein lies the message of our historical account of the marriage of experimental method with computers in the social domain.

3.2 THE IMPACT OF WORLD WAR II

Babbage had the concept of the modern digital computer, but he did not have the technology to carry it through. The technology required evolution from mechanical to electromechanical to electronic devices, which occurred in the first half of the twentieth century. Computers progressed from special-purpose analog machines to more general-purpose digital devices as electronics improved. World War II was the catalytic agent that precipitated the electronic computer out of the technological suspension where its elements were floating freely.

Vannevar Bush developed a series of electromechanical analog computers from 1925 through World War II. In 1937 H.H. Aiken of Harvard University, in collaboration with International Business Machines, formulated concepts derived from punched-card equipment and digital switching networks to build a fully automatic calculator. The Automatic Sequence Controlled Calculator (the Mark I) was an electromechanical machine which was operational in 1943; it was used throughout the remainder of World War II up to 1948 to produce mathematical tables. This computer was functionally equivalent to Babbage's analytical engine.

It should be emphasized that special-purpose analog and digital computers were built during World War II in many countries, particularly in Britain and Germany, as well as in the United States. For example, many servicemen worked with analog fire-control computers on ships and on land-based antiaircraft batteries coupled to radar equipment. With the notable exception of predecessor digital telephone devices, computers were transformed from a scientific oddity before the war to an indispensable and widely-used tool during the conflict. In the fiery crucible of World War II computerized Furies issued forth for the first time.

The challenge of a much faster and more powerful electronic calculator with no moving parts spurred many to experiment with new techniques. The first large electronic computer was the ENIAC (Electronic Numerical Integrator and Calculator) designed by Eckert and Mauchly in the United States. The ENIAC, completed in 1946, had some 18,000 vacuum tubes which operated with sufficient reliability and adequate synchronization to produce useful results. Computer instructions were laboriously set up on a plugboard, as with punched-card machines, for each new job.

The first stored-program electronic computer, one which held both program instructions and data in computer memory, was initially developed in England in 1948 by Williams and Kilburn at the University of Manchester. In the United States, conceptualization of the stored-program computer was associated with Goldstine and von Neumann (1946). The stored-program feature, eliminating the need to wire programs for each new computer run, made more versatile programing possible over a new vista of applications.

3.3 SAGE

While World War II ushered computers onto the world scene, the atom bomb thrust computer development into its most spectacular and greatest achievement—the birth and rise of real-time computing systems. These are computer-serviced systems which are designed to shape and control events in a given environment according to specified system objectives while such events are taking place. The real-time system is the technological embodiment of direct man-machine control over the environment.

When the Soviet Union exploded its first atomic device in 1949, the race was on for the development of a highly improved North American air defense system that could meet and neutralize the nuclear threat. The concept of SAGE (Semi-Automatic Ground Environment) emerged as a real-time, computer-aided air defense network to detect, identify, and destroy manned enemy bombers over North American airspace. A schematic of the key elements of SAGE is shown in Figure 3.1.

Billions of dollars and top-priority scientific and technological manpower were poured into SAGE. Computer developers, of both hardware and software, were pushed to the limits of their ingenuity and inventiveness to ward off the threat of nuclear holocaust. The initial SAGE Air Defense Direction Center was installed in the New York area in 1958, nine years after the detonation of the first Soviet atom bomb. The last SAGE installation was in Ottawa, Canada in 1963. By that time the intercontinental ballistic missile armed with thermonuclear warheads was amply stockpiled in the Soviet arsenal, and SAGE was virtually obsolete at the time it became fully operational. Although SAGE could counter the manned bomber threat, and although this deterrent was and is adequate justification for its continued existence, it was powerless against the ICBM.

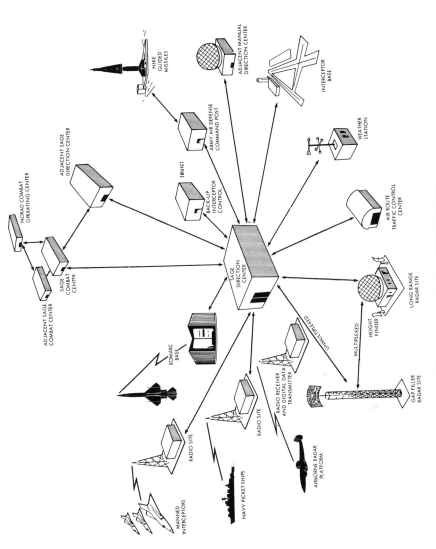

Figure 3.1. SAGE SCHEMATIC

SAGE has provided a remarkable and often unrecognized pioneering legacy in the principles and practice of real-time computing systems.

- It has demonstrated the power of real-time systems to monitor and control complex and very fast-moving events on a continental basis, and by extension, on a worldwide basis.
- SAGE is the first computerized subculture in the world, when this term is interpreted to mean distributed and interconnected computing centers, with a common mission and standardized ground rules, managed by a well-defined social hierarchy with a formal division of labor, and possessing the means to sense, communicate, and control changes in a highly complex environment.
- SAGE is the first of the large-scale systems to extend the principles and practice of online and real-time man-computer communication over a significant segment of social affairs as opposed to specialized scientific and technical uses.
- SAGE was the first system to introduce simultaneous mass training of thousands of personnel in highly realistic, computer-simulated situations, as, for example, in continental system training exercises involving up to 10,000 personnel in the air defense network.
- SAGE, for better or worse, established many of the mores and folkways of large-scale computer system development, a mixed legacy of technique and values, that is deeply and often unconsciously embedded in real-time system development today.

There are other firsts for SAGE which are developed in detail by the author in another book (1967). Suffice it to say that the large-scale real-time computing system, the technological embodiment of the application of social knowledge to action, emerged first in SAGE; it was marked by many brilliant successes, and, as we shall later see, by many false starts and obstructive failures.

SAGE was soon followed by the Mercury-Gemini-Apollo manned spaceflight project which represents, among other things, a remarkable example of rapid experimental evolution in real-time command and control systems. Military real-time information systems were developed concurrently in each of the services and appeared in other countries. Commercial real-time systems subsequently appeared in air reservation services, banking, stock market activities, and in other areas in the early 1960's. The emerging computer utility was a direct offshoot of online man-computer communication as practiced in pioneering real-time systems.

3.4   RECENT DEVELOPMENTS

The growth of computer installations has been phenomenal. Between 1945 and 1950, some 20 electronic digital computers were produced, primarily as experimental prototypes. By 1955, the figure jumped up to 1000 as commercial production was initiated, and as the computer industry was rapidly skyrocketing up to the billion-dollar mark. In 1960 some 6000 computers were available; and in 1965 the figure was 30,000. In 1970, the computer industry topped $10 billion annually for goods and services.[1] In 1975, well over 100,000 computers will be available, and the total market is expected to exceed $20 billion. The rest of the world possesses some 20,000 computers, as the United States leads the way in quantity and quality of computer power. In the 1980's, many predict that the computer industry will be the largest industry in the United States and the world.

The phenomenal growth of the computer industry has been spurred by great advances in computer speed and capacity, with a steady decline of costs. Computation speeds have progressed from approximately one second in World War II, to millionths of a second (megaseconds) in the 1950's, to billionths of a second (nanoseconds) in the 1960's, to trillionths of a second (picoseconds) in the 1970's. High-speed, central computer storage has progressed from 150 words or machine registers at the end of World War II (ENIAC), to tens of thousands in the 1950's (for example, the SAGE computer had 69,000 words of high-speed storage), to hundreds of thousands in the 1960's, to millions of words and perhaps some dramatic breakthroughs in the 1970's. Medium- and low-speed storage can be organized in files containing billions of words, as in the computer-accessible files for Social Security administration in the United States. These rapid strides in storage, accessing, retrieving, and modifying computerized information have made vast concentrations of organized information possible, and they have raised perplexing questions such as the purpose and desirability of national data banks.

Computer size has gone down from the multiroom dimensions of the ENIAC and SAGE vacuum-tube computers (the SAGE computer has 58,000 tubes) to compact, transistorized computers, to the miniaturized, brain-sized computers that are being developed as integrated electronic circuits achieve high operating reliability in low-cost mass production. Advances in materials and ceramic research, in magnetic and photochemical phenomena, and in polymer research on the one side, and in information theory, linguistics, and bionics on the other side, may lead to radical transformations in computer organization and design which many believe to be long overdue. With all due respect to Babbage, we should soon be able to improve substantially on his nineteenth-century concept of computer design.

Analyses of computer costs vs. computer power, such as those conducted by Knight (1968), reveal that not only are computer costs plummeting downward, but that the rate of decline in cost was more rapid in the 1960's than it was in the 1950's. In contrast, personnel costs to service computers, to design, write, checkout, and maintain programs, have steadily gone up. As a result, the dominant consideration in computer system cost-effectiveness is no longer hardware; software eventually counts most. The cost-effectiveness equation is dominated by the human equation, and the trend is expected to continue, perhaps for the indefinite future.

The effectiveness of software is essentially the effectiveness of man-computer communication, not just for programmers, but for all computer users. And here comes the rub: man-computer communication, as we shall see throughout this book, is the least understood and, in many respects, the most sorely neglected area in the computer world.

Computer languages have progressed from binary computer language, to symbolic machine language (e.g., add, multiply, and shift commands), to higher-order languages which are beginning to approach natural English (e.g., LOGIN, DEBUG, DISPLAY, and HELP). There are well over 1000 computer lanuages in use, and the more popular languages have developed distinct dialects (such as PL/1, FORTRAN, ALGOL, COBOL, and JOVIAL). The problem of language standardization has been particularly vexing since no single language stands head and shoulders above the others. In view of the vast quantitative and qualitative differences between users and among their problems, perhaps none ever will. Little objective evaluation of computer language effectiveness has been made, as is the case in so many other areas of man-computer communication. Experimental method and findings for comparative computer language effectiveness is, as we shall see, virtually nonexistent; current knowledge is very primitive.

The statistics for computer communications are even more mind-boggling than those for computers as computer utilities generate increasing thrust. Cordtz (1970) cites the following figures which give us some estimates of the early development of mass information utilities (p. 69): "At present, 10,000 general-purpose computers are connected to an estimated 190,000 terminals by means of leased lines or over the common-carrier network. But by 1974 more than half of the 98,000 computers then in operation are expected to be linked by transmission facilities to 1,200,000 terminals." The National Bureau of Standards is studying standardization of user procedures to avoid confusion and waste in the binary babble that is sure to come. Eventually computer terminals are expected to become coextensive with television and telephone service.

The main outlines of the computer breakthrough in this century are easy to see. In just one generation since the end of World War II, electronic computers have increased from 1 to 100,000; speed and storage capacity of computers have improved as much as a billion-fold; computerized subcultures have appeared in the form of distributed real-time systems dealing with complex environments; the computer business has advanced from an insignificant dwarf to an economic giant at a magnitude approaching tens of billions of dollars—even while computer costs move steadily downward; and the marriage of computers and communications in the form of mass information utilities promises to be the most spectacular growth of all.

3.5 THE COMPUTER JUGGERNAUT

When painted in these broad strokes, the computer picture is progress incarnate. But this picture, which is typically projected by computer enthusiasts, shows only the rose-colored half of the computer world—the machine side. This stereotype misrepresents, and misrepresents grossly, because it does not give any idea of the most vital side of the computer world, the human side. Like Oscar Wilde's portrait of Dorian Gray, the older it gets, the more monstrous it becomes. Only occasional hints have been given of these problems, but they will become increasingly apparent as we delve into the human use of computers. The subsequent chapter, which deals with the history of man-computer communication, the development of time-shared systems, and the spectrum of computer services, will help redress the lopsided perspective created by the shiny machine view of the computer world.

Concurrent and intertwined with this humanistic lag is the experimental lag in the human use of computers. The real-time computing system has not been recognized as a massive breakthrough in experimental method that makes it possible, for the first time, to study real-world social behavior in a well-defined, operationally specified system setting. The real-time system makes it possible to extend experimental method to social affairs in a manner almost inconceivable just one short generation ago. This awesome breakthrough has almost been strangled because of the deep-rooted neglect of human behavior in computer-aided systems. The humanistic-experimental lag is a fundamental stumbling block in the path of what Norbert Wiener (1954) described as the human use of human beings in a cybernetic world.

Although social revolution is sweeping through the United States and most of the world, and although it is stirring up a storm in many of our key institutions and in the physical, biological, and social sciences, it has hardly touched the citadel that is at the focal point of much contemporary social change—computer science and technology. Physical scientists, appalled at the power of their nuclear genie, have recognized the grave urgency of their social responsibilities and have made notable efforts toward arms control and international peace. Biological scientists, recognizing the social implications of deciphering the genetic code, have vigorously pursued international and national population control, global ecology and environmental control, and the prospects of biological engineering. More recently, social scientists have responded to the Black Revolution, the Student Revolution, and the abortive War on Poverty; they are becoming increasingly involved in the hard-core problems of urban society. Computer scientists, who are spawning perhaps the greatest revolution of them all, the information revolution—the reconstruction of human knowledge—have yet to respond in a socially significant manner to the imminent extension of mass information services for the general public.

The human use of computers remains an enigma. The computer juggernaut vaunts a pious amorality when it should be motivated by a democratic ethic. The computer juggernaut follows the dictates of crude technology rather than scientific method; it does not pursue systematic and open testing and evaluation of user information services. In a misanthropic vision of things to come, the computer juggernaut prizes machine intelligence above human intelligence. Will computer professionals be the first or the last to respond to the human ramifications of the social upheaval of their own making?

4

THE HUMANISTIC CRISIS
IN
COMPUTER-SERVICED SOCIETIES

COMPUTERS in all their early forms were for counting, calculating, and measuring. Now, in the short space of only one generation, we have discovered that computers may be applied to nonnumerical information, to practically any form of information and human knowledge. This breakthrough into a new human era is a projection of Pythagoras's cryptic dictum that all things are numbers—an eerie projection of things to come. But habits die hard; and we continue to think about mathematics and machines rather than about people and human problems, while the growing imbalance assumes grotesque forms.

4.1 MISANTHROPIC MAN-COMPUTER COMMUNICATION

The current condition of man-computer communication stems from the needs and the background of the professional mix that originally developed and used computers. These initial users were the mathematicians, engineers, and "hard" scientists who pioneered electronic digital computers. The World War II applications were laborious and time-consuming mathematical problems, as in the computation of tables of ballistic trajectories or in analytic problems concerning atomic reactions. John von Neumann, for example, was initially attracted to computers by the same motivation that inspired Babbage—to relieve the tedium and extend the range of large-scale computation.

Industrial applications were esoteric and highly specialized, as in digital switching devices for telephone communications, or in process control industries such as petrochemicals and food processing. For the initial digital devices, man-computer communication consisted of formulating problems, designing computerized solutions, wiring computers, feeding them with punched-card inputs, and printing outputs such as mathematical tables.

These early man-computer communications were closely tied to the constraints of machine circuitry, and were tightly bound to logical and mathematical symbology. The early computer languages were conceived and used by small coteries of specialists, and they were not designed or intended for widespread use. These scientists and engineers were professionally trained in the use of the symbolic tools of their trade, and the small number of computers and computer users made for intimate, person-to-person working relations. (Recall that only about 20 electronic computers were produced between 1945 and 1950.) The ensuing history of man-computer communications has largely been an attempt to escape from the restricted confines of esoteric symbology into the freedom of natural language.

With the advent of the stored-program computer in the late 1940's, which made possible the incorporation of instruction sets in computer circuitry and internal storage of operating programs, and the subsequent appearance of commercial electronic computers on the open market in the early 1950's, and with the concomitant rise of large-scale real-time systems for military command and control, a grave shortage of trained personnel was generated. People who could design and produce computer programs were desperately needed, but they were nowhere available. These rapid extensions of computers into military and commercial areas could not be serviced by the small numbers of pioneering engineers, scientists, and mathematicians who understood and knew how to communicate with computers, and who had other jobs to perform.

An unplanned division of labor took place, and "professional" programers appeared, in rapidly growing numbers, to translate the verbal specifications of system analysts into workable computer language. The trend in man-computer communication was from part-time professional specialists, such as scientists and mathematicians, to full-time specialists who were exclusively concerned with the bread-and-butter activities of coding, debugging, and maintaining programs. The initial tradition of specialization in esoteric computer language was maintained for the second formative decade through the 1950's. The infancy of man-computer communication was nurtured on the cold and bitter milk of machine code and symbolic notation.

In response to growing pressures to provide more programers for more computing applications—military command and control requirements, for example, exerted pressure on the order of hundreds of millions of dollars per year—programer indoctrination was kept at the bare essentials of mastering machine code and learning debugging fundamentals. Attempts to professionalize programing proved abortive as the demand continued to race ahead of the supply, with people virtually picked off the streets and trained on the spot for quickie applications. Knowledge of users and computer program applications was acquired in a haphazard manner, on-the-job, largely in the production of workable machine code. Programers selected and trained under these conditions had little exposure to human-engineered programs or user-oriented program products. Most programers tended to view accommodations for users as costly and disconcerting in the larger and more urgent business of building programs and making them work within limited resources. By common agreement, virtually no one particularly cared how well computer programs worked, just so they would cycle under minimal operational loads without "hanging up." In the hurly-burly world of chronically lagging schedules in crash projects, a scientific tradition of systematic man-machine performance testing never had a chance to see the light of day.

As mentioned in the previous chapter, the first radical breakthrough in interactive man-computer communications occurred in real-time military command and control systems. In SAGE, military operators had consoles equipped with alphanumeric keyboards and verbally tagged dials and switches for composing and sending messages to the central computer. The consoles had two types of cathode ray tube displays, and they were equipped with a light gun in conjunction with pushbutton switches to select and control displayed information. The console and its controls had to be designed to permit the average enlisted man to master its operation.

Even though a wealth of empirical data was being ground out every day in SAGE man-computer operations, very little of it was experimentally systematized and organized for the computer community. This unfortunate situation developed for a variety of reasons, including military security, proprietary industrial information, and an effective lack of appropriately trained human engineers and social scientists who had access to SAGE man-computer communications.

Consider, now, the user tradition developed by the hypertrophied computer community in response to these historical trends. For three critical, formative decades—the 1940's, the 1950's, and most of the 1960's—the social scientists, the human engineers, and the human factors specialists, the people professionally trained to work with human subjects under experimental conditions, were only indirectly concerned with man-computer communications, largely at the knobs, buttons, and dials level rather than at the interactive problem-solving level of the user. In all fairness, there were exceptions to this rule, but they were too few and too sporadic to make a significant and lasting impact on the mainstream of user development. Since there was, in effect, an applied scientific vacuum surrounding man-computer communication, it is not at all surprising that there does not exist a significant scientific tradition for investigating and understanding the human use of computers.

After a human generation of computer development, we now find a vast gap between the ubiquitous promises of "user-oriented" computerized systems of every conceivable kind, and the substantive scientific work on user performance that is needed to back up the glowing claims. In the absence of sustained, responsible criticism from scientific and humanistic quarters, it is the hawker of computerized wares who talks most and loudest about user performance in the public forum. And the gap continually widens under the mounting pressure of innovation without evaluation. Curious rituals are being institutionalized, characterized by universal lip service to the user, and marked by pious professions on humanizing the impact of computers on society, but with the user coming out of it all, in the end, as the forgotten man.

It would be misleading to say that man-computer communication in the computer world was neglected due to a perverse attitude of engineers, "hard" scientists, programers, and mathematicians toward the human use of computers. Part of the problem, as we have just seen, lies in the historical fact that computers were originally created to count and measure, and that the professionals who spawned and used the first computers were interested in abstract ideas and in their embodiment in hardware rather than in human behavior in using such devices. Had social scientists been deeply and extensively involved in the creation of electronic computers the story might have been different. They weren't.

The heroes of the computing world include such figures as Eckert, Mauchly, Aiken, Goldstine, Wilkes, and Hopper—John von Neumann is the now legendary super-hero. (See, for example, Angeline Pantages' article, "Computing's Early Years," in 1967.) The archetype of excellence is the creative mathemathical genius who can take seven-league strides through computerland. In a curious identification with the new golden calf, the hero is the human embodiment of the ideal qualities of the computer. This ideal still inspires computer science curricula, which are oriented toward mathematical and logical prowess rather than toward a sensitivity to real-world problems and social responsibility. In the pursuit of excellence, the computer world aspires toward technical heroes—there are no humanistic heroes.

Another offshoot of this pervasive humanistic lag stems from the manner in which computers were first used and continue to be used today. The batch, or offline computing system, is the evolutionary predecessor of time-sharing; it has been the plodding, operational workhorse of most data processing. The early computers were virtually one of a kind, very expensive to build and operate, and computer time was far more costly than human time. Under these constraints, it was essential that computer efficiency come first, with people last. Thus, under early batch systems and up to this day, the trick is to keep the computer working uninterruptedly with maximum throughput (useful computation time). To achieve this goal, user jobs are stacked and done one at a time on a waiting line arrangement. The user typically has only indirect contact with the computer, and turnaround time (the interval between submission and completion of a computer job) often takes days in conventional batch systems.

The batch system forces users to put up with interrupted problem-solving and unpredictable delays in services. It reinforces the notion that computer time is supreme and that human time is expendable. During the formative era in the rise of computers, the message was propagated, with drum-beat monotony, that computer needs are more important than user needs. The user approached the computer room with great trepidation, as if it were a shrine; and he considered himself lucky if the digital deity, as it dispensed its random favors, would service the user's supplication in due order.

This subservient attitude toward the almighty machine took hold in pioneer designers and users of computer systems and was transmitted to their disciples. Their main energies were directed toward getting working programs and reliable computers rather than understanding and helping people to put information processing to work. The dehumanization of computer services struck deep roots and spread throughout the computer world.

The developing computer ethos assumed an increasing misanthropic visage. Technical matters turned computer professionals on; human matters turned them off. Users were troublesome petitioners somewhere at the end of the line who had to be satisfied with what they got, because, after a substantial investment, they usually couldn't go elsewhere. Low quality and often abominable computer services were offered and accepted in a rapidly growing field where there were virtually no professional standards and no tradition of objective system testing for designers or users. Garbage in, garbage out (GIGO) became a sardonic joke—it was too often a fact of life. Computer professionals lived in an esoteric world of their own that became increasingly isolated from the human and social needs they were serving. And why not? Demand for computer services continued to rise exponentially, salaries kept going up, sheer experience reigned supreme, and the vicious cycle became self-sustaining. This is the Dorian Gray portrait of the other, the hidden, side of the computer coin. The public side showed the astronomical rise and spread of resplendent machine brains creating new miracles and fat profits, while the working side, conveniently out of sight, hid a misanthropic imbalance between hypertrophied technology and atrophied human needs.

4.2 THE CHALLENGE OF TIME-SHARING

Time-sharing systems, the technological basis for computer utilities, arrived on the scene at a critical historical juncture. As indicated in the previous chapter, the early 1960's witnessed remarkable advances in computer power, in computer storage capacity, in higher-order computer languages, in computer engineering and reliability, and in computer communications, which pushed computer system costs steadily downward in the intense competition for the computer pie in the sky. It became apparent that computer costs would soon be secondary to human costs. The realization began to dawn, but not without considerable resistance, that the *new* name of the game was user information service rather than central computer efficiency. The race was on for improved software packages and diversified computer services.

The basic techniques for time-sharing were previously developed in the 1950's in real-time command and control systems for military and space applications. Time-sharing was practiced in the sense that many users were simultaneously served by the same computer as they solved problems on the spot. In time-sharing the users are a more or less random and changing collection of people at any point in time, typically but not necessarily working on unrelated tasks with different computing programs, entering and leaving the system independently of one another, and using it for varying and largely unpredictable periods of time; such use approaches that of a public utility, roughly analogous to the quasi-random pattern of telephone traffic.

Experimental time-sharing systems were sponsored by the Advanced Research Projects Agency of the Department of Defense in the early 1960's. These pioneer prototypes accelerated the development of computer utilities through public funds. The Massachusetts Institute of Technology developed the Compatible Time-Sharing System (CTSS) used for Project MAC (Corbató, Merwin-Daggett, and Daley, 1962); the System Development Corporation developed TSS, their Time-Sharing System (Schwartz, Coffman and Weissman, 1964); and RAND came up with JOSS, the Johnniac Open-Shop System (Shaw, 1964). Commercial applications, building upon the invaluable legacy of these publicly supported prototypes, have subsequently sprouted and are rapidly spreading with practically all computer manufacturers marketing or developing some version of time-sharing hardware, software, and support facilities.

According to time-sharing advocates (see, for example, the above references) the user has fast and direct access to the computer when he wants it, provided that guaranteed access is available; he can get what he wants in minutes rather than hours or days for many types of jobs; he may exert continual online control over his program; and he is free to change his mind and do things differently as he interacts with the computer. Time-sharing means expense-sharing among a large number of subscribers with reduced costs for many applications; and time-sharing permits direct man-computer communication in languages that are beginning to approach natural language, at a pace approaching human conversation, and in some applications, at graded difficulty levels appropriate to the skill and experience of the user.

The critics of time-sharing point to higher costs and lower machine efficiency in time-sharing, to impressive advances in job shop scheduling, to mass servicing of users, and faster turnaround in the latest batch systems (for example, see Emerson, 1965; Macdonald, 1965; Patrick, 1963; and Lynch, 1967). Time-sharing advocates respond by emphasizing the compensatory savings in human time for online operations, the convenience to the user, and more rapid program development. The critics counter by insisting that users develop lazy and careless attitudes under time-sharing by going to the computer with poorly designed and untested programs in an effort to trade off computer time for human time.

The online/offline controversy is a gargantuan contest to dominate the multibillion-dollar software industry. This competition has major implications for a much larger future industry with the imminent rise of computer utilities for the general public. Here, then, we have a pressing and far-reaching confrontation between the two generic types of computer systems, a contest in which the human factor increasingly plays the dominant role. Which type of man-computer communication is better? In what respects is it better, by how much, and under what conditions? These are applied scientific questions best solved by system testing and evaluation under appropriate experimental controls. What is the experimental evidence to date? Part II of this book is addressed, in part, to these and related questions.

Chapter 2, which describes the proliferation of time-sharing systems and the contest over the role of computer communications between communication carriers, computer hardware, and computer software firms, points out the current state of man-computer communication. The main theme that runs through this account of the internal development of man-computer communication in the computer world, and the account of the two previous chapters bearing on computers and public utilities, is that the public interest continues to be the last, not the first consideration, and that the individual user is still the forgotten man. At best, the public has the equivalent of a disinterested tradition working against it, and at worst, an active misanthropic stance in the computer milieu, with the vested interests of very big business aimed at profits first and foremost, with lip service for the public weal.

It is ironic that vast public sums—and we are talking about billions of dollars of public funds—were used to develop the concept and the practice of real-time computing systems (in military command and control for national defense and manned spaceflight) which led directly to the development of computer time-sharing and computer utilities. It is even more ironic that the first experimental time-sharing systems were also sponsored by public funds from the Department of Defense which enabled commercial firms to leapfrog over and profit from the worst and most expensive mistakes that are inevitably committed in pioneering ventures. The citizen can easily invoke the one-for-one economic argument: the public paid for most of the development of computer utilities and the public is entitled to its money's worth. But the stakes are much higher than immediate economic considerations, because the overriding promise of the information utility is the enhancement of human intelligence and the realization of a more humane world. If the public doesn't regulate and control mass information utilities, narrow vested interests will. The social stakes are too high to let the information revolution pass as just another economic opportunity to be resolved by the vagaries of the marketplace. Informed public knowledge could lead to concerted action in the public interest, hopefully before it is too late. These and related arguments are developed in detail in Part IV.

4.3 THE VARIETIES OF COMPUTER SYSTEMS AND COMPUTER SERVICES

It is commonplace to cite the growing use of computers in all walks of life. Computer matching and mating, dining and dating, are among the latest fads. Like the legendary song of the Sirens, the dramatic exploitation of computers in society, in a culture that worships novelty, casts a magic spell that disarms our critical faculties. The unwary consumers, like the adventurous but impressionable Argonauts of old, are easily seduced by intimations of sweet things to come. The cold fact remains that no one has conducted a comprehensive census of computers and their applications. As a result, we are in the dark as to how and with whom computers are proliferating and where they are headed.

In the absence of sound empirical data, many have tried to rationalize computer trends by setting up classification schemes. Without empirical checks and balances, such schemes shrivel up and fade away. For example, Ilger (1964) made a preliminary attempt to classify computer systems. He developed a double-classification scheme, matching five types of users against six types of information systems with one example in each of the 30 cells. His five key users were: industrial, business, military, government, and institutional. The six types of information systems included acquisition, control, regulation, decision-making, transformation, and generation systems. In 1965 the Bureau of the Budget worked out a two-way classification matrix, operational environment vs. system response. Tuggle (1968) has developed a classification scheme for computer programs consisting of six attributes: primary system process, system complexity, primary data type, manpower ability, machine capacity, and language class.

The swiftly moving computer field confounds these and similar attempts to classify computer attributes. New and different systems are continually arising. The trend toward general-purpose computer facilities defies clear-cut categorization. It is very difficult to construct independent, mutually exclusive, and exhaustive categories. The main shortcoming is not a paucity of classification schemes, but the lack of empirical follow-up, of iterative experimentation in the field where the action is to see if such schemes are internally consistent and useful in practice.

Computing Reviews and *Computers and Automation* have evolved classification schemes of computer applications over a period of many years. The applications category for *Computing Reviews* (1968) emphasizes the sciences, humanities, and technology, as shown in Table 4.1. In contrast to the above academic approach, *Computers and Automation* stresses business applications. The key application categories used by *Computers and Automation* are listed in Table 4.2; this outline served as the framework for listing over 1400 computer applications (1968). These two classification schemes provide contrasting notions of the extensive and intensive use of computers in many walks of life.

Another way to describe the use of computers in society is to identify and sketch leading trends. Several of these trends have been mentioned earlier in this and the previous chapter. One is from offline to online data processing, from batch processing to interactive man-computer communication. Another is from the dedicated computer facility for the large organizational user (e.g., SAGE) to semidedicated computer systems for specific groups of users (e.g., university computer centers) to the relatively nondedicated, general-purpose system for individual users (e.g., computer utilities). A socially significant trend in computer communications is from local, to regional, to national and international computer networks. (See, for example, the pioneering interactive networks sponsored by the Department of Defense described by Licklider and Taylor, 1968.) The related general trend is the move from private to public computer services.

As impressive as these applications and trends are, they still fall far short of computer service for every individual. If we make the crude assumption that there will ultimately be, on the average, one computer terminal for each individual in the United States (either at home, school, or at the job), and if we make the further assumption that 200,000 terminals exist in 1970, then only one-tenth of one percent of the population has access to online computer services in 1970. No claims are made for these estimates. They illustrate that the surface has hardly been scratched in extending computer services to the general population. Further, with such extremely small proportions of the total population, it is quite hazardous to project trends for future information services with much confidence.

However, because of steady decreases in computer costs, a breakthrough in computer services may occur within the next five years which could radically change the current picture of computer applications. Table 4.3, describing commercial time-sharing systems (adapted from the Computer Research Corporation, 1968), shows that lowest computer terminal rates are already approaching ordinary telephone rates on an hourly and monthly basis. Minimum charges are in the neighborhood of $100 per month and are as low as $5 per terminal/hour. These charges are competitive with overall, life span rates for small, free-standing computers. For example, a small computer at $5000 with a useful life of five years costs

Table 4.1. APPLICATION CATEGORIES USED BY
COMPUTING REVIEWS

3. APPLICATIONS

3.1 Natural Science
  3.10 General
  3.11 Astronomy; Space
  3.12 Biology
  3.13 Chemistry
  3.14 Earth Sciences
  3.15 Mathematics:
      Number Theory
  3.16 Meteorology
  3.17 Physics:
      Nuclear Sciences
  3.19 Miscellaneous

3.2 Engineering
  3.20 General
  3.21 Aeronautical; Space
  3.22 Chemical
  3.23 Civil
  3.24 Electrical; Electronic
  3.25 Engineering Science
  3.26 Mechanical
  3.29 Miscellaneous

3.3 Social and Behavioral
    Sciences
  3.30 General
  3.31 Economics
  3.32 Education; Welfare
  3.33 Law
  3.34 Medicine; Health
  3.35 Political Science
  3.36 Psychology;
      Anthropology
  3.37 Sociology
  3.39 Miscellaneous

3.4 Humanities
  3.40 General
  3.41 Art
  3.42 Language Translation
      and Linguistics
  3.43 Literature
  3.44 Music
  3.49 Miscellaneous

3.5 Management Data Processing
  3.50 General
  3.51 Education; Research
  3.52 Financial
  3.53 Government
  3.54 Manufacturing;
      Distribution
  3.55 Marketing;
      Merchandising
  3.56 Military
  3.57 Transportation;
      Communication
  3.59 Miscellaneous

3.6 Artificial Intelligence
  3.60 General
  3.61 Induction and
      Hypothesis-Information
  3.62 Learning and
      Adaptive Systems
  3.63 Pattern Recognition
  3.64 Problem-Solving
  3.65 Simulation of Natural
      Systems
  3.66 Theory of Heuristic
      Methods
  3.69 Miscellaneous

3.7 Information Retrieval
  3.70 General
  3.71 Content Analysis
  3.72 Evaluation of Systems
  3.73 File Maintenance
  3.74 Searching
  3.75 Vocabulary
  3.79 Miscellaneous

3.8 Real-Time Systems
  3.80 General
  3.81 Communications
  3.82 Industrial Process Control
  3.83 Telemetry; Missiles; Space
  3.89 Miscellaneous

3.9 Miscellaneous

Table 4.2.   OUTLINE OF COMPUTER APPLICATIONS FROM
COMPUTERS AND AUTOMATION

I. *Business and Manufacturing*
in General
1. Office
2. Plant and Production

II. *Business—Specific Fields*
1. Advertising
2. Banking
3. Educational and
Institutional
4. Finance
5. Government
6. Hospitals
7. Insurance
8. Labor Unions
9. Law
10. Libraries
11. Magazine and Periodical
Publishing
12. Military
13. Oil Industry
14. Police
15. Public Utilities
16. Publishing
17. Religious Organizations
18. Sports and Entertainment
19. Steel Industry
20. Telephone Industry
21. Textile Industry
22. Transportation
23. Miscellaneous

III. *Science and Engineering*
1. Aeronautics and Space
Engineering
2. Astronomy

3. Biology
4. Chemical Engineering and
Chemistry
5. Civil Engineering
6. Economics
7. Electrical Engineering
8. Geology
9. Hydraulic Engineering
10. Marine Engineering
11. Mathematics
12. Mechanical Engineering
13. Medicine and Physiology
14. Metallurgy
15. Meteorology
16. Military Engineering
17. Naval Engineering
18. Nuclear Engineering
19. Oceanography
20. Photography
21. Physics
22. Psychology
23. Sociology
24. Statistics

IV. *Humanities*
1. Archeology
2. Anthropology
3. Art
4. Games of Skill
5. Genealogy
6. Geography
7. History
8. Languages
9. Literature
10. Music

roughly $100 per month. More significantly, direct costs for human time at the console are beginning to exceed direct costs for machine time. Would you believe that it already costs less to talk to your computer than it does to talk to your analyst?

The application of computers to social affairs grows wider and deeper with every passing day, and is becoming as broad as human endeavor. Many of these applications are on dedicated computers for private tasks and services. Many applications are semiprivate, and, with the advent of computer utilities, the most rapidly growing segment of computer applications lies in the public domain. Intelligent regulation of computer utilities requires definitive empirical data on data banks and information services in the public domain, those in the private domain, those that overlap, the conditions specifying such overlap, and their rates of change. This information needs to be classified and quantified in regard to cost, benefits, and problems relating to the public interest.

In the absence of a descriptive, empirical census of computer facilities and services, neither the public nor the computer industry can know who the users are, what tasks and problems they have, how well they are being solved, and what new services or improvements to seek. Such information would be invaluable both for public regulation of computer utilities and for consumer-oriented industrial planning in the growing computer market.

Many side benefits would accrue from a periodic computer census. Computer power is linked to information power—we would learn more about the dimensions and nature of this new force and how it is growing, in quantitative as well as qualitative terms. Computer power is an indispensable asset for local and national emergencies, in war, insurrectionary movements, or in natural disasters. Knowledge of pertinent information banks and available computer resources could help alleviate human suffering and social dislocation during such periods. Centralized and decentralized data banks could be compared on cost and social effectiveness. Litigation over computer services could be correlated with recurrent problems that have not been successfully handled by existing legal procedures. Work on computer communication standards and conventions could be greatly facilitated to reduce wasteful redundancy and confusion in information services. Without reasonable standardization of information procedures based on working practice, the growing din of clacking computer tongues could become the electronic Tower of Babel. The census could provide early warning of unforeseen problems and new trends that may have a major impact on the public interest. As with

Table 4.3. COMMERCIAL COMPUTER UTILITIES

ORGANIZATION	COMPUTER	LANGUAGES	TERMINALS	NO. OF USERS
Allen-Babcock Computing, Inc. Palo Alto, California	IBM 360/50	PL/1 (on-line subset)	IBM 2741, 1050 TT-33, 35, 37 Friden 7100 Datel Thirty 21	90
Applied Logic Corp. Princeton, New Jersey	DEC PDP-6, PDP-10	FORTRAN IV, DDT, AIDE, BASIC, LISP, MACRO-10, SNOBOL-6 Compact COBOL	TT-33, 35, 37 CRT, PLT IBM 2741	40
Bolt Beranek and Newman Inc. Cambridge, Massachusetts	PDP-10 PDP-7(3)	TELCOMP-10, LISP, FORTRAN IV, MACRO, SNOBOL	TT-33, 35	32
CDC-CEIR Washington, D.C.	GE-235, 420	BASIC, ALGOL, FORTRAN II, IV	TT-33, 35 Friden 7100	40
Call-A-Computer Raleigh, North Carolina	GE-265	ALGOL, BASIC, BIICAC, FORTRAN II, FORCAC, EDIT	TT-33, 35 PLT, CRT	40
Computer Network Corp. Washington, D.C.	B-5500	FORTRAN IV, ALGOL, BASIC, COBOL	TT-33, 35, CRT	32
Computer Sharing, Inc. Bala Cynwyd, Pennsylvania	SDS-940	CAL, BASIC, QED, TAP, DDT, FORTRAN II, IV	TT-33, 35	32
Computer Sharing Services Denver, Colorado	GE-265	BASIC, FORTRAN II	TT-33, 35	see remarks
Computer Time-Sharing, Inc. Bloomington, Minnesota	CDC-3300	FORTRAN II, EDIT, DEBUG, BASIC	TT-33, 35	64
Com-Share, Inc. Chicago, Illinois	SDS 940	BASIC, CAL, QED, FORTRAN II, IV, DDT, TAP, SNOBOL	TT-33, 35, 37, PLT	32
Data Central, Inc. St. Louis, Missouri	SDS 940	BASIC, FORTRAN II, IV	TT-33, 35	32
Data Network Corp. New York, New York	SDS 940	BASIC, CAL, FORTRAN II, IV	TT-33, 35	32
DIAL-DATA, Inc. Newton, Massachusetts	SDS 940	CAL, DDT, QED, ALGOL, FORTRAN II, IV, BASIC, SNOBOL, ARPAS, LISP	TT-33, 35, 37, PLT, CRT	40
Direct Access Computer Corp. Southfield, Michigan	B-5500	ALGOL, BASIC, COBOL, FORTRAN IV	TT-33, 35	48
Fulton National Bank Atlanta, Georgia	GE-420	BASIC, FORTRAN IV	TT-33, 35	30
General Electric Co. Information Service Dept. Bethesda, Maryland	GE-265, 635	BASIC, ALGOL, FORTRAN II, IV	TT-33, 35, PLT, Friden 7100, 7102	40
Graphic Controls Buffalo, New York	GE-235	BASIC, ALGOL, EDIT, FORTRAN, PACER, TSAP, LAFFF, LISP	TT-33, 35, Friden 7100, 7102	40
IBM Information Marketing Dept. White Plains, New York	IBM 7044 360/40, 360/50	QUIKTRAN, 360 BASIC, 360 DATATEXT	IBM 1050, 2741, TT-33, 35	

HOURLY TERMINAL RATE	PROCESSOR TIME PER MINUTE	DISC STORAGE/ CUSTOMER	MINIMUM CHARGE PER MO.	REMARKS
None	$5.00-$10.00	0+	None	360/50 has been modified.with special operation codes for efficient conversational interaction. CPU charges are dependent on amount of core used.
$10-$25	see remarks	10K+	None	Processor time is charged at $.015 for each 10,000 instructions executed.
$10-$15	$0-$25.00	50K+	None	TELCOMP available now — all other languages available in early 1969. No CPU charge for PDP-7, CPU charge for PDP-10 is $25 per minute.
$6.25-$12.75	$2.00	0+	$0-$250	A maximum of 30 users can be accommodated on a GE-420.
$6.50-$9.00	$3.00	0+	None	Special rates for high schools and colleges.
$7.00-$10.00	$12.00	75K+	None	System has capability of interfacing with high speed CDC 200 terminals.
$7.00-$10.00	$2.50	60K+	None	Terminal rates are increased by $3 per hour for the use of QED, BASIC, CAL, FORTRAN IV and DDT.
see remarks	see remarks	see remarks	see remarks	Rates are not presently available.
$10.00	$4.80	0+	None	Special rates available for large storage requirements and for heavy usage.
$10-$20	$2.50	60K+	$100.00	Com-Share Southern, Inc., an affiliate of Com-Share, Inc., has a different rate structure.
see remarks	see remarks	see remarks	see remarks	Rates are not presently available.
$9.00-$18.00	None	0+	$100.00	
$10-$12	$3.00	60K+	None	Special applications packages for Electronic Circuit Design and Analysis, Statistics, Linear Programming, etc.
see remarks	see remarks	see remarks	see remarks	Rates are not presently available.
$10.00	$3.00	0+	$350.00	I/O time is charged at the rate of $.03 per second.
$10.00	see remarks	0+	$100.00	ALGOL available with 265 only. FORTRAN IV available with 635 only. 64 users with 635 CPU rate for 265 is $24 per minute. 635 rate is $.40 per second.
$10-$13	$3.00	0+	$50.00	
see remarks	see remarks	0+	$100.00	Rates: Terminal/QUIKTRAN — $10/hr., DATATEXT — $2.15/hr., BASIC — $11/hr.; Processor/QUIKTRAN — $2/min., BASIC — $7/min., DATATEXT — $.008/7 I/O Transfers or 120 ms of processor time.

Table 4.3. COMMERCIAL COMPUTER UTILITIES (Cont.)

ORGANIZATION	COMPUTER	LANGUAGES	TERMINALS	NO. OF USERS
ITT Data Services Paramus, New Jersey	IBM 360/50, 360/65	FORTRAN IV, BASIC	TT-33,35 IBM 1050, 2741	50
Intinco Limited London, England	UNIVAC 418(2)	Stockbrokers Language	TT-33, 35	see remarks
John P. Maguire & Co., Inc. New York, New York	IBM 360/40	BTAM, DOS	IBM 1050, 2740	60
Keydata Corp. Watertown, Massachusetts	UNIVAC 491	KOP III, SPURT	TT-28	200
McDonnell Automation Co. St. Louis, Missouri	GE-420	BASIC, FORTRAN	TT-33, 35, Friden 7100	30
On-Line Systems, Inc. North Hills Pittsburgh, Pennsylvania	GE-255	BASIC, ALGOL, FORTRAN	TT-33, 35	20
Philco-Ford Corp. C. & E. Division Computer Services Network Willow Grove, Pennsylvania	B-3500, GE-265, Philco-212	BASIC, ALGOL, TUTOR, COBOL, FORTRAN II, IV	TT-33, 35, 37, Univac 1004, 1005, 1130	40
Pillsbury Management Systems Phoenix, Arizona	DATANET-30	TRAC	TT-33, 35, 37, IBM 2741	15
Rapidata New York, New York	GE-425 DATANET-30	BASIC, RITE, FORTRAN IV	TT-33, 35, Friden 7200, IBM 2741	40
REALTIME Systems, Inc. New York, New York	B-5500	FORTRAN IV, COBOL, ALGOL	TT-33, 35	24
Remote Computing Corp. Los Angeles, California	B-5500	COBOL, ALGOL, FORTRAN, BASIC	TT-33, 35	48
Time-Sharing Systems, Inc. Milwaukee, Wisconsin	B-5500	FORTRAN IV, ALGOL	TT-33, 35	32
TYMSHARE, Inc. Los Altos, California	SDS 940	CAL, BASIC, ARPAS, SUPER BASIC, QED, FORTRAN II, IV	TT-33, 35, 37, PLT, CRT, CR	42
U.S. Time Sharing, Inc. Washington, D.C.	IBM 360/50	360 ASSEMBLER, PL/1, FORTRAN IV, COBOL, RPG, ALGOL	TT-33, 35, IBM 1050, 2740, 2741, 2780, DURA 1021, 1041, CRT, Datel Thirty 21	67
Univac Information Services Div. Blue Bell, Pennsylvania	1108, 418, 9300	FORTRAN, COBOL SIMSCRIPT, GPSS	Univac 1004	see remarks
VIP Systems Corp. Washington, D.C.	IBM 1460	IBM ATS	IBM 2741, DATEL, DURA	40
White, Weld & Co. New York, New York	SDS 940	FFL, QED, DDT, FORTRAN II	TT-33, 35	24

HOURLY TERMINAL RATE	PROCESSOR TIME PER MINUTE	DISC STORAGE/ CUSTOMER	MINIMUM CHARGE PER MO.	REMARKS
$12.00	$7.00	0+	$150.00	Application packages for Consumer Credit Record Retrieval, Finance Accounting, and Mutual Fund Shareholder Accounting.
see remarks	see remarks	see remarks	see remarks	Methods of charging vary; the rate is approximately $5000 per year plus a usage charge of $.05 per inquiry.
see remarks	see remarks	see remarks	$1,500.00	All prices negotiated according to storage and processing requirements. System used for accounting and management services.
see remarks	see remarks	see remarks	see remarks	Charges based on message transmissions, processor time and storage. System used for accounting and management services.
$10.00	$3.00	0+	$100.00	
$12.50	None	0+	None	PDP-10 system under development.
$5.00-$15.00	$2.40-$5.00	0+	$100.00	Philco 212 system has no disc or drum storage.
$5.00	$.60-$1.20	0+	$100.00	System includes Test Editors, Management Information Systems and computer-assisted learning programs. Processor rates vary according to system used.
$9.00-$11.00	$3.00	0+	$100.00	I/O is charged at the rate of $.03 per second based on disc swap time.
$15.00	$6.65-$8.35	0+	$500.00	Several background jobs can be initiated by user to run concurrently.
$5.00	$6.00	0+	None	
$11.00	$7.20	see remarks	$75-$350	60K character of storage included in $350 per month minimum rate.
$13-$16	None	60K+	$80.00 or $390.00	Applications packages include COGO, ECAP, EASYPLOT, APT and CSMP.
$4.00-$6.00	$6.00-$9.00	0+	None	50,000 bytes of storage available at no additional cost for each $100 of usage per month.
see remarks	see remarks	see remarks	see remarks	Rates and user information not available at this time.
$5.00-$10.00	None	0+	$125-$800	Several rate plans available depending upon usage and terminal location. IBM 360/40 system is being planned.
see remarks	see remarks	see remarks	$1,500.00	Rate and storage information not available.

democracy and freedom, the price of growing information power is nothing less than eternal vigilance.

The case for empirical feedback on the use of computers has only been broached in this section. Suffice it to say at this point that there can be no intelligent public experimentation without public description and useful quantification of computer services. And, further, in the absence of definitive real-world data on computer use, it is the hawkers of computer wares who set the stage, and, in the confusion that follows, it is the self-seeking opportunist rather than the public who benefits most from growing information services.

4.4 THE PROBLEMATIC POTENTIAL OF COMPUTER-SERVICED SOCIETIES

The frontiers of computer technology are shifting constantly and computers are proliferating in many directions at once. The high-speed electronic computer is constantly being driven and perfected toward the ultimate limit of molecular information storage with speed-of-light transmission. Offline services are steadily evolving toward online information delivered in real time to help solve human problems as they arise. Computerized subcultures have appeared in military applications and are spilling over into civilian life in the form of regional, national, and international computer communications networks. While only a minuscule proportion of the general population has direct contact with computer services, few doubt that computer applications will eventually influence the daily life of all citizens and, some day, the entire world. The computer-serviced world is apparent in principle if not yet in fact.

If present experience is any guideline, the trend is toward pluralistic and openly competing information services rather than monolithic, centralized giant brains. The play of pluralistic checks and balances in computer services may be observed everywhere on the computer scene. Even in highly centralized command control systems in a military setting such as SAGE, each central computer in the network has unique adaptation parameters, its own set of special-purpose programs, and unique input/output requirements custom-tailored to its particular defense configuration. Commercial real-time systems strike out on their own system design paths even though they borrow heavily from military predecessors. Computer hardware and software competition is fierce and diverse. Computer languages proliferate, almost uncontrollably.

Alexis de Tocqueville was astounded more than a century ago by the spectacle of restless energy and the buzzing, blooming confusion of the American economic scene—if he could retrace his steps once more, he would see the same spectacle in the rampant exuberance of computer developments in the United States today. The American lesson, at least in this respect, is encouraging—computer services can lead to unprecedented diversity in human information and knowledge in a pluralistic social setting.

But deification of diversity for its own sake is mindless allegiance to a disembodied concept. It is fruitless to try to prove the absolute superiority of diversity over unity, of decentralization over centralization, of public over private interests. The choices are not abstract, they are concrete for particular issues, in particular situations, at particular times. The resolution of such arguments will vary with the unique case in question. The critical point is that there be an open forum for vigorous exploration of alternatives to permit intelligent selection. The incredible diversification of actual, possible, and conceivable information systems and services, for good and for evil, raises the challenge of effective social inquiry. The challenge is whether the public will develop the effective intelligence to contribute to and make such choices, or whether, as with virtually all major technological revolutions in the past, a new elite will arrogate such power and make such decisions on their own behalf. A leading objective of this book is to present the case for the solution of choice in this dilemma—the uplifting of effective public intelligence through the extension and institutionalization of new and improved social knowledge in social affairs. First and foremost, the computer revolution is a revolution in human knowledge; computer-serviced reconstruction of human knowledge can be the means for progressing to a flowering of worldwide human intelligence.

PART II

PROTOTYPE
CASE HISTORIES

5

BIOGRAPHY OF A
COMPUTER UTILITY

IN PART I of this book the information utility was viewed from various vantage points—as a public utility (Chapter 2), in the light of its historical development (Chapter 3), and in the context of emerging computer-serviced societies (Chapters 3 and 4). In the two chapters of the second part, these broad aspects of computer utilities are contrasted against the concrete experience of a pioneer time-sharing system, and against individual experience with such systems. This contrast serves several useful purposes. First, general issues can be more directly related to the working operations of current systems which serve as precursors for mass information utilities. Second, the reader can become familiar with the features of a particular computer utility that has elements common to most computer utilities. Third, virtually nowhere in the literature do we find case-history reviews of long-term evolution of particular time-sharing systems and of individual user experience—comparative case histories are urgently needed so that future users may benefit from the lessons that have been learned and discover the pitfalls that should be avoided. Finally, an understanding of a working system in some detail, from both the designer and user viewpoints, is necessary to appreciate the problems of scientific test and evaluation of man-machine system performance that are treated in Part III. This chapter is a case history of a prototype information utility, and the subsequent chapter is an experimental case history of individual user experience.

The computer utility described in this chapter was one of the first to appear. The System Development Corporation Time-Sharing System (TSS) has a history of almost a decade of service for a great variety of users; it is one that has spawned a second-generation system that is being widely implemented. The author has had firsthand experience with both of these systems; some of the experimental studies discussed in Part III were performed on TSS. The development of TSS and its continued operation have been supported by the Department of Defense and accumulated experience with this system is primarily in the public domain.

5.1   ORIGINS

The first time-sharing systems grew out of convergent technological trends that would have inevitably yielded such systems sooner or later. No one can really assume prior credit for "originating" the concept. Digital time-sharing was practiced in switching circuits of telephone systems before World War II. The electronic digital computer, as we have seen, arose from World War II technology. The stored-program computer followed shortly afterwards. SAGE was the first system in which many users, including those at remote stations, as in the Remote Combat Center, shared the same computer in real time. The steady advances in computer power, the reduction of computer costs, and the development of more versatile input-output equipment, together with the above technological precursors, all converged toward the first time-sharing system. The first general-purpose time-sharing system, the Compatible Time-Sharing System (CTSS), was developed at the Massachusetts Institute of Technology, and the first public demonstration of time-sharing was held at MIT in November 1961. CTSS has since exerted a leading impact on the computing world in the design and development of time-sharing systems. Unfortunately, an authoritative account of the historical development of CTSS has not yet been written.

Other time-sharing systems were soon developed, many of them sponsored by the Advanced Research Projects Agency (ARPA) of the Department of Defense. The SDC Time-Sharing System, under ARPA sponsorship, was conceived in 1962 and became operational in 1963. Glauthier (1967) has reviewed the origins and development of time-sharing systems and has documented the multiple scientific and technological inputs that have contributed to their exponential rate of growth. Parkhill (1966) has described key technical characteristics of the main first-generation time-sharing systems, and he has sketched the divergent lines of evolution that characterize the second-generation systems that are proliferating today. Although scattered references may be found on specific applications of time-sharing in various systems, there is no intensive literature on cumulative experience for user populations for a large, general-purpose system—for a computer utility. As in other computer developments, the machine side comes first and the impact of computers on people is lost in the shuffle.

5.2 SYSTEM DESIGN

To understand time-sharing system design, it is helpful to have some idea as to how a user works with the system. User programs are stored on magnetic tapes or on disk files. Typically, when a user wants system services, he goes to a typewriter terminal connected to the central computer. He "logs in," that is, establishes his identity as a bona fide user by typing in an authorized identification code that is recognized and accepted by the control computer. Then the user calls for the program he wishes to operate, again via the typewriter console, often by simply typing in the name of the program. The computer loads the program from its inactive state in disk storage and activates it by placing it on magnetic drum storage. All other active programs are also located on drum storage. Each operating program is transferred, one at a time, in serial order, from the drum into central high-speed storage. When the user's program is reached in this "waiting line," the user gets computer service. Since only a fraction of a second is typically devoted to each turn for each "interactive" user, the computer is said to be "time-shared." He sees the results of his interaction with his program in the form of an automatic printout at his typewriter initiated by the computer.

The basic user cycle is fundamentally a three-step cycle: 1) user input; 2) computer output; 3) user "think" time; and a new cycle with the next user input. The user types in his command. The computer picks up the input message, processes it when the user's program is operated, prepares the output message, and sends it to the user's terminal. The user then "thinks" about his next command, starts typing his next message, and the cycle starts all over again.

As we enter into experimental studies of users of time-sharing systems in these chapters, we will find that the step from the user input to the computer output has been the one that has received the greatest amount of study. That is, the step representing the machine side of the cycle. The other side, the step from computer output to the user's next input, the "thinking" step, has received the least amount of study. This cerebral link is the most significant part of the user cycle since it represents the directive human intelligence that guides the interactive problem-solving process.

Returning to the machine side, the user's program is transferred to core memory only if it requires processing. Otherwise, it is passed up for that turn. Thus, theoretically, the user may spend as much time as he needs thinking about what to do next without wasting the computational time of the machine. Although a time-sharing system processes programs sequentially and discontinuously, it gives users the illusion of simultaneity and continuity because of its high speed, particularly if the computer response bounces back at a rapid conversational pace.

Figure 5.1, adapted from Coffman and Wood (1965), blocks out the main elements in the flow of TSS information. Reading from left to right, users at remote terminals compose messages to be sent to the central facility. These messages are routed to a Digital Equipment Corporation PDP-1 computer acting as the focal input/output station for receiving, storing, monitoring, and transmitting messages from the various online devices to the central computer. The IBM AN/FSQ-32 is the central processor of the system, shown with its main types of peripheral equipment.

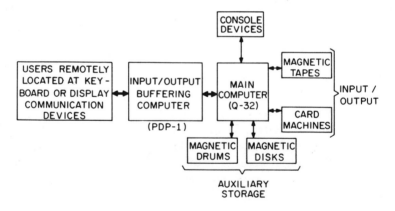

Figure 5.1.   SDC TIME-SHARING SYSTEM CONFIGURATION
(from Coffman and Wood, 1965)

The equipment configuration for TSS is shown in Table 5.1 under three main heads, the central computer, associated computers, and the main input/output devices. In this table, "ips" is inches per second, "cpm" is cards per minute, "wpm" is words per minute, "K" is thousands, and "lpm" is lines per minute. Note that secondary storage (disks and tapes) is quite large to accommodate user programs and data—a central requirement for computer utilities.

The associated or satellite computer provides a critical system service by handling much of the routine traffic chores concerned with receiving, storing, and forwarding messages from the users to the central system and in routing responses from the main computer back to the users. Thus, input/output traffic functions are overlapped with central computer operations to allow the central system to perform more useful computations on user programs per unit time, resulting in more efficient throughput. One of the main criticisms levelled at time-sharing systems by batch advocates is that time-sharing leads to poor throughput. Experience with the MIT system has shown an effective throughput of 61 percent at high-capacity loads (Scherr, 1967); and the SDC Q-32 Time-Sharing System has shown comparable throughput efficiency at approximately 70 percent (Schwartz and Weissman, 1967); experience with the time-sharing system at the University of Massachusetts has also shown effective machine throughput at 70 percent (Gonter and Smith, 1970). These figures approach the levels of machine efficiency characteristic of many batch systems.

The last category of Table 5.1 lists the main types of input/output devices for communications between users and the central system. These are subdivided into typewriter and cathode ray tube consoles. With the typewriter terminal, the user types in his messages and receives automatic printouts from the computer in response to his queries. With the CRT, the user may employ a light pen, a graphic tablet, or a keyboard to send messages to the computer, by pointing, drawing figures, or activating keyboard switches, respectively. The computer response appears on the display scope at a message rate, as shown in Table 5.1, essentially an order of magnitude faster than the rate for typewriter terminals. While typewriter terminals are slower than CRT terminals, they are also much less expensive with respect to hardware and software, often considerably less expensive. But CRT terminal costs are steadily decreasing (see, for example, Theis and Hobbs, 1968), and the long-term competition between the two main types of terminals promises to be fierce.

Table 5.1.   Q-32 TIME-SHARING SYSTEM EQUIPMENT

Component	Number	Capacity/Speed	Total
AN/FSQ-32 COMPUTER			
Main Core Memory	4	16,384 words	65,536 words
• Cyle time 2.5 μsec.			
• 48-bit word			
Input Core Memory (Buffer)	1	16,384 words	16,384 words
• Cyle time 2.5 μsec.			
Drum	5	139,264 words	696,320 words
• Access time 11.5 ms.			
• Word transfer rate 2.75 μsec.			
Disc File	2	4,194,304 words	8,388,608 words
• Access time 225 ms.			
• Word transfer rate 12 μsec.			
Tape Drives (729-IV)	11	112½ ips	
Card Reader (714)	1	250 cpm	
Card Punch	1	100 cpm	
Typewriter	2	100 wpm	

ASSOCIATED COMPUTERS (ON/OFF-LINE)

PDP-1			
• Shares input core memory of Q-32			32K words
• Cycle time 5 μsec.			
• 18-bit word main core memory	1	4K words	4K words
1401-D			
• Core memory	1	4K char.	4K char.
• Printer	1	600 lpm	
• Tape drives (729-IV)	2	112½ ips	
• Card reader (Uptime)	1	850 cpm	

I/O DEVICES

Teletypes and Typewriters		
• Model 33 Teletypes	34	100 wpm
• TWX data sets (remote users)	6	100 wpm
• Soroban typewriters	3	90 wpm
• Telex data sets	1	100 wpm
• Data-Phone sets	6	100 wpm
• IBM 1051-1052	1	150 wpm
• Communications testboard	1	
Display Consoles	6	2K char. max.
• Light pens		(per console)
• Vector-generator capability		
• Graphic tablet	1	5K points/sec.
• Keyboard	2	100 wpm

5.3 INFORMATION SERVICES

When TSS became operational in 1963, the only information service available was programing and checkout, just enough to put the system together and to get "the show on the road." By 1964 the number of user applications had grown rapidly to include military, simulation, information retrieval, natural language processing, and information management programs. The initial users included educational, state, and federal organizations such as Stanford University, The RAND Corporation, the Los Angeles Police Department, and the Veterans Administration. By mid-1968, according to a survey by Spierer and Wills (1968), there were roughly 175 different application programs running under TSS each week.

The user community in 1963 consisted of some 50 individuals located at SDC in Santa Monica, California. The initial version of TSS was able to service eight users simultaneously. By 1966 the total number of authorized users reached a peak of about 500, and the maximum capacity of the system was 30 users working with the system at the same time. These users were located in many parts of the United States and, in some instances, in other countries, including Mexico, Finland, and Denmark, as shown in Figure 5.2.

Since 1966, when ARPA sponsorship was reduced and when TSS became largely self-supporting, the number of users dropped to 200, with special arrangements providing for guaranteed service to subscribers. In 1969 the system operated 15 hours per day, from 5 A.M. to 8 P.M. six days a week. The early morning hours were primarily used by the East Coast subscribers.

Authorized users are guaranteed access to the system for specified periods of time. They are assured of up to 48,000 words of drum or "swap" storage, commensurate with core storage capacity. Disk storage may be as high as 200,000 words, and each subscriber is permitted the use of at least one tape drive. Users log in with accounting control numbers, which are authenticated and checked against the system access schedule. Software resources for the users include the executive or control program which resides permanently in core memory, many utility and service programs, and diversified application programs, the programs that are typically prepared and operated by users.

The executive program controls the allocation of computer system resources, performs accounting services, manages system loads and as-

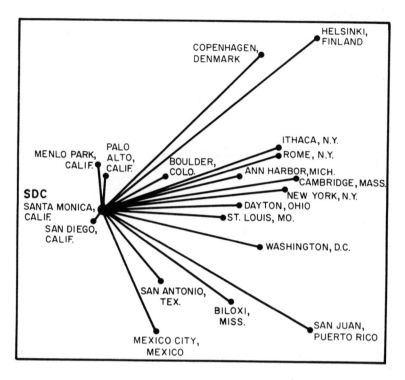

Figure 5.2.   REMOTE USERS OF THE SDC TIME-SHARING SYSTEM

sociated priorities, and handles error detection and recovery procedures. The utility programs cover functions such as language processors which include JOVIAL, IPL-V, and LISP compilers, TINT (an interpretive language), assemblers, such as SCAMP, and metacompilers, including META and DBL. In addition, utility services include many routines that facilitate editing, debugging, information retrieval, and file maintenance. These routines were designed primarily for programers.

The application programs have been reviewed by Spierer and Wills who classify them into the following eight broad areas: online programming and debugging, data base management, information retrieval, document retrieval, natural language processing, behavioral gaming and simulation, data reduction and analysis, and educational applications. Table 5.2 shows a simple lesson-building sequence from PLANIT, an interactive language designed for educational purposes (Feingold, 1967).

Table 5.2. LESSON-BUILDING SEQUENCE FROM PLANIT

	Dialogue	Explanation
User†:	*CO	Commence operation in the lesson-building mode. The asterisk is printed by PLANIT when a user input is required.
PLANIT:	P/Q/M/D/C	PLANIT is asking the user —in the concise form—to select the type of lesson frame he will build.
User:	*?	The user requests explanation of the above printout.
PLANIT:	(P)ROBLEM/(Q)UESTION/(M)ULTIPLE CHOICE/(D)ECISION/(C)OPY	PLANIT lists the available lesson frame types.
User:	*Q	The user specifies the Question frame.
PLANIT:	1. FRAME 25.00 LABEL = * HISTORY	PLANIT assigns a number to the lesson frame (25). The user assigns a label (HISTORY).
PLANIT:	2. SQ.	Specify Question.
User:	*WHO INVENTED THE ELECTRIC LIGHT?	
PLANIT:	3. SA.	Specify anticipated student answers.
User:	*A+ EDISON *B MARCONI *C BELL	The + after A indicates to the program that this is the correct answer.
PLANIT:	4. SAT.	Specify Action to be Taken, depending on answer given by the student.
User:	*A+ F: GOOD WORK. B: 5 *B R: THAT WAS THE WIRELESS TELEGRAPH. TRY AGAIN. *C R: BELL WAS THE TELEPHONE MAN. TRY AGAIN. *— C: B: 1	The user specifies a Feedback message ("GOOD WORK") to be presented if the student answers correctly; then the program is instructed to Branch to Lesson Frame 5. A Repeat command is given in case student gives answer B or C. If student gives any other response, the program is instructed to print the Correct answer and to follow this by Branching back to Lesson Frame 1 for remedial instruction.

† The user is typically a teacher or lesson-designer.

5.4   SECOND-GENERATION SYSTEM

In January 1967 work began on a successor system to the Q-32 TSS. The new system, called ADEPT (no acronym, although many printable and some unprintable names have been devised), was supported by ARPA with the understanding that it be tested and evaluated in a National Military Command System environment. The design of ADEPT capitalized on the prototype experience of the Q-32 TSS, leading to improvements in four key areas.

Economy. Whereas the Q-32 system ran on a large computer, ADEPT was planned to provide the same types of sophisticated time-sharing services on a less expensive, "medium"-sized computer (the IBM 360/ 50). This transition took advantage of engineering advances in "third generation" computers which spurred the growth of commercial time-sharing systems toward the end of the 1960's.

User Self-Service. In spite of the breakthrough in conversational capability offered by the pioneering time-sharing systems, most computer languages utilized by programers were still too difficult and costly to learn for the lay user, and continuing pressure was maintained to approach the ease and simplicity of natural language. ADEPT was required to incorporate more ostensibly flexible and versatile information services such as the Time-Sharing Data Management System (TDMS) for the nonprogramer.

More Flexible Central Control. The Q-32 TSS featured a "closed" executive system in which all basic system commands were integrated into the executive program. The modification of such commands (such as entering or leaving the system, loading, and terminating program operations) was a difficult and costly process. Accordingly, the concept of the central executive was revised to incorporate a Basic Executive (BASEX) and an Extended Executive (EXEX), in which the Extended Executive contained system commands that could be more easily deleted, augmented, or modified in response to evolutionary system changes.

Security. The Q-32 TSS was primarily a public operation with security controls mainly for subscription and accounting purposes. Military requirements for varying levels of security, organizational requirements for the protection of proprietary information, and individual requirements for "privacy" led to a more elaborate design in ADEPT for specified degrees and types of security.

Table 5.3 describes the main hardware components of the ADEPT time-sharing system on the IBM 360/50 computer. The items and abbreviations are essentially the same as those listed in Table 5.1 for the Q-32 TSS. One difference is that various capacities are listed as "bytes" rather than machine words. A byte is eight bits, and four bytes comprise one word in the 360/50. Except for the absence of buffer computers in the initial version of ADEPT, and for hardware advances, the general configuration of equipment for the Q-32 TSS and ADEPT is similar. The difference between the larger Q-32 computer and the medium-sized 360/50 is reflected in the comparative capacities of the two systems. TSS can handle up to 30 simultaneous users compared to 10 for ADEPT. The ratio will be changed, however, when ADEPT is adapted to larger and more powerful computers, as is currently planned.

Figure 5.3 shows the basic sequence of operation for an individual user from the point of view of the executive. Program control initiates service in response to an activity request. The user's program is scheduled, swapped into core from drum storage, and executed. The operation of the user's program (object program) is terminated either by completion of the program, expiration of the user's "quantum" (usually less than a second) in the round robin, or in an error condition. The object program is then swapped out of core back to drum storage and control is returned to the scheduling algorithm.

The three main components of ADEPT are the executive or control program, the data management system, and the programer's package. The scheduling function of the executive has been described above. The executive handles file security to prevent unauthorized access to restricted files and it has features to prevent accidental damage or destruction of stored data and programs. The control program is designed to permit any mix of batch and time-sharing operations, a feature that was only indirectly attainable in the Q-32 TSS.

The Basic Executive (BASEX) is responsible for hardware resource management, interrupt controls, memory allocation, and system-user scheduling. It resides permanently in core. The other part of the executive, the Extended Executive (EXEX) is a flexible, open-ended collection of semiautonomous programs. EXEX is treated by BASEX as if it were a user program with certain privileges. This dual structure permits relatively easy modification and custom-tailoring of user-system interfaces.

The Time-Shared Data Management System (TDMS) evolved from prior work on an earlier system called LUCID. TDMS has been designed as a data management system that provides nonprogramer users with a variety of techniques to handle large volumes of structured data. De-

Table 5.3.   ADEPT TIME-SHARING SYSTEM EQUIPMENT

Component	Number	Capacity/Speed	Total Bytes
360/50 COMPUTER			
Main Core Memory • Cycle time 2 μsec • Accesses 4 bytes (one word) in parallel	1	262,144 bytes	262,144
Drum (2303) • Average access time 8.6 ms. • Data rate 312,500 bytes/sec. • Rotates at 3,500 rpm	1	4,000,000 bytes	4,000,000
Disc (2311) • Average access time 75 ms. (1 ms. min. to 135 max.) • Data rate 156,000 bytes/sec. • Maximum number of bytes/track 3625 • Number of tracks 2000	4	7,250,000 bytes	29,000,000
Disc (2302) • Average access time 175 ms. (1 ms. min. to 214 ms. max.) • Data rate 143,000 bytes/sec.	1	226,000,000 bytes	226,000,000
Tape Drives (2402-3, 9-track) • Tape speed 112.5 ips • Density 800 bytes/in. • Data rate 90,000 bytes/sec.	7	21,000,000 bytes	147,000,000
Tape Drives (2402-3, 7-track) • Tape speed 112.5 ips • Density 800,556,200 bytes/in. • Data rate at 800 Density 90,000 bytes/sec.	1	20,450,000 bytes	20,450,000
I/O DEVICES			
Display Console (2250) • Light pen • Character generator • Vector generator • Alphameric keyboard • Function keyboard	1	8,000-byte buffer	
Display Console (2260) • Character generator • Alphameric/function keyboard	1	960-byte buffer	
Communication Terminals (2741)	4	14.8 char./sec.	
Operator Communication Terminal (1052)	1	14.8 char./sec.	
Model 33 Teletypes	4	100 wpm	

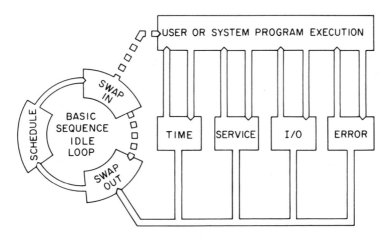

Figure 5.3. ADEPT SEQUENCE OF OPERATION

signed for operation on IBM S/360 computers, TDMS represents gains over its predecessor in data storage capacity, more versatile data structures, easier manipulation of such data, and more options in generating reports.

With TDMS the user is enabled to construct his own data base using his own jargon rather than programing terms. He can modify his data base either online through a terminal, or offline if batch operations are preferable, as with large transactions. He can retrieve items from his data base through online inquiries. And he can manage his files by subsetting, merging, and sorting his data. TDMS has various error-detection and tutorial features to help the user. Translation programs are available to convert data from initial format to TDMS format. Provision is made for combining and rearranging the data, and for reduction and analysis of data. Finally, the user can request hard-copy reports derived from his data base or he can work with CRT displays of his data. Figure 5.4 shows graphic manipulation of TDMS data for a real estate application.

The programer's package includes a JOVIAL compiler, an editing system, and an online debugging facility. Allowance has been made for augmentation of language capability with other compilers, such as FORTRAN and COBOL. As in the Q-32 TSS, ADEPT incorporates TINT, a time-sharing interpreter. TINT is a simplified version of JOVIAL that includes many tutorial and error-checking procedures. The editor permits online composition, modification, deletion and insertion of text for

Figure 5.4.   AN EXAMPLE OF GRAPHIC DATA MANAGEMENT

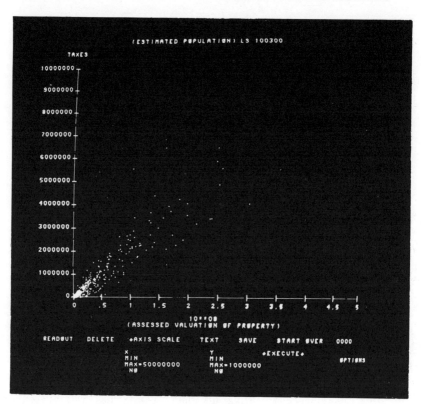

The user has light-penned "Execute" and received the above display. From the analysis options available beneath the graph, he chooses "Axis Scale" and specifies a maximum of 50,000,000 on the X-axis, and 1,000,000 on the Y-axis, in order to scale down the display.

programs or data. The debugger facilitates interactive description, tracing, and modification of programs and their data. The programer is free to select online or offline options in coding and debugging his programs.

5.5   USER EXPERIENCE

At the outset, it should be appreciated that it is quite difficult to write about user experience when most of the documented records are

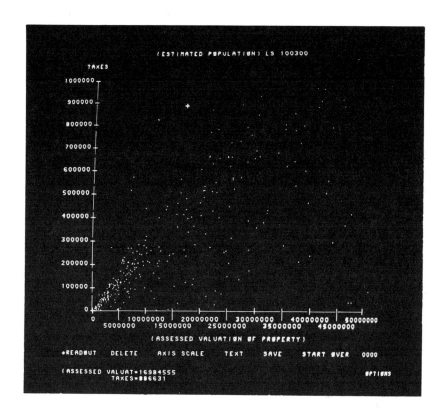

The rescaled display appears. With the "Readout" option, the user can light-pen any point to get its value. Here, the user has light-penned a city (identified by the program with a cross), which is shown (at bottom) to have an abnormally high ratio of taxes to assessed valuation.

concerned with central system experience and technical design considerations. What is needed are definitive, case histories of individual and group users, particularly those who have used these systems over long periods of time. While users have had such experiences, they have not distilled the essence of such experiences and put them down on paper, and as a result, it is necessary to reconstruct user trends indirectly and with many gaps. Although the sociology of information utilities may become a significant discipline in its own right, perhaps within the next decade, an awareness of user history in time-sharing communities was not part of the pioneering experience nor has it struck roots in current computer utilities. Current accounts of user history are still in the predisciplinary, anecdotal stage, including the present account.

It should be recalled that the Q-32 TSS was designed as an experimental prototype to demonstrate the technical feasibility of time-sharing. The design orientation was directed toward a viable working system rather than one tailored to incorporate user needs and requirements for specified user populations with well-defined tasks. As a result, the sample of users for the Q-32 TSS initially consisted of experienced programers; it then spread to include scientists and technicians working in specialized areas requiring familiarity with data processing. Except for a small percentage of applications, the users of these systems were specialists and cannot, by any stretch of the imagination, be considered as representative of the general population. Extrapolations to public use have to be made with great caution.

Three stages may be discerned in the evolution of computer utilities from the user's point of view—design, installation, and ongoing operations. The design stage is marked by the initial trial operations of the newly assembled system on a small number of "in-house" users, more often than not programers working on the system. In this stage, the system "hangs up" frequently from numerous hardware and software errors (mutual recrimination between overworked and embattled hardware and software types may reach paranoid heights); the executive goes through rapid gyrations from one week to the next; documentation is often absent; and the game is sheer survival—keep the system on the air. Nonprogramer users are mercifully shielded from the pandemonium of system birth.

In the installation stage, the first clients, including nonprogramer users, are introduced to the system; they are preoccupied with "getting on board." This is the equipment-griping and software-complaining stage. The system is still shaky and fails often, and it is more convenient to blame the equipment and the software than it is to blame one's own shortcomings. Users on the one side, and central system personnel on the other side, are often sensitive and defensive, looking for flaws in the opposing camp to placate the anxiety generated by the unreliability of system operations. Documentation may improve dramatically, since the system designers have to communicate in understandable English with users outside of the original design circle.

Numerous procedural changes are made in system services as users literally debug their way through the system with their exploratory, trial-and-error behavior in mastering time-sharing tools. A fair share of the credit should be given to users who carry system debugging to a point that programers could not possibly achieve on their own, either by deliberate intent or by inadvertent "goofs." Instead of programers and users working together as an integrated team to improve system operations, they often work at odds with much mutual suspicion. A frequent user stance is to try to "beat" the system.

An arrangement whereby user experience could be formalized and cultivated would lead to better understanding of fundamental system evolution on all sides. It would be recognized that numerous errors, omissions, and inconsistencies will unavoidably make their appearance in the central system and its tools, and such findings could be exploited for overall system improvement. Unfortunately, the computer world has not yet learned that the user must be comprehensively and meticulously tested together with the computer facility, and the user world has not yet learned to insist on thorough human testing of information services before they accept such services. This double blinder leads to inferior information services and an effective abdication of working management, resulting in a delegation of authority and responsibility for system effectiveness to the vagaries of technicians who are mostly concerned with "not rocking the boat."

The third stage, ongoing system operations, is characterized by improving system performance, consolidation of system services, a reduction in programing overhead to maintain the system, and the preoccupation of users with their application problems rather than with central system problems. Although these three stages are highly simplified stereotypes, they probably occur in some form for most systems. Some trouble-plagued time-sharing systems never reach productive operations and remain impaled on the second stage. Others, like the Q-32 TSS reach the third stage, in this case at a point where only one programer is necessary to maintain the system at a steady state.

Significant user experience can be profitably extracted during the third stage when the user has had sufficient opportunity to pursue and solve his problems and to start "taking over" the system to make it fit his own changing needs. For example, Fano and Corbató (1966) made some observations on three years of working experience with the MIT time-sharing system. They compared this system to a growing organism, largely because of the increasing tendency for the user community to exchange and share files, programs, and techniques. The users have "taken over" in the sense that they are the focus of system direction and change—most of the object programs were written by users rather than system programers. The users organized their own editorial and referee boards to decide on new commands and revised conventions, and to decide which information should be stored in public files. Joint problem-solving was starting to take place between users at different remote stations working with the same program and data base, as it did with students and teachers and with members of the same research team. Fano and Corbató predicted that user communities may tend to evolve toward closely knit real-time systems. This observation suggests a possible major evolutionary pattern for computer utilities—a trend away from individual online problem-solving toward team problem-solving, to cooperative real-time control.

The Dartmouth Time-Sharing System as described by Kemeny and Kurtz (1968) has undergone a similar evolution to that described for MIT. The Dartmouth system has been operating since May 1964. The similarity is strongest in regard to enthusiastic acceptance and widespread use by faculty and students, who comprise the basic user community. Kemeny and Kurtz claim that over 80 percent of the student population knows how to produce computer programs. Many other colleges are also aiming at eliminating computer illiteracy in their entire undergraduate curriculum. The United States Air Force Academy, for example, requires all cadets to take introductory computer science courses involving successful preparation and checkout of student-assembled programs. At Dartmouth the users apparently did not "take over" as extensively as at MIT. The modus vivendi was more in the form of a working partnership between faculty and undergraduates who developed the system as a team. This account, like the others, is largely anecdotal and is oriented toward central system development rather than the evolving experience of the user community.

To what extent has the MIT and the Dartmouth pattern of user evolution occurred in the SDC time-sharing systems? The trend from individual online problem solving to team problem-solving has occurred, but along different organizational lines corresponding to differences in the user communities. For example, SDC has a larger proportion of programer users who tend to use larger programs with longer running times than nonprogramer users at SDC. The MIT user statistics collected by Scherr, and the SDC user statistics described by McIsaac (1966), show considerably larger program jobs at SDC. McIsaac's statistics reveal that SDC users learned to exploit the system more fully within a one-year period—the same programs expanded and grew more complex, and their users consumed more computer time for their tasks. Clearly, user learning adaptation took place, leading to greater exploitation of system resources with increasing user experience, for all types of users.

Here is a fundamental property of computer utilities that often escapes the machine-minded system designer: the user is not a stationary consumer target, he is forever adapting and changing, and, with increasing experience and skill, he levies greater and more complex demands on system services. This explains why time-sharing systems typically operate at maximum capacity, lagging behind demand wherever they are in operation. The SDC experience is no exception to this rule.

Qualitative changes in problem-solving style occur as well as sheer quantitative changes in exploiting central system resources. Schwartz (1965) pointed out a suggestive example in programer problem-solving that occurred relatively early in the evolution of the Q-32 TSS. This trend was observed in the programer's use of memory dumps (the printout of the contents of large segments or blocks of computer memory). In initial Q-32 TSS operations, programers characteristically extracted large memory dumps while checking their programs and had them printed out offline. Requesting voluminous printouts is a buckshot approach that provides extra insurance for the programer who might lose some useful data if he didn't have complete records. In time, as programers got used to requesting and getting the information they needed online, they found that it was not really necessary to hoard all the information they could get. Eventually the use of memory dumps tapered off to the point where the feature was dropped. Online debugging, with selective rather than indiscriminate outputs, has proved adequate for most purposes.

Team problem-solving occurred in the general areas of linguistics, information retrieval, educational applications, graphics and display development, gaming and simulation, and in management information systems, corresponding to organizational entities at SDC. The emergence of real-time control over user applications could be found in computer-assisted instruction, man-computer bargaining and negotiation studies, and in Los Angeles Police Department applications. As at MIT, most of these examples are in the experimental stage.

The evolutionary trend from online applications for individual users, to team problem-solving, to real-time control has occurred only with highly specialized users; there is no experience in the full cycle of this evolution for individuals representing a significant segment of the general public for matters that involve public participation. Public use of mass information utilities still remains virgin territory for scientific exploration, even though we have had almost a decade of experience in pioneering time-sharing systems.

6

SELF-TUTORING:
AN ONLINE CASE HISTORY

6.1 INTRODUCTION

IN THIS CHAPTER we turn our attention from the system as a whole to the individual user and his personalized experience. Emphasis is also placed on experimental studies of human performance in computer utilities; as such, this chapter helps introduce Part III, which is concerned with scientific studies of the human use of information utilities. The example selected is indicative rather than representative of problems faced by computer users. It has the advantage of allowing the reader to understand how it feels to be a user, and how we might go about studying such individual experience in a systematic manner amenable to scientific test and evaluation.

This study was concerned with the effectiveness of individual user performance for an extended self-tutoring task in a time-shared computing facility. The investigation was an experimental case history of one individual (the author) following the TINT self-tutoring user manual from beginning to end in the SDC Q-32 Time-Sharing System at a Teletype console. (TINT is a user-oriented dialect of JOVIAL, an interpretive language adapted to time-sharing with many self-teaching features.) The methodology featured measurement of natural user behavior in which the user served as his own control in successive console sessions. The sample included 1861 user input commands collected over 18 hours at the teletypewriter terminal.

The quantitative results revealed some evidence for systematic learning and reinforcement effects; there were progressive tendencies toward higher productivity and lower error rates with increasing experience. The qualitative findings revealed that the numerous and diversified exercises facilitated familiarity with the elements and the varied services of the language. The chief drawback was exclusive reliance of the tutoring method on literal reproduction of the text by the user at his console. The chapter concludes with recommendations for more genuine interactive involvement between the user, the central system, and self-tutoring aids. This study is indicative of the predisciplinary experimental status of man-computer communication, reviewed in Part III, and of the need for a vast expansion of such research to meet the serious challenge of mass information utilities.

6.1.1   Objectives of the Study

A leading claim of the proponents of time-sharing systems is the alleged superiority of user effectiveness in a system environment that permits immediate knowledge of results and selective reinforcement of user behavior. Have these potential advantages been realized with the first generation of user-oriented languages? In a preliminary effort to bridge this experimental gap in the areas of user languages, the present study was designed to explore and measure individual performance in self-tutoring.

The objectives of this study fall under two key cateories, methodology and learning behavior. Methodologically, the basic problem was to observe, record, and measure normal user behavior in self-tutoring over an integral and coherent learning experience in a longitudinal manner, as opposed to a cross-sectional investigation in an artificial laboratory environment. The approach used was to adopt an experimental case-history technique, to study a single individual intensively throughout all the lessons of a self-tutoring user manual. The contents of the selected manual were designed as an integrated set of exercises leading to presumably adequate mastery of the object language so that the user could venture out by himself to solve his own problems. Natural behavior could be experimentally tapped by following the course of user performance in his progress through the exercises in the manual. Through the design and use of suitable behavioral units and associated measures of performance (as described below), the user serves as his own control. A guiding principle in the development of this methodology was to capitalize as much as possible on the normal resources of the system to provide records of user behavior and measures of his performance so that there would be minimal interference with his spontaneous pattern of learning.

The basic objective with regard to learning behavior was to test a number of hypotheses bearing on the presence or absence of learning and related effects using a variety of exploratory techniques. These include trend analyses of user productivity, error analyses, and tests for warmup and fatigue effects. Subjective reports were also collected to provide additional insight into attitude and motivation. In view of the limiting constraints of a sample of one, and the fact that the author is the sample, this study is put forth as strictly exploratory and suggestive.

6.2 METHOD

"The TINT Users' Guide" (Kennedy, 1965, with more recent addenda and corrections) was selected as the self-tutoring manual. TINT is an outline interpretive language, a dialect of JOVIAL oriented toward nonprogrammer users. TINT enables the user to compose and execute JOVIAL programs online at a Teletype. The manual includes 32 lessons covering TINT services and system facilities with numerous exercises ranging from programs only a few lines long to programs with approximately 30 statements. The first three lessons start with basic system commands (the SDC Q-32 Time-Sharing System, TSS) and then proceed to introductory TINT commands. Lessons 4 through 6 cover JOVIAL variables, some operators, and values. Lessons 7 through 10 are concerned with frequently used TINT commands such as PRINT, INSERT, and COPY, including a review exercise. Lessons 11 through 19 cover JOVIAL operators, arrays (tables), indexing, and various types of declarations. TINT debugging and input/output procedures are reviewed in lessons 20 through 22. Specialized JOVIAL functions and subroutines are covered in lessons 23 through 27, such as procedure declarations and trigonometric equations. The next two lessons provide an introduction to display scope capabilities and the last three exercises are given over to review. Numerous examples are usually presented in each exercise. They are diversified and often interesting and cover a broad range of applications. Figure 6.1 shows a sample page taken from "The TINT Users' Guide." User inputs are underlined; computer outputs are not underlined; explanatory notes appear under the Comments column. The mortgage illustration is straightforward and informative, and gives some indication of the versatility and limitations of TINT.

EXERCISE 17

REVIEW—ERWIN BOOK'S FRIENDLY FINANCE AND FACTORIAL
PROGAMS FEATURING FORMAT DECLARATIONS

Examples: Comments:
? START
✳   1.00 ITEM RATE F;   Erwin Book's friendly finance program.
✳   2.00 FORMAT MORTGAGE, 13, 3FII.2;
✳   3.00 READ RATE, PAYMENT, BALANCE, N;
✳   4.00 FORMAT HEADER, C✳MONTH INTEREST PRINCIPAL BALANCE✳; The character
✳   5.00 PRINT HEADER;   following the C serves as a bracketing
✳   6.00 FOR K=1, 1, N;   character. In this example, the ✳ is the
✳   7.00 BEGIN   bracketing character. Only the characters
✳   8.00 I=(RATE✳BALANCE) /12. +.5; P=PAYMENT−I; between the asterisks will
✳   9.00 BALANCE = BALANCE−P;   appear in the print line.
✳   10.00 PRINT MORTAGE, K, I/I00., P/I00., BALANCE/I00.;
✳   11.00 END
✳   12.00 ?EXECUTE
           RATE = ? 0.06
   PAYMENT = ? 5000 $ 50.00 / mo.
   BALANCE = ? 500000 $ 5000 loan
           N = ? 36

MONTH	INTEREST	PRINCIPAL	BALANCE
I	25.00	25.00	4975.00
2	24.87	25.13	4949.87
3	24.75	25.25	4924.62
4	24.62	25.38	4899.24
5	24.50	25.50	4873.74
6	24.37	25.63	4848.11
7	24.24	25.76	4822.35
8	24.11	25.89	4796.46
9	23.98	26.02	4770.44
I0	23.85	26.15	4744.29
II	23.72	26.28	4718.01
I2	23.59	26.41	4691.60
I3	23.46	26.54	4665.06
I4	23.33	26.67	4638.39
I5	23.19	26.81	4611.58
I6	23.06	26.94	4584.64
I7	22.92	27.08	4557.56
I8	22.79	26.21	4530.35
I9	22.65	27.35	4503.00
20	22.51	27.49	4475.51
21	22.38	27.62	4447.89
22	22.24	27.76	4420.13

(continued)

Figure 6.1.   SAMPLE PAGE FROM "THE TINT USERS' GUIDE"

In the introduction the user is told that it should take about eight hours to complete the lessons in the manual. He is instructed to copy the input messages for each example and wait for the appropriate computer response, both of which are indicated in the manual. If the user gets an error response from the system or if the computer output does not match the output in the text, the user is expected to examine his own inputs for possible errors and to correct them whenever he can so that his record will correspond verbatim with the text. The user is not given any exercises to perform on his own, nor any scoring technique to measure and evaluate his own progress.

The author, who is not a programer, served as the sole subject for this study. Although he had read about TINT in various publications previously, he never had any intensive experience working with TINT online. Neither did he have any substantive experience with JOVIAL, of which TINT is a subset. His attitude toward TINT and toward the users' manual at the start of the experiment was essentially positive.

The experimental procedure basically consisted of the subject going through the TINT manual, following each lesson in the order presented. The only systematic difference from normal usage consisted in intermittent querying of TSS to obtain a permanent record of the time (for performance measurement), and informal verbal recording of "critical" events as they occurred, inserted into the Teletype output so that all data —human and computer-produced—would be registered online in a single record. Thus the time-tagged Teletype record served as both the objective and subjective data base for this study.

All exercises were completed except for the last in the manual, which was a routine verbal review of TINT procedures, and except for a few instances in which some system facilities were not available during peak loads (e.g., tape drives), or when inexplicable machine, program, user, or combination errors occurred that could not be corrected. The author followed the self-tutoring sequence in the manual and did not solicit help or advice on technical content from anyone except for administrative matters relating to logging in and out of TSS. In this respect, the learning experience was strictly self-tutorial.

Twelve console sessions were required to go through the manual. As the end came into view, there was a tendency to have double sessions in the same day to complete the manual earlier. A session was terminated only at the end of a lesson to minimize uncontrolled user warmup effects. When all lessons were completed, the records were analyzed. In view of the exploratory objectives of this study and the limited time and resources available, the data were analyzed manually.

The basic behavioral unit was the user's input command, operationally defined as a new, discrete line of Teletype input terminated by a carriage return from the user. Examples include simple system commands such as !LOAD TINT to more complex inputs such as compound statements occurring on a single line, for example: A = 56; B= 34; C =3.45; D = 32.13; E = 4H(WORD); F = 5H(WORDS)—all having single line input and depression of the carriage return key in common. Each such user input was numbered successively for each session and was manually scored for errors. If an error was detected—either by an error message from the computer, or by mistyped characters, cancel or rubout indicators, or by comparison with the standard in the users' manual—the error was recorded and classified. Two types of errors were noted: typing errors (misspelling, cancel, rubout, or incorrect copy), and comprehension errors (all others, such as incorrect commands, illegal formats, or unsuccessful attempts to correct previous errors). Using the itemized responses for each session as indicated above, together with time tags and error indications, a variety of measures were derived that were related to performance. These are listed and described in Table 6.1.

Items 1 through 8 in Table 6.1, which are concerned with user commands and types of errors, have been explained above. The remaining entries in Table 6.1, starting with Frequency Distribution of Errors, stem from various hypotheses that were explored in this study. Item 9 refers to the raw score frequency distribution of strings of errors, varying in the observed data from isolated single errors to eight erroneous input lines in succession. This data is necessary to make comparisons against theoretical error models such as the Poisson distribution. Items 10, 11, and 12 refer to measures derived from observed frequency distributions of errors for each console session, including the mean, the variance, and the ratio between them. For the Poisson model, the mean is equal to the variance, and the observed variance in excess of the mean is useful in providing an estimate of maximum theoretical correlated variance for predicting user errors. This simple model is used widely in accident and human error research and in queuing theory, where the occurrence of given classes of events is associated with relatively low probabilities (see Machol, Tanner, and Alexander, 1965).

The last four measures are concerned with hypotheses on fatigue and warmup effects during the course of a console session. The fatigue hypothesis essentially states that the user is comparatively fresh and alert at the beginning of his console session and becomes progressively more bored and tired toward the end of the session, with such fatigue marked by lower productivity and higher error rates in the last part as compared to the first part of the session. The warmup hypothesis predicts an opposite response in user performance; it essentially states that the user forgets many of the fine details of console operation between sessions, and that only after a suitable warmup period using the console can he work up to his own optimal productivity and fewer errors in the second

Table 6.1. PERFORMANCE MEASURES

Name	*Description*
1. Total Commands	Number of discrete user input lines per console session.
2. User Commands per Minute	Index of user productivity.
3. Typing Errors	Rubouts, cancellations, grammatical and mis-spelling errors.
4. Comprehension Errors	All other types of errors.
5. Total Errors	Sum of typing and comprehension errors.
6. Percentage Typing Errors	Typing errors divided by total commands.
7. Percentage Comprehension Errors	Comprehension errors divided by total commands.
8. Percentage Total Errors	Total errors divided by total commands.
9. Frequency Distribution of Errors	Frequency counts of errors occurring singly, in doublets, three in a row, etc., for comparison against theoretical frequency distributions.
10. Error Distribution Mean	Observed empirical mean.
11. Error Distribution Variance	Observed empirical variance.
12. Mean/Variance	Ration of mean to variance—index of random occurrences of errors.
13. Errors in First Half	Errors occurring in the first half of all user commands for the given console session.
14. Errors in the Second Half	Errors occurring in the last half of all user commands for the given console session.
15. Commands in the First Half	Discrete user inputs occurring in the first half time period of the console session.
16. Commands in the Second Half	Discrete user inputs occurring in the last half time period of the given console session.

half of a console session. Obviously, both effects, among many others, influence user performance. The last four variables in Table 6.1 provide measures to obtain empirical feedback as to which of these effects is dominant over the other or whether they essentially cancel each other out.

6.3   RESULTS

Table 6.2 contains the basic empirical data for all performance variables for each of the 12 console sessions. In addition, means and standard deviations are listed for each variable. All measures have been described previously and none should offer any difficulty except perhaps for item 9, Frequency Distribution of Errors. The first entry reads "77/0; 5/1; 3/2; 2/4," which means that 77 user commands were correct; five user commands occurred as single, isolated errors; in three instances there were strings of two errors in a row; there were no instances of three errors in succession, and in two cases four errors in a row were observed. The mean and standard deviation for this variable were calculated by pooling all the data into a single frequency distribution.

Table 6.2 represents the raw data of the experiment. Each of the 17 performance measures are now reviewed with respect to descriptive statistics, relevant tests of hypotheses, and noteworthy points concerning methodology or findings.

6.3.1   User Productivity

The first performance measure, the duration of each console session, has several notable properties. Most sessions varied between one and two hours. Total console time for going through the exercises in the users' manual is 17.8 hours. Approximately 12 additional hours were spent in reading the exercises in advance or in reading related documentation from other sources.

Items 2 and 3 in Table 6.2, total commands and user commands per minute, are measures of user productivity. The entire self-tutoring sequence involved 1861 user commands with a mean of 155 commands and a standard deviation of 60.2 per console session, as shown in Table 6.3. Note that user commands per minute started at a slow rate, close to one per minute at the initial session, and rapidly climbed up to about two commands per minute by the fifth session and then bounced around the two-command rate thereafter. The rank-order correlation between user commands per minute and console session is .43; that is, user productivity rises with increasing experience. If the low score of 1.06 user commands per minute for session 10 is not included in this calculation—the only session with most of a long string of scored errors associated with central system deficiencies (at saturated system capacity levels) rather than user errors—then the same correlation without this anomalous session jumps up to .63, which is statistically significant at the 5 percent level, even with the small sample of 11 console sessions.

6.3.2 User Errors

Items 7, 8, and 9 in Table 6.2 refer to typing, comprehension, and total error rates (expressed as percentages) in the self-tutoring sequence. The overall average error rate is 13.8 percent, which represents about one erroneous user command for each seven that the system receives. The variability of error rates is large, ranging from 4 to 27 percent with a standard deviation of 6.6 percent, which is almost half as large as the mean. User productivity and user error rates are highly intercorrelated (product-moment correlation of —.88); that is, higher error rates are associated with fewer commands per minute. This high correlation is significant at the 1 percent level.

Learning effects may be tested with these error scores. For example, one would expect reduced error rates with increasing experience. The rank-correlation between total error rates and the sequence of console sessions is —.33 (decreasing error rates with increasing experience); with the anomalous session 10 removed (the "system error" session), the correlation goes up to —.56 which is significant at the 5 percent level, corroborating the hypothesis that error rates of a beginner tend to diminish with increasing experience. Typing and comprehension error rates show similar decreasing rates with increasing experience, but at low and nonsignificant correlation levels (rank-correlations of —.13 for both variables for all the data, and —.33 with session 10 deleted).

An interesting finding in the comparative results for typing and comprehension errors lies in the obtained standard deviations. Note in Table 6.2 that while average comprehension and typing error rates are similar (6.1 percent and 7.6 percent, respectively), the standard deviation for comprehension errors is almost twice as large as that for typing errors (5.1 percent and 2.6 percent, respectively). A statistical test for the correlated mean difference between these two standard deviations shows a *t*-value of 2.27, significant at the 5 percent level, which corroborates the hypothesis that the variability of comprehension errors is larger than the variability of typing errors. This finding supports the hypothesis that typing errors tend to be stable and consistent, independently of task or lesson

Table 6.2. EXPERIMENTAL PERFORMANCE

Performance Variables	Console Sessions 1	2	3	4	5	6	7	8	9	10	11	12	Mean	Std. Dev.
Session Time (min)	86	116	93	122	40	73	113	62	113	53	94	104	89.0	27.2
Total Commands	89	165	144	206	91	149	231	99	213	56	231	187	155	60.2
User Commands (min)	1.02	1.41	1.55	1.69	2.27	2.04	2.02	1.60	1.89	1.06	2.46	1.80	1.73	.43
Typing Errors	8	7	8	17	2	12	13	5	14	6	7	10	8.9	3.9
Comprehension Errors	11	21	9	18	2	5	6	15	8	9	8	9	10.1	5.5
Total Errors	19	28	17	35	4	17	19	20	22	15	15	19	19.1	9.1
Percentage Typing Errors	9.0	4.2	5.5	8.3	2.2	8.1	5.6	5.1	6.6	10.7	3.0	5.4	6.1	2.6
Percentage Comprehension Errors	12.4	12.7	6.2	8.7	2.2	3.3	2.6	15.1	3.8	16.1	3.5	4.8	7.6	5.1
Percentage Total Errors	21.4	16.9	11.7	17.0	4.4	11.4	8.2	20.2	10.4	26.8	6.5	10.2	13.8	6.6
Frequency Distribution of Errors	77/0; 5/1;2/3; 3/2;1/4;1/5; 2/4	137/0; 5/1;2/3; 1/4;1/5; 1/8	133/0; 9/1; 1/2; 1/6	171/0; 19/1; 8/2	87/0; 2/1; 1/2	132/0; 13/1; 2/2	212/0; 10/1; 4/1;1/2; 3/2; 3/3;1/5; 1/3	79/0; 4/1;1/2; 3/3;1/5;	191/0; 18/1; 2/2	41/0; 5/1; 2/2; 1/6	216/0; 6/1; 3/2; 1/3	168/0; 12/12;2/2; 1/3	.128	.526
Error Distribution Mean	.22	.19	.12	.18	.044	.166	.084	.228	.105	.306	.066	.104	.147	.077
Error Distribution Variance	.57	.87	.36	.22	.065	.129	.130	.637	.112	.926	.116	.147	.357	.326
Ratio of Mean/Variance	.39	.22	.35	.82	.68	.90	.65	.36	.94	.33	.58	.71	.577	.238
Errors in First Half	12	18	12	20	3	9	11	11	7	6	7	7	10.2	4.9
Errors in Second Half	7	10	5	15	1	8	8	9	15	9	8	12	8.9	3.9
Commands in First Half	38	65	87	104	41	61	101	51	119	26	121	89	75.2	35.3
Commands in Second Half	51	100	57	102	50	88	130	48	94	30	110	98	79.8	31.8

differences, whereas comprehension errors fluctuate more widely with task differences. This and related hypotheses can be examined more closely by looking at the comparative frequency distributions of errors.

Variables 10, 11, 12, and 13 in Table 6.2 are concerned with the frequency distributions of strings of errors, and some statistical properties of these error distributions. Two key hypotheses are examined with this data: to what extent does the data fit into a Poisson model of error distributions, and are there any systematic differences in the pattern of successive errors between typing and comprehension errors?

The full frequency distribution for occurrences of successive errors is given in Table 6.3. Note the Poisson-like structure of the frequency distribution, with highest scores at the low end rapidly tapering off to zero scores at nine successive errors. The first entry in Table 6.2 indicates that no errors occurred with 1644 input commands; the next that isolated single errors occurred in 108 commands; the next that errors were found in two successive commands in 28 instances, and so on up to the maximum string of eight erroneous commands in a row which occurred once. The mean of this distribution is .128, and the variance is .276. The mean and variance of the Poisson distribution are equal. Fitting the Poisson distribution to the observed mean, the Poisson model accounts for 46.4 percent of the observed variance. Theoretically, the maximum correlated variance obtainable from this data is the remaining 53.6 percent of the variance, which is equal to a correlation coefficient of .73 (calculated by taking the square root of .536). This preliminary analysis indicates that about half of the variance in the observed succession of errors varies randomly whereas the other half may be attributed to nonrandom effects. What bearing does this generalization have on the comparative pattern of typing and comprehension errors?

An examination of the observed frequency distributions reveals that typing errors tend to be distributed in short error strings, whereas comprehension errors account for the relatively nonrandom, longer error strings. Stated psychologically rather than statistically, typing errors tend to occur in short strings as more easily recognizable and quickly correctable errors. While comprehension errors can also be of the short string variety, and can often be quickly corrected, they may also occur as stubborn problems requiring extended testing of alternatives until an adequate solution is found—the extended testing is revealed in longer error strings.

It has been previously determined that increasing experience is associated with reduced error rates. Is increasing experience also associated

Table 6.3.   FREQUENCY DISTRIBUTION FOR OCCURRENCES
OF SUCCESSIVE ERRORS

Successive Errors	Observed Frequency
0	1644
1	108
2	28
3	8
4	3
5	2
6	2
7	0
8	1
9	0
Sum	1796

with reduced variation of errors? That is, does the variability of errors tend to diminish with increasing familiarity with the task? Item 12 in Table 6.2, the variance of errors for each console session, permits a test of this hypothesis. The rank-correlation between ordered sessions and observed variance is —.26 for all 12 sessions—later sessions tend to be characterized by smaller variance. If the "anomalous" session 10 is deleted, the correlation jumps to —.50, which is significant at the 5 percent level for a one-tailed test, for the hypothesis as stated above. From the viewpoint of user errors alone, as distinct from user and system errors combined, the data appears to support the twin contentions that individual learning is marked by reduced variability of errors as well as reduced levels of errors.

6.3.3   Warmup and Fatigue Effects

The last four measures in Table 6.2 permit contrasting tests for warmup and fatigue effects. The data show an average of 10.2 errors in the first half of each session, against an average of 8.9 in the second half. This small difference in favor of the warmup hypothesis is not statistically significant (correlated mean-difference t-value of 1.1). The productivity measures show a similar trend—higher productivity in the second half of each session as compared to the first half (79.8 vs. 75.2 commands, respectively). The mean difference again is not statistically significant (correlated t-value of .77). These results indicate that one individual sitting at the console for periods usually varying between one and two hours, will have a small, consistent, but nonsignificant tendency toward higher productivity and fewer errors in the second half of such sessions as compared to the first half.

6.3.4 Qualitative Results

The qualitative results essentially consist of the open-end verbal comments inserted into the Teletype record at the time they occurred during any given console session. These results, after some preliminary editing and classification of responses, are assembled in Tables 6.4 and 6.5. The responses are subsumed under two major categories—(1) task problems (Table 6.3), in which the comments are directed primarily toward correct user inputs or to understanding the substantive content of the exercise, and (2) attitudinal problems (Table 6.5), which are more concerned with motivational factors and changing subject evaluation of the self-tutoring sequence. These categories were arrived at inductively after all the comments were assembled and reviewed. It was quite obvious that together with the ongoing commentary on task problems there was also an ongoing evaluation of the self-tutoring sequence and the central computing system, a kind of pitting of the user against the "system." Tables 6.4 and 6.5 list the main comments under task and attitudinal headings in essentially chronological order.

6.4 INTERPRETATION

The interpretation is approached from viewpoints of the objectives, methodology, and learning effects. Each is broken down into key areas oriented toward extensions of time-sharing user studies in self-tutoring.

6.4.1 Methodological Interpretation

The claim was made in the introduction that this investigation was designed as an experimental study of natural user behavior. To what extent is this allegation valid? The study was conducted with a known and reproducible set of stimulus inputs, the lesson sequence of the TINT users' manual. User and system responses were recorded on the Teletype output and collected over essentially the entire set of exercises

Table 6.4. CHRONOLOGICAL LISTING OF OPEN-END TASK
            COMMENTS

1. Learning how to snag a console and log into the system successfully was a key problem for the first few sessions.
2. Lots of trouble with punctuation and omission of end-of-statement symbols (; and $ for TINT).
3. Continual trouble with conflicting use of " and ? symbols to address TINT after interactions with the central system.
4. Problems with inconsistent rules on allowable spaces between symbols; e.g., equations may have spaces between symbols but such commands as ?EXECUTE and some parentheses may not.
5. Some errors in the text had to be corrected for proper solutions.
6. Punctuation and grammatical errors persist.
7. TINT and system errors occur often enough to throw the user off stride.
8. Development of single glance, complete input line typing technique replaces haphazard symbol and phrase hunting and pecking at the Teletype.
9. Repetition of basic procedures and commands leads to abbreviations and shortcuts.
10. Lessons are not graded or ordered according to difficulty levels and require unequal time for completion.
11. Had to quit system when HALT and other techniques could not break into an endless factorial loop.
12. Considerable trouble with alternate tape procedures and with computer operator communication.
13. Use of product-moment correlation example very helpful in seeing alternate possible approaches and solutions.
14. Tendency toward increasing substitution of own examples and use of different values for examples than those given in the text.
15. Graphic displays were a welcome change of pace from straight typing.

in the manual. Recorded user behavior was subjected to various operationally defined scoring techniques to extract quantitative measures bearing on user performance. These measures were statistically analyzed to determine whether they satisfied various hypotheses on user productivity, error behaviors, and warmup-fatigue effects. All of this was done within the framework of an applied set of user tasks for a self-tutorial manual, on a time-sharing system under normal operations, and with a frequently used program system (TINT) for this facility. These above characteristics comprise an application of experimental method to real-world activities as opposed to an esoteric experiment conducted within the artificial confines of a laboratory.

Further characteristics of this type of real-world experimentation should be noted. One is the test of a wide variety of hypotheses—an

Table 6.5. CHRONOLOGICAL LISTING OF OPEN-END ATTITUDINAL
COMMENTS

1. Initial fear of making errors was soon dispelled by system permissiveness.
2. Initial expectation that TINT is an easy language was soon replaced by a growing conviction of its difficulty.
3. TINT manual based entirely on rote copying of material.
4. User ease and training time underestimated; 8-hour claim for console time does not hold for nonprogramers.
5. Many examples presume extensive knowledge of previous programming.
6. Good manual for learning how to type TINT messages, but not for learning how to use the language on your own.
7. Learning rules, symbols, punctuation, and techniques are lost rapidly if not used often.
8. No user problems or performance scores in text; knowledge of progress hard to evaluate.
9. Variety of examples are impressive, but explanations of steps and method of solution almost nonexistent—have to check out documented sources.
10. Decided to drop direct copying of text and start to experiment with related examples on own.
11. Definite feeling of having to feed inputs to the system continually while on the air—relief of this pressure was noticed when system was temporarily down.
12. Complete reliance on self-tutoring is an extreme position; easy availability of knowledgeable teacher in conjunction with manual would accelerate learning enormously.
13. Errors involving the computer operator can be embarrassing.
14. Printed text in manual is preferable to explanations clattered out by Teletype which are hard to read and study with all the noise and physical obstructions; the last question-answer exercises were almost entirely worthless when explanations of questions were easily accessible in the text.

omnibus test approach bearing on many facets of user performance, as opposed to the single critical hypothesis approach. The orientation of this study was exploratory and open-ended rather than a test of a fixed set of preconceived hypotheses. Subjective responses were collected in addition to objectively scored measures of performance to extend the base of the study and to provide independent qualitative checks and balances on the quantitative findings. Another distinctive methodological feature was the use of the case history approach. As mentioned in the introduction, this longitudinal approach has not been applied to user studies in time-sharing and is a necessary step for intensive study of individual behavioral changes in the time-sharing milieu. As demonstrated in this study, numerous measurements on a single individual (almost 2000 input commands) permitted extensive statistical tests to be applied to a variety of hypotheses in which the individual effectively serves as his own control. While it unquestionably would have been preferable to apply such tests to more than one case history to determine whether results are generalizable, it is nevertheless worthwhile to put forth the findings on one individual as a methodological and exploratory contribution to facilitate the work of others.

Turning from general to specific methodology, several limitations and areas for improvement may be noted. A basic premise on the quantitative side of this study is the assumption that all discrete input commands are equal and linearly additive in measuring user performance. This assumption has great simplifying power which permits the investigator to pool all user commands into a single sample for comparative analysis. But it courts the risk of adding apples and oranges. For example, simple "read" values for many tables and equations were each counted as separate input commands, providing that they were accompanied by a carriage return; on the other hand, complex input commands consisting of compound statements were also counted as one command. It would seem appropriate in future studies to distinguish between different types of input commands to see whether systematic differences hold between such commands with respect to various measures of user performance. For example, higher error rates are probably more likely to occur with complex than with simple user inputs.

A similar limitation may be directed at the measures of user errors in this study. Typing errors and comprehension errors may be broken down into finer categories. A thoroughgoing inductive approach would be ideal, one in which unique types of errors are separately tabulated and then combined into larger aggregates as warranted by the empirical data and by logical considerations. A large sample of users and errors would be essential for such work to arrive at stable quantitative findings. The total sample of 230 errors in this study preclude fine-grain analyses of different varieties of errors.

Another methodological limitation of this study stems from the reliance on manual scoring techniques for user performance. Frequency counts of user input commands, classification of commands, error indications, error tabulations, time tagged data, and measures of computer time are usually available within existing time-sharing systems or can be obtained from raw data through appropriate recording and reduction programs. The exploratory nature of this study and the limited time and budget constraints did not permit such program developments to occur.

The manual scoring effort would have been prohibitive if a diversified sample of users were employed in this study.

6.4.2. Learning Behavior

Even within the methodological constraints of this study, as noted above, systematic learning effects were identified. User productivity progressed from roughly one command per minute to two commands per minute throughout the course of the self-tutoring sequence. (These figures are consistent with average user productivity rates found in larger user samples; see Sackman, 1967.) User errors decreased with growing experience, very roughly from 20 percent to 10 percent error rates. Error rates were highly and inversely correlated with user productivity levels. This inverse relationship between errors and productivity has been observed in other time-sharing systems (Sackman and Gold, 1968). It was also found that earlier sessions were characterized by higher variability in the occurrence of successive errors whereas error fluctuations became more stabilized in later console sessions. Even though considerable variation in performance was seen in different console sessions, most of these learning effects were statistically significant.

The analysis of errors into typing and comprehension categories also revealed systematic learning effects. Typing errors tended to occur more randomly and in isolated instances whereas comprehension errors were consistently associated with longer successions or strings of error. This finding fits into the simple interpretation that typing errors are usually easier to detect and correct than comprehension errors.

These somewhat theoretical observations have practical bearing on the effectiveness of the Teletype terminal for man-computer communication in time-shared facilities. They suggest that each user, for better or worse, may exhibit a fairly consistent level of typing errors. The typing errors, which comprise perhaps half of all user errors, represent a hard core of errors that occur more or less randomly and unpredictably and are not easily subject to change. Comprehension errors, on the other hand, represent the more variable segment of user errors, fluctuating with task differences and subject to reduction as the user becomes increasingly familiar with the object problem. Comprehension errors are potentially more predictable and more amenable to training—they tend to disappear when the underlying problem is solved and to be replaced by new problems. The Teletype console, then, carries the twin burden of a relatively slow, character-by-character input rate, and for each user, an added penalty of a relatively unpredictable and virtually unavoidable typing error rate. The limitations, in conjunction with problem-oriented comprehension errors, are apparently key factors in determining effective user productivity at his console, at least as far as the data in this study is concerned, since productivity was highly related to error rates.

The qualitative findings help cast the results of this study in broader perspective. Perhaps the most critical of these factors is the basic design and structure of the TINT self-tutoring sequence—the ready-made, "cookbook" instruction sequence in which the user simply retypes at his console the input lines that are literally spelled out for him in the text. What kind of learning does this technique provide?

Several types of learning do in fact occur. One learns to get on the system, to converse with TINT, and get off the system. One also learns many of the mechanics of the language—the basic input statement, frequently used commands, the vagaries of grammar and punctuation, the omnipresence of various types of user errors, ways to identify and correct them, the overall structure and the various services in the TINT repertoire, and a broad range of simple applications of TINT. Rote copying of the self-tutoring sequence facilitates the above skills. When it is taken into consideration that the original TINT users' guide was conceived, designed, and produced in only one month, the above payoff for the user is impressive and the overall cost-effectiveness of this manual is comparatively high.

This case history illustrates an anachronistic lag in the evolution of time-sharing: time-sharing systems are still using well-established batch-processing habits to formulate and solve man-computer problems. Such formulation and problem solving are still being done basically at the desk, away from the computer, as they were and are still being done with batch systems. The computer run in both systems still serves essentially as an external machine test for ideas conceived and organized away from the computer.

The qualitative results in Tables 6.4 and 6.5 mention some desirable changes to improve the self-tutoring effectiveness of TINT. These include exercises of graduated difficulty levels, problems that the user has to solve on his own, definitive statements of problems and specification of desired solutions, objective scoring techniques to measure and evaluate user progress, encouragement of self-experimentation with system techniques, some kind of access to a knowledgeable expert to compensate for self-tutoring pitfalls, elimination of descriptive online tutorial material that can be presented more cheaply and effectively in book form, and allowance for more leisurely reflection and exploration of alternatives online with less pressure on the user to keep feeding the computer. While some self-tutoring programs, such as the BASIC system at Dartmouth (Becker, 1967), use graduated difficulty levels, some branching techniques, and provide some performance sources for users, there is no system yet available that incorporates all the above features for self-taught programing.

It was previously mentioned that the qualitative results have an important bearing on the qualitative findings. We are now in a position to state what that relationship is. In essence, the quantitative results of this study apply primarily to the online mechanics of implementing well-formulated and previously solved problems; they do not apply to genuine user problem formulation and problem solving. The learning effects, the error analyses, and the tests for warmup and fatigue effects are primarily concerned with mechanical implementation of problems that had been completely conceived and spelled out before they ever reached the console. Studies devoted to the more fundamental processes of formulation and solution of problems remain to be done; if such studies are to exhibit any validity, they should include relevant user behavior away from the console as well as at the console. Perhaps most online tasks are mechanical runs and routine tests of well-formulated problems, rather than cooperative man-computer ventures into the unknown. Perhaps Rodin's nineteenth-century "Thinker" is still the prototype for human problem-solving. Even in the world of computers, online human behaviors are still secondary tributaries to the primary mainstream of "manual" decision-making. Part III will spell out how embarrassingly little we know about how to use a computer as an active real-time partner to help people grapple with problems.

PART III

EXPERIMENTAL INVESTIGATION OF HUMAN PROBLEMS IN INFORMATION UTILITIES

7

THE SCIENTIFIC STATUS

OF

MAN-COMPUTER

COMMUNICATION

THE PRINCIPAL CHALLENGE of public information services lies in consecrating its use for social excellence. This is not merely an exhortation toward moral rearmament; it means that each level and facet of society has a responsibility and share in formulating the goals and specifying the means to achieve social excellence in the implementation and evolution of computerized information services. No single individual, organization, group, or professional class has the necessary knowledge, wisdom, and resources to do the job on its own—an open, cooperative endeavor is required. And such cooperative social action should be guided by the best method available—scientific method applied to open social experimentation.

The thesis developed in the following pages is that, for a great variety of reasons, conventional scientific traditions and techniques to test the human use of computers are inadequate to meet the challenge of public information services. A much broader program of social experimentation, involving extensive cooperation of technological, municipal, and participating groups, is urgently needed to study and formulate principles for the human use of computer utilities. The knowledge necessary for effective interaction of man and machine will not become available under current arrangements.

The nature and the basis of the above position is developed in the two chapters of this section. First, the status and prospects of the scientific study of man-computer communication are reviewed, with special emphasis on problems and pitfalls. The next chapter is a statement of leading research priorities for emerging public information services.

Over the single human generation that electronic computers have been on the social scene, technological developments in computer communications have been evolving inexorably toward mass computer services. But, as indicated earlier, parallel growth of effective man-computer communication has lagged far behind. This chapter traces the background of man-computer communication, reviews the techniques that have been developed to study man-computer communication, the scope and nature of available findings, and the critical gaps that need to be filled in to move toward the information utility.

The author has previously reviewed a substantive part of the material that follows. The reviews have appeared in an earlier book (1967) and in other publications. A description of the main points of all studies that are cited is beyond the scope of this chapter. Instead, the original studies or the reviews in which they are found are cited, and then only key contributions are briefly described. This procedure makes it possible to follow leading trends in experimental studies in man-computer communication without bogging down in details. For the more controversial areas, the detailed reviews and original sources should be consulted.

7.1 THE COMMAND CONTROL LEGACY

As the first of the large-scale real-time systems, SAGE air defense pioneered in online man-computer communication and produced the earliest studies involving large subject samples. In SAGE, military operators had consoles equipped with alphanumeric keyboards and verbally tagged dials and switches for composing and sending messages to the central computer. The consoles had two types of cathode ray tube displays; they were equipped with a light gun in conjunction with pushbutton switch actions to select and control displayed information. The console and its controls had to be designed to permit the average enlisted man to master its operation (see Figure 7.1). Even though a wealth of empirical data was being ground out every day in SAGE man-computer operations, relatively little of it was experimentally systematized and organized for the computer science community—for a variety of reasons, including military security, proprietary industrial information, and a lack of appropriately trained human engineers and social scientists who had access to SAGE man-computer communications.

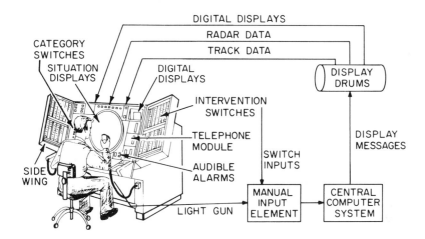

Figure 7.1. MAN-COMPUTER COMMUNICATION IN SAGE

In its role as pioneer in real-time systems, SAGE made many brilliant starts and suffered from abysmal failures. For example, Figure 7.1 represents an online man-computer configuration that was designed and working as a prototype for SAGE in the early 1950's. Yet this is conceivably a sneak preview of the public information utility of 1984. The use of a rapidly updated geographic display, the option of a light gun to pinpoint data, and the depression of a small number of pushbuttons to request display information for each human message sent to the computer have not been fundamentally improved upon, even today. On the other hand, the relatively slow response to human requests, the crude error indicators (operators knew about errors, but were given no information on the nature of the errors), the lack of computer feedback to many human actions, and the neglect of computer-assisted instruction in training individual operators (this cultural lag has only recently been corrected), all betray primitive aspects of man-computer communication which are now considerably refined and perfected.

The experimental studies reviewed are three by the author and a fourth by Murphy, Katter, Wattenbarger, and Poole (1962). These studies include a large-scale field test involving some 800 military personnel at Air Defense Direction Centers and Combat Centers in the northeastern part of the United States (Sackman and Munson, 1964), a follow-on test of the 58,000 man-computer messages collected in the original field test, and a field test comparison of improved computer programs for SAGE man-computer communication (Sackman, 1964). The Murphy study was a field test comparing alternative modes of automated operator feedback in composing messages for the computer.

These studies revealed the great behavioral complexity of online man-computer communication in SAGE, and sketched many of the experimental parameters. From the point of view of overall system performance, problems in man-computer communication were rated on a par with problems in equipment, man-to-man communication, and with the simulation techniques used in the large field study. The percentage of notable problems reported in each of these four areas was approximately the same. This finding stresses the importance of relating man-computer problems to the total system context, including the surrounding social environment.

As might be expected from the general literature on human error, individual differences were rampant. They covered the entire scale from almost error-free performance to the error-prone types who were continually frustrated by illegal messages. Error rates rose for all individuals as the rate of man-computer messages rose and as the human work load increased. Clearly the detection and remedial training of error-prone individuals is a major task in the design and development of a man-computer communication systems, particularly those that involve users with large skill differences, as in public information utilities.

The design of user feedback for error messages turned out to be critical in SAGE. When a military operator activated an illegal message, he would receive an audio and visual signal (e.g., a tinkling bell and the letter "I" on his display) which told him in no uncertain language that his message was illegal. However, he was not given any clue as to why his message was erroneous. The computer program had this information (e.g., a nonexistent track number or an interceptor heading greater than 360°) but did not pass it along to the operator. Left to his own devices, the operator frequently could not find out what he did that was wrong, and he had to try another tack or just do something else. If the system has explicit remedial information on human error, it should get that information to the user as directly and clearly as possible. This piece of commensense information is given mere lip service today.

The types of man-computer errors that were uncovered raised many questions. An empirical classification of errors was difficult to arrive at because of the confusing variety of errors. They varied with crew position, load levels, and individual differences. An empirical taxonomy of user errors, cross-validated across systems, is sorely needed for generalized computer utilities.

Certain types of systematic errors occurred under heavy load conditions. For example, as individual work load rose with very high man-computer message rates, all positions showed a sharp increase in the proportion of useless, repetitive messages. This occurred when operators had more work to do in a shorter period of time and at the same time that the computer program gave longer display response times. As a result, operators would irritably bang away at their activate buttons or shoot their light guns, repeating the same message over and over again. This example of computer-induced repetition-compulsion reveals the close relationship between system response time and user error rates.

The experimental results on SAGE system response time in relation to operator needs highlighted the variability and adaptability of the human user. The findings conclusively showed that computer responses on the order of five seconds were better liked and more operationally effective than response times on the order of 10 or 15 seconds. But the findings also showed that with adequate training and exposure, crews learned to adapt to and live with longer response times, particularly if they received cues from the computer as to how long they would have to wait and whether their message was legal. The lesson that emerges is that users like a fast conversational exchange from the computer if they can get it, but that they can also learn to work with long response times if they receive adequate training and appropriate cues from the system.

To round out the response time picture, the Murphy study showed that very fast outputs from the computer (which spurred the crew to work at excessive speed) resulted in great increases in error rates. And these exaggerated error rates remained abnormally high even with corrective design features to help the operator. These various findings point to an underlying psychological pattern of real-time pacing on the part of the user for a given task, a type of real-time behavioral dynamics we have only begun to tap in man-computer communication.

The study conducted by the author on the field sample of 58,000 operator messages was the only systematic sample of SAGE man-computer messages that was gathered for a credible combat setting. A simple tabulation of message frequencies revealed many messages that were never used by air defense crews. Others were used with extremely high frequencies. There are roughly 500 unique messages for SAGE operators.

Systematic and stable differences in man-computer message rates were found among the various crew positions. Of particular importance was the correlation between military rank and message rates. The command staff had lower message rates than the operational staff, and the Sector Commander typically showed the lowest man-computer communication rates of the entire crew. Other studies, including IBM investigations in management information systems (Dunlop, 1968), reveal a similar reluctance on the part of executives to communicate directly with computers, particularly if there are subordinates available to get the desired information.

Even when artifacts of the test situation were taken into account, numerous positional messages were uncovered that were apparently nothing more than deadwood, messages that took up valuable program space and computer time but produced nothing in the real user world. Other switch actions were used extremely frequently; many of these could have been broken down into more refined, special-purpose messages. The lesson here should now be apparent: a continuing empirical census of user message traffic should be taken in man-computer systems to cultivate and enhance useful features and to eliminate deadwood and stumbling blocks. No designer or team of designers is so clever that they can anticipate in advance what the user will actually work with among all the options available, nor how well each feature will work, unless they get continuing feedback from real-world system experience. The acid test of reality is the indispensable guide for continually improved system design throughout the life-cycle of the object system.

Some significant methodological advances accrued from this early SAGE experience in techniques for investigating man-computer communication. These are discussed under three general areas: the collection and analysis of man-computer data; online questionnaire techniques; and real-world system testing.

Although computers have opened new vistas in the collection and analysis of system data, techniques for recording and reducing digital data are still primeval. The lack of an empirical scientific tradition in computer system development looms large in explaining this sorry state of affairs. In SAGE, recording and reduction facilities were grafted onto the operational computer program after its configuration had been fully established. Every new recording/reduction scheme had to be gerrymandered to find a place in the operational program system.

With regenerative recording, described in Figure 7.2, it became possible to capture completely all digital events pertaining to man-computer interaction, and to play these events back in real-time for unlimited experimental exploration and manipulation at the leisure of the experimenter. Since regenerative recording deals with man-computer communication in real time—the way it is as it happens—we had a powerful new capability to conduct real-world experimentation.

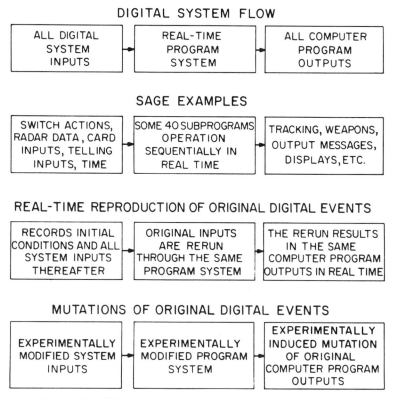

DIGITAL SYSTEM FLOW

| ALL DIGITAL SYSTEM INPUTS | REAL-TIME PROGRAM SYSTEM | ALL COMPUTER PROGRAM OUTPUTS |

SAGE EXAMPLES

| SWITCH ACTIONS, RADAR DATA, CARD INPUTS, TELLING INPUTS, TIME | SOME 40 SUBPROGRAMS OPERATION SEQUENTIALLY IN REAL TIME | TRACKING, WEAPONS, OUTPUT MESSAGES, DISPLAYS, ETC. |

REAL-TIME REPRODUCTION OF ORIGINAL DIGITAL EVENTS

| RECORDS INITIAL CONDITIONS AND ALL SYSTEM INPUTS THEREAFTER | ORIGINAL INPUTS ARE RERUN THROUGH THE SAME PROGRAM SYSTEM | THE RERUN RESULTS IN THE SAME COMPUTER PROGRAM OUTPUTS IN REAL TIME |

MUTATIONS OF ORIGINAL DIGITAL EVENTS

| EXPERIMENTALLY MODIFIED SYSTEM INPUTS | EXPERIMENTALLY MODIFIED PROGRAM SYSTEM | EXPERIMENTALLY INDUCED MUTATION OF ORIGINAL COMPUTER PROGRAM OUTPUTS |

Figure 7.2.   STANDARD REGENERATIVE RECORDING

Figure 7.2 summarizes the basic operation of standard regenerative recording and introduces the notion of regenerative mutations. The first row provides the main headings for the rest of the diagram, showing the basic digital system flow of inputs-program-outputs. The second row indicates examples of these three components for SAGE. The third row illustrates direct playback of the referent real-time computer run. The fourth row shows that experimental modifications of inputs, or changes in the program system, or both, result in mutations of the original program outputs. The technical details of regenerative recording are discussed in the author's book (1967).

A powerful property of the generalized regenerative mutation illustrated in Figure 7.2 is that it represents a paradigm of a controlled digital experiment. Program outputs from direct playback comprise an objective, rigorous standard against which the experimental changes may be measured. The modified inputs or revised portions of the computer program are the experimental changes, the two main sources of independent variables. The unchanged portions of the input and the unchanged programs are the experimental controls in the mutation rerun. The change in outputs is the dependent variable, or the experimental results of the mutation rerun. Simple regenerative reruns are direct experimental replications of real-time digital events. Thus any modification of a regenerative rerun is, in principle, an automatic controlled experiment in relation to simple playback, an experimental variation of a set of original real-world events. Both simple playback and systematic mutations were successfully used in SAGE, and these applications can be generalized, in principle, to any online man-computer system.

Paper and pencil questionnaires provided cheap, fast, and valuable insight into human attitudes and overall system performance. The questionnaire results provided valuable checks and balances against the reliability and validity of automatically collected data. A simple rating scale on system service correlated substantively with system load levels, frame time, and known system malfunctions. Open-end items provided valuable leads on program and equipment defects and on improved display format and presentation. Objective questionnaire items lend themselves easily to online polling techniques. Such techniques automatically allow the system to get on-the-spot fedback from the users, which is of vast interest for computer utility development, but which has been consistently neglected in man-computer communication.

The next major phase in the development of scientific method could be the emergence of real-world experimentation—the systematic test and evaluation of real world events in living social context. This trend is being reinforced from many diverse sources, technological and social, catalyzed by the computer, which makes it possible to collect and analyze not only unprecedented amounts of data, but also qualitatively new species of data. An example is regenerative recording, which makes it possible to capture live system events in the raw for unlimited playback and analysis at a later time. Operational simulation techniques, as employed in SAGE, make it possible to conduct numerous controlled experiments on a large scale in the field, using the operational system as its own test bed, at low cost in time, effort, and money. The command and control experience, as in SAGE and in the manned spaceflight programs, is a preview of a broad panorama of possible and potential social experimentation, conducted in real time in the real world. The implications of this experimental philosophy are developed later in working toward a framework for real-world social experimentation with computer utilities.

7.2 BEHAVIORAL IMPLICATIONS OF TIME-SHARING USER STATISTICS

The pioneering time-sharing systems were breaking new ground and had to develop empirically a whole set of statistics for user traffic, scheduling efficiency, and central system accounting procedures. They worked out a number of simulation and recording procedures to time and measure various characteristics of users and the central system. These procedures led to preliminary descriptive data on users, problem tasks, and man-computer effectiveness in system timing and system capacity. The leading studies from which these data were gathered include Scherr (1967) and Raynaud (1967) at MIT, using the Compatible Time-Sharing System; Totscheck (1965) and McIsaac (1966) using the SDC Time-Sharing System; and Shaw (1965) and Bryan (1967) at RAND with the JOSS system. A summary of user findings is found in Table 7.1.

Some of the more striking aspects of user behavior in time-sharing from Table 7.1 should be stressed. First, the vast part of the user's time is spent away from the terminal. This means that man-computer problem-solving is predominantly a human-directed process, involving mostly introspection or man-to-man communication. Man-computer symbiosis may be a semantically and behaviorally misleading concept in this context. These descriptive data suggest that the user formulates and imaginatively rehearses solutions to problems at his desk, and that the computer is primarily employed for follow-up implementation, test, and verification of human ideas. According to this interpretation, the computer and its information services represent a tactical tool in human problem-solving, with the user as the directive source of strategic intelligence—hardly a symbiotic relationship between man and machine.

The other data on user pacing seem to fit into the suggested human problem-solving scheme. The single day seems to be the basic unit for user self-scheduling. Most of the day is apparently employed in figuring out new or revised problem strategy and tactics, coupled with a single session at the terminal to try out the new variations and see if they work. The single day seems to emerge as the basic working unit for human turnaround time.

Table 7.1. PRELIMINARY SUMMARY OF USER CHARACTERISTICS IN TIME-SHARING *

Timing and Pacing

1. More often than not, the time-sharing user will employ a terminal only once a day, and not every day; this rule is subject, however, to numerous exceptions for individual users and between different users.
2. The typical user spends between half an hour to an hour at his console at each session; this rule is also subject to great intra- and inter-subject variability.
3. Approximately 10% of the typical user's total working time is spent in man-computer communication at his console, whereas 90% of his working time is spent away from the console.
4. His median input rate is at the general order of one request every half minute, whereas his average input is roughly one per minute at the terminal.
5. Half of the time he will insert a new command some 10 seconds after he has received a complete output from the computer; only on comparatively rare occasions will he wait as long as a minute before making a new request after receiving an output.
6. The ratio of human time to central proessor time is at the general order of magnitude of 50:1; that is, approximately 50 seconds of elapsed human time is associated with one second of computer operating time on the user's program.

System Effectiveness

7. Users with tasks requiring relatively small computations become increasingly uncomfortable as computer response time to their requests extends beyond 10 seconds, and as irregularity and uncertainty of computer response time increases. Users with problems requiring much computation tolerate longer intervals, up to as much as 10 minutes for the largest jobs.
8. As system load rises with increasing numbers of users, system response time increases, and, at high-load levels, both central system effectiveness and user performance tend to deteriorate.

Individual Differences

9. The computer is generally more verbose than the human; each line of human input tends to be accompanied, roughly speaking, by about two lines of computer output. New users tend to be more verbose; more terse responses occur with increasing experience.
10. Programmers seem to use, on the average, larger object programs and more computer time than nonprogrammers.
11. As the central system matures, and as users become more experienced, there is a tendency for object programs to grow in size and complexity, and for experienced users to require more computing time and a larger share of system capacity. Experienced users are more adept in exploiting central system resources.

    * SOURCE: Harold Sackman, *Man-Computer Problem Solving* (Princeton: Auerbach, 1970).

As described in Chapter 6, the author (1970) conducted an experimental case history study of individual performance at a time-sharing terminal for an extended self-tutoring task. The results reinforce the interpretation that rapid conversational interaction with the computer implies routine rather than innovative decision-making and problem-solving at the console. No claims are made at this point for the validity of what might be called the humanistic problem-solving hypothesis—the hypothesis that man-computer problem-solving is primarily a human-directed phenomenon that is individually unique and highly personalized. The hypothesis is introduced at this point as a key behavioral issue, a problematic issue that may be operationally defined and critically tested when further user data under controlled experimental conditions becomes available.

Raynaud has demonstrated that users are willing and able to live with delays in online computer response up to as much as 10 minutes, depending upon the type of job submitted. Figure 7.3 shows the results of his online poll of user satisfaction on a scale varying from 0 to 9 for various job categories ranging from small to large jobs at the MIT time-sharing system (CTSS). Raynaud's findings hint at the great potential of online polling. The data in Figure 7.3 supports the previously mentioned conclusion from command and control experience that user satisfaction with system response time is a complex function of the user's skill, attitudes, his task, and the job setting, subject to modification by training.

Another noteworthy feature of these early statistical and accounting studies is the striking learning and adaptation that takes place among users with increasing time-sharing experience. More experienced users—programers and nonprogramers—learn how to exploit the central system more effectively. Unless constrained by the system, more experienced users tend to use larger programs, more primary and secondary storage, and more central processor time. How many time-sharing systems, current and projected, have a built-in evolutionary capability to expand and adapt to more sophisticated information services with increasing user experience?

7.3 ONLINE VS. OFFLINE PROBLEM-SOLVING

Within the last several years, 10 experimental studies have appeared, each comparing some form of online and offline data processing with respect to man-machine measures of system performance. These studies comprise the first substantive data base for comparing and evaluating the

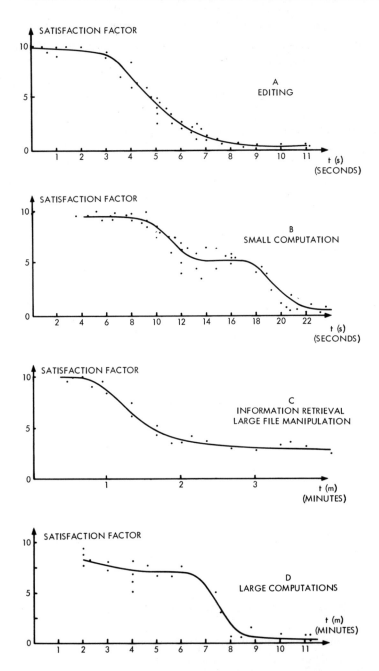

Figure 7.3.   USER SATISFACTION WITH SYSTEM RESPONSE TIME
FOR DIFFERENT TASKS (from Raynaud, 1967)

growing and changing competition between time-sharing and batch processing (Adams and Cohen, 1969; Erikson, 1966; Gold, 1967; Grant and Sackman, 1967; Sackman, 1970; Schatzoff, Tsao, and Wiig, 1967; and Smith, 1967). (One of these studies is derived from 1968 data made available to me by Col. Monti Callero from a preliminary experiment at the Air Force Academy.) Since it is beyond the scope of this report to enter into technical details, only a highly summarized account can be given from an updated version of the author's detailed survey of this field (1970). Table 7.2 shows the pooled results for all 10 studies for key measures of man-computer effectiveness—man-hours, computer time, costs, and user preference.

7.3.1 Basic Results

- Time-sharing seems to require fewer man-hours than batch processing for completion of experimental tasks. The median value for the pooled results of all 10 studies shows a 20 percent advantage for time-sharing.

- The results on computer time tend toward more machine time under time-sharing than in batch processing for the pooled set of experimental tasks, with almost twice as much machine time under time-sharing as the median value.

- The tendency toward fewer man-hours and more computer time under time-sharing suggests the hypothesis that time-sharing users tend to trade off computer time for human time—more exploratory computer runs with less polished programs—which may be interpreted positively as more effective exploration of a wider variety of problem alternatives, or negatively as careless use of computer resources, or both.

- Comparison of man-machine system costs on available data seems to show a tendency toward somewhat lower costs under batch attributable to lower computer facility costs for the offline mode.

- When ratings were formally collected, a decided user preference was demonstrated for time-sharing over conventional batch. Independently of the relative cost-effectiveness of online vs. offline programing for particular installations, the computer facility manager may well have to reckon with a burgeoning bandwagon

Table 7.2.   COMPOSITE RESULTS: ONLINE VS. OFFLINE
PERFORMANCE FOR TEN STUDIES

	Man-Hours	Computer Time	Costs	User Preference
Air Force Academy (1968 Pilot Study)	Time-Sharing * 1.2:1	Batch 1.7:1	Approx. Same	Approx. Same
Air Force Academy (1969 Pilot Study)	Batch 1.2:1	Batch 1.8:1	Batch	Approx. Same
Air Force Academy (Main Study, 1969)	Batch 1.1:1	Batch 1.9:1	Batch	Time-Sharing
Adams and Cohen (1969)	Approx. Same (1:1)	Batch 3.8:1	Batch 6.7:1	Batch
Erikson (1966)	Time-Sharing 1.9:1	Time-Sharing 3.4:1	Time-Sharing	Time-Sharing
Frye and Pack (1969)	Unknown	Batch 3.8:1	Batch 3.4:1	Time-Sharing
Gold (1967)	Time-Sharing 1.2:1	Batch 5.7:1	Approx. Same	Time-Sharing
Grant and Sackman (1967)	Time-Sharing 1.6:1	Batch 1.4:1	Approx. Same	Time-Sharing
Schatzoff, Tsao, and Wiig (1967)	Batch 2.1:1	Time-Sharing 1.1:1	Batch 1.5:1	Not Reported
Smith (1967)	Instant 1.2:1	Batch 1.5:1	Approx. Same	Instant
Median for All Studies	Time-Sharing 1.2:1	Batch 1.9:1	Batch	Time-Sharing Preferred

---

* The mode showing a reported *advantage* appears in each box together with its favorable ratio; e g, this entry shows less man-hours for time-sharing at a 1.2:1 ratio.

"Instant" batch is treated in this table as a simulated version of time-sharing.

SOURCE: Harold Sackman, *Man-Computer Problem Solving* (Princeton: Auerbach, 1970).

effect for online services if he wishes to attract and keep better programers and more users over the long haul.

- Wherever data was available on individual differences in subject performance, such individual differences usually overshadowed online/offline computer system differences. Computer-aided problem-solving almost seems to magnify individual differences, creating many new problems in fitting information services to the unique needs and capabilities of users. Only initial, exploratory probes were conducted to determine the nature and basis of the large variations in individual man-machine effectiveness.

- Available data indicated no practical differences in final program size or running time when produced under online vs. offline conditions.

- Preliminary and tentative evidence was obtained indicating a higher-quality and better understood end product under time-sharing.

7.3.2 Interpretation

It should be apparent that man-computer problem-solving is a highly complex area, an area whose surface has hardly been scratched by sustained experimental effort. The methods and findings presented in the previous sections should accordingly be taken as tentative and subject to rapid alteration as the technology of man-computer communication swiftly changes.

The limitations of these studies should be made explicit. First, there are only 10 studies and most of them are exploratory rather than definitive. Sample sizes were generally small, only two studies had over 100 subjects. User tasks may or may not be representative of tasks in the general data-processing community. None of the investigators made any claim for the generality of their experimental problems and none would be able to make such claims until empirical surveys are made of data-processing tasks with the aim of establishing a rational and viable classification scheme.

Subjects were not always equally trained in both modes, nor were they equally favorably disposed in their pre-experimental attitudes toward the competing computing systems. In fact, subjects with a stronger background in batch tended to do better with batch, whereas those steeped in time-sharing tended to do better in the online mode, an effect notable in most of the studies.

Online and offline conditions were typically not comparable; often one of the modes had to be simulated. Service in one mode tended to be more reliable than service in the other mode, depending upon the tradition and resources of the computer facility. Except for two studies, turnaround time was uncontrolled and was not recorded, a key factor in interpreting the results. Computer languages and debugging tools were often not comparable. One might make a case for unwarranted experimental bias for some of the studies in guaranteeing access to terminals under time-sharing while leaving offline subjects to the vagaries of the real-world batch system. Guaranteed access whenever you want it is an elysian myth in overworked, capacity-filled time-sharing systems.

The continuing challenge in these fast-moving changes is in the more fundamental evolutionary changes in human problem-solving and human creativity. A large number of human and man-machine parameters have already been teased out of the studies on hand; more are bound to come with new studies. (The author [1970] includes detailed results of a large-scale study comparing time-sharing and batch processing at the United States Air Force Academy on a sample of approximately 400 cadets.) It is entirely possible that the computer utility will usher in new types of man-machine tasks and new problem situations unprecedented in the behavioral literature that will greatly transform our understanding of human problem-solving as we perceive it today.

7.4 OTHER STUDIES

The development of real-time command and control systems, the collection of time-sharing user statistics, and the online/offline experiments represent three fairly well-defined areas of inquiry in man-computer communication. Each of these has at least an initial cluster of studies associated with it and a recognizable body of issues and findings. There are other highly relevant areas that have only been lightly touched upon by experimental effort that are nevertheless vital for any balanced scientific approach to man-computer communication. Two such areas are covered in this concluding section of the literature review—computer language comparisons and user terminal comparisons.

7.4.1 Computer Language Comparisons

Large efforts have been expended on computer language development, with well over 1000 languages and dialects alive and reportedly well. Many claims and counterclaims have been made for the advantages of newcomers against the alleged anachronisms of established languages. Allegations abound, and innovation appears to be more important than verification. To add salt to the wounds, virtually every language has, as its main claim to fame, the ubiquitous subtitle "user-oriented."

Experimental efforts in the computer language area have been abortive, at best. For example, Rubinoff, et al. (1968) conducted a study described as a triple experimental evaluation of an interactive retrieval language at the Moore School. The experimental design is nowhere to be found, the number of subjects is not mentioned, no statistics are cited, but the interpretation bristles with advice, conclusions, and platitudes on behalf of the local language.

An earlier Air Force attempt to compare competitive computer languages against an experimental problem (AFADA, 1963) ended in embarrassing ambiguity. The experimental task was a relatively simple command and control problem concerned with allocating rescue resources under specified emergency conditions. Ten different languages were used to produce a solution to this problem through different firms operating on an "honor" system to keep accurate and valid records. There was no testing of individual differences and the quantitative results were admittedly noncomparable. The report concluded with a ringing endorsement of the desirability of careful experimental design together with various suggestions for future work.

Rubey (1968) formulated a well-intentioned study—a comparison of PL/1 against COBOL, FORTRAN, and JOVIAL. This effort fared almost as badly as the Rubinoff study as far as experimental design and experimental controls were concerned. Rubey simply had each programer solve the same problem with PL/1 and with a comparison language. He had seven programers and six problems (two programers worked on one of the problems). Various measures such as man-hours, computer time, and program errors were tabulated. There was no statistical design and no rationale for subject or problem sampling except for a bootstrap appeal to face validity. The evaluation group and programer supervisors interacted freely with the subjects while they were solving problems. This "Comparative Evaluation of PL/1" was sponsored by the Air Force

Electronic Systems Division and was widely reported (e.g., *Datamation, Computerworld,* and *Data Processing Digest*).

The fact that each subject solved the same problem twice was shrugged off as a minor inconvenience by the experimenters, who believed that all the real action was in the coding and debugging. This "experiment" prohibited any meaningful analysis of problem-solving behavior. The vast individual differences that showed themselves were dismissed as one of those perverse characteristics of human subjects that could not be avoided. The uncontrolled intervention of evaluators and supervisors with programer problem-solving was viewed as a desirable technique to tap subjective experience with the languages. Language experience and language preference were not considered important enough to mention, measure, or control.

As an experiment, the Rubey study is an unmitigated flop. As an exploratory report of the experience of seven programers using PL/1 and various comparison languages on a standard set of problems, the study has value in raising and suggesting possible useful leads for future study; several broad hypotheses may be culled. One is that a more complex and flexible language such as PL/1 tends to be associated with longer learning time, more debugging effort, and more computer time to solve standard tasks. A second hypothesis is that experienced programers (average of six years) tend to be willing to live with the disadvantages of a more complex language if it can give them greater programing power and flexibility, and that they would probably continue to prefer such complexity over the long run. (The subjects unanimously preferred PL/1.) A contrasting hypothesis is that the neophyte is more likely to prefer a simple and easily mastered language, providing that it meets his needs. This hypothesis is supported by the wide acceptance and extensive use of "easier" languages for the nonprogramer user such as BASIC, JOSS, and TINT. Finally, system service, or the joint effectiveness of compiled and operating system characteristics, can "completely" override language considerations—system service is a critical control variable in assessing computer language cost-effectiveness.

The nonexperimental literature is filled with potential hypotheses concerning computer language effectiveness. The above suggestions from the Rubey study are only fragments to be fitted into a broad conceptual framework for the systematic study of computer languages. This field is so threadbare, and the computer world is so hungry for objective findings, that substantive experimental study is likely to make a significant impact on computer practice and perhaps even trigger a burst of related studies, as has occurred in the online/offline arena.

7.4.2 Comparison of User Terminals

The area of user terminal configuration, or manual inputs and displays, has not progressed significantly beyond the bleak assessment made by Pollock and Gildner in 1963. These authors reviewed the literature on user performance with manual input devices for man-computer communication. Their extensive survey, covering large numbers and varieties of switches, pushbuttons, keyboards, and encoders, revealed "inadequate research data establishing performance for various devices and device characteristics, and incomplete specification of operator input tasks in existing systems." There was a vast experimental gap between the hundreds of manual input devices surveyed and the small subset of such devices certified by even a primitive attempt at user validation. They recommended an initial program of research on leading types of task/device couplings, and on newer and more natural modes of inputs such as speech and handwriting.

In an extensive review of human factors problems in graphic displays for man-computer communication, Barmack and Sinaiko (1966) arrived at similar conclusions. Their review covered various types of keyboards, cathode ray tubes, display codes, light pens, switches, and pushbuttons. Innovation studies were widespread for graphics; evaluation of user effectiveness was virtually nonexistent.

Some of the practical problems encountered in developing effective user performance with a new computer-aided graphic system were described by Barmack and Sinaiko for the Culler-Fried system at the Space Technology Laboratories of TRW. The Culler-Fried system is among the more sophisticated systems available that permit student, scientific, and engineering users to obtain graphic portrayals on a CRT for a wide variety of mathematical functions. Over 400 of the TRW technical staff received an indoctrination program on this system. Less than 100 used the equipment for project work for 10 or more hours over a half-year period. The major constraint was the requirement for considerable mathematical skill. There were also problems in understanding the instruction manual, a lack of self-tutoring features for users with different skill levels and interests, and inadequate dissemination of system changes. This illustration highlights the critical value of user testing as an integral part of system development in man-computer communication. The added time and cost of user testing with system prototypes could result in great improvements in system design and in user performance even with the most carefully engineered devices.

Barmack and Sinaiko made various recommendations for future research on human performance with computer-aided graphics. For displays, empirical data on representative user populations was recommended with regard to learning, speed, error, and accuracy measures—research that would make possible a display designer's handbook. Traditional human engineering data on non-computerized displays were considered inadequate by these authors for the requirements of computer-driven displays. Recommendations for research on manual input devices centered around the collection of normative performance data from representative user populations. Performance measures included speed and accuracy of typing, block printing, script writing, and effectiveness in pointing to data, in conjunction with measurement of training time and effort to achieve desirable levels of performance. These authors urged that alternative input methods should be experimentally evaluated for solving standard problems. The results of such tests would indicate which types of problems are optimal for particular types of manual inputs. Principles and procedures for developing instructional systems for indoctrinating new users were also recommended, based on cumulative empirical data from user performance.

Comparative effectiveness of competing display systems represents a significant line of applied experimentation in man-computer communication. Using a time-shared computer with both typewriter input consoles and cathode ray tube display (CRT) with light pen input, Swets et al. (1966) found that the speed with which data was displayed, the amount of data, and the quality of data displayed did not significantly affect subject performance. He stated that "performance was not substantially improved by what appeared to be a more efficient mode of response and feedback, as supplied by the scope and light pen," and concluded that "these variables were not critical." (This does not, however, prove that they are "not critical" in another setting.)

Morrill, Goodwin, and Smith (1968) compared typewriter with light pen input modes for 20 students learning to use a management information system at Mitre Corporation. Their results tended to show superior performance for subjects using the typewriter terminal, although the performance differences were not statistically significant. Once again, observed individual differences were very large, overshadowing input mode differences.

In a more recent experimental study, Jones, Hughes, and Engvold (1969) compared typewriter and CRT terminals against paper-and-pencil manual techniques on a sample of 32 production managers and schedulers for a small, hypothetical job-shop task. The results showed a performance superiority of the computer-aided techniques over the conventional paper-and-pencil approach. While there were no statistically significant performance differences between typewriter and CRT terminal users, those who had used both types of terminals preferred the CRT display. As in the online/offline studies discussed previously, individual differences overshadowed computer system differences, in this case for types of terminal configuration. A suggestive positive by-product of the results revealed that marginal performers were substantially helped by computer-aided techniques, more so with display terminals than with typewriter terminals.

Although the above three studies hardly constitute experimental grounds for the superiority of one type of console over the other, they suggest that the competition between the two modes is one that should be closely followed by careful experimental studies. There are many varieties of typewriters, keyboard configurations, and graphic displays, and these need to be experimentally matched against representative user tasks. Dolotta (1970) after comprehensively reviewing the status of typewriter terminals for user ease, convenience, and effectiveness, concludes (p. 29):

> The chief faults in present terminals . . . lie in the areas of human factors and applications. It is as though the manufacturers were content to make, market, and deliver a piece of equipment without the most thorough field test. Such a field test should be performed by a number of *actual,* knowledgeable and critical *users,* and should involve extended use of the terminal's prototype in a sizeable number of truly typical tasks.

7.5 SOCIAL SCIENCE AND THE COMPUTER UTILITY

This concluding section is addressed to certain aspects of the intersection between social sciences and information utilities. The implications of social science for computer utilities are described in three areas, starting from educational applications where computer services have already made a significant impact, to behavioral research and theory, where computer effects are less pronounced, to social science broadly considered, which is only beginning to be tapped by computer science and technology. Primary emphasis is placed on methodological problems in conducting social research and on the promise of social science support for information utility development.

7.5.1 Computer-Assisted Education

The application of computers to education assumes many forms. Types of users include students, teachers, researchers, and administrators. Tasks include computer-assisted instruction, information retrieval, online experimentation in a variety of disciplines, writing and debugging computer programs, and a host of data management and scheduling activities related to educational administration. Computer facilities vary from general-purpose, time-sharing systems in which education is but one application as in Project MAC (Fano and Corbató, 1966), to online facilities dedicated to educational applications, as with the PLATO system at the University of Illinois (Bitzer, 1968), to fast, remote-batch systems to service student problems (Lynch, 1966), to a variety of special-purpose teaching machines featuring programmed instruction with the aid of medium and small-sized computers. Future applications will incorporate networks of communicating computers as envisaged for library services in Project Intrex (Overhage and Harman, 1965) and in generalized educational information utilties as described by McCartan (1969).

A vast market has opened up in computer-assisted and programed learning. Many large and small organizations are entering this field, and there are bewildering arrays of new educational aids and services for the growing spectrum of users. Evaluation is fragmented and incomplete in the face of the rising flood of educational goods and services.

Unlike the computer sciences, the educational field has had a long tradition in experimental testing of human performance. With the advent of computer-assisted instruction (CAI), many traditional educational problems were transferred to the computerized setting, such as: forced vs. self-pacing; comparisons of CAI, lecture methods, and noncomputerized programed instruction; massed vs. spaced learning; multiple-choice vs. constructed response modes; comparisons between different programed instruction procedures for step size, sequencing and branching; comparisons between various reinforcement schedules and prompting techniques; graphic vs. symbolic displays, and comparisons among various types of audio-visual presentations. The list of gross experimental problems can be extended almost indefinitely. There is a vast experimental literature on educational performance and much of it overlaps and interpenetrates the mounting literature on computer-aided performance as automation grows and proliferates in the educational setting.

No attempt is made to review and summarize the experimental literature pertaining to computer-aided educational performance—a task that is beyond the scope of this chapter—except to comment briefly on two leading problems for experimental *method* raised by the online environment. These problems include the cost-effectiveness of online computing systems, and the collection and analysis of online performance data.

Although many experiments show a superiority of some form of CAI over a presumably comparable traditional educational technique, the cost of developing, installing, and maintaining CAI software may be prohibitive. Such costs often are not mentioned or may be deliberately withheld as proprietary information, or may be misleadingly reported at an excessively low figure if a commercial interest is at stake. Although effectiveness data might be accurately presented, cost data is often unreliable, and objective cost-effectiveness comparisons cannot be made. A related factor is that the lion's share of the experimenter's time and attention is often devoted to the innovative computerized method, whereas the traditional method gets perfunctory treatment. Objective experimental comparisons of user performance in computer-based educational methods require cost-effective experimental designs.

The problem of recording and reducing computer-generated educational data is already assuming major proportions. This problem is not endemic to education; in 1966 NASA congressional testimony revealed that, even with advanced data compression methods, computerized telemetry inputs were being collected at a much greater rate than they could be reduced and analyzed; the problem has since grown worse as more Earth satellites and deep-space probes are launched. Response time between data collection and completed analysis was stretching out over longer intervals and increasing amounts of data had to be discarded with minimal or no examination of their value or contents. Suppes (1966) anticipated a similar situation for computer-assisted education. At Stanford University, for example, computerized data output for 5000 students ran as high as 1000 pages a day. He claimed that pedagogical intuition and traditional data reduction procedures from the social sciences are inadequate to cope with this flood of data.

A major upheaval is taking place in the broad field of data analysis, largely as a result of the new opportunities and problems associated with computerized data recording, reduction, and analysis. Major developments are taking place in data filtering, data compression, real-time recording, online data exploration, online data sampling, human monitoring of ongoing data streams, computerized graphic portrayal of data, interactive statistics, and iterative, multivariate analyses of data subsets—all geared toward more efficient detection, selection, and reduction of computerized data.

The third problem is concerned with the adequacy of traditional experimental method to meet the challenge of computer-aided human behavior. This is a wide-ranging problem extending well beyond the realm of education, with broad implications for all social sciences and for the philosophy of science. This problem can only be briefly mentioned at this point. Criticism has been heard in many quarters that the tradition of formal research in psychology and education has not provided the techniques and materials that educators need to get better instruction in the classroom. We have previously noted Suppes' (1966) rejection of traditional experimental guidelines for effective recording and analysis of student behavior in a computer-serviced environment. Silberman (1966) claims that the austerely controlled, abstract conditions of laboratory experiments have little applicability for the real educational world, where conditions are quite different. He claims that most educational research effort is geared toward professional publication rather than direct and immediate application in a live setting. He recommends less effort on abstract models and general innovations, and more effort on iterative "cut and fit" system engineering of instructional methods and aids—efforts that culminate in direct application to a specific educational setting. These, and related criticisms reflect a growing pragmatic temper in educational circles for new experimental techniques—for more applied rather than pure research, for more timely implementation of improved methods, and for more immediate, tangible results to meet rapidly changing problems.

7.5.2 Behavioral Theory

Only fragmentary efforts have been made to relate the mainstream of behavioral theory to man-computer communication. No discernible body of systematic experimental literature has arisen, even though computer usage is rising exponentially in the behavioral sciences (see Borko, 1962, for the initial impact; also Bowles, 1967, and the March 1969 issue of the *American Psychologist* for more recent trends). Those who have written on the subject deplore the lack of behavioral experimentation in man-computer communication and tend to believe that earlier theories are inadequate to meet the challenge of new forms of human perception, problem solving, and creativity in computer-serviced environments.

Barmack and Sinaiko, as mentioned earlier, look to new behavioral theories to interpret man-computer problem-solving. Various research recommendations stemmed from Barmack and Sinaiko's analysis of the nature of .creative work and its relation to computer-aided innovation. Although the interest level is high throughout computer and user communities on the potential for computers to enhance creative effort, virtually no experimental evidence is available to determine whether current systems facilitate or hinder the development of new ideas. They urged that detailed case histories of the problem-solving process be conducted for representative users to help determine the extent to which interactive computer-aided graphics aids the development of significant ideas, particularly in the early, formulative stages.

Miller (1968) has attempted to relate human thinking processes with user response time in an online computer environment, but without the benefit of any follow-on experimentation. Nickerson and others (1968) sketch various human factors problems in the design of time-sharing systems, but do not offer a behavioral theory to approach such problems. Although Fitts (1967) attempted to link a theory of human information processing with cognitive factors and traditional learning theory, his experimental data did not involve man-computer communication.

In contrast to these fragmentary efforts along conventional social science lines, a growing pragmatic temper is reflected in trends toward large-scale social experimentation. Some of these trends were previously discussed in the educational setting. Suchman (1967) has reviewed the concept and practice of social experimentation in the field of public health, and he has generalized the methodology that has evolved to other forms of social test and evaluation. Argyris (1968) and Campbell (1969) have surveyed many of the experimental problems and pitfalls associated with social field experimentation and social evaluation. At the national level, parallel efforts are underway to develop a variety of quantitative social indicators, in certain respects analogous to the national economic indicators that were introduced during the 1930's. A significant body of methodology and findings is being developed on large-scale social experimentation that may be profitably employed in planning for experimental computer utilities.

Although much has been proclaimed on the impact of computers on human and social intelligence, we find ourselves in an embarrassing theoretical and conceptual vacuum. It is almost as if the introduction of online man-computer communication has confronted behavioral theory with un-precedented new power and a bewildering variety of alternatives, beckon-ing toward a future that is only dimly perceived. The time is ripe for major connecting links betwen burgeoning computerized capability and the social sciences.

7.5.3 The Role of Social Science in Computer Utility Development

The development of computer technology has been largely the work of engineers, mathematicians, hard scientists, information specialists and computer programers. Generally speaking, social scientists have been involved only in a marginal manner. The advent of the computer utility is likely to involve social scientists on an unprecedented scale. This sec-tion briefly sketches some of the implications for social science in the development of public information services.

The prior review of the history and state-of-the-art in man-computer communication reveals an instructive pattern. By and large, the rigorous, professional, productive studies have been performed by social scientists (usually psychologists), and the relatively crude and primitive studies with ambiguous results have been done by other types of computer pro-fessionals, such as systems analysts and programers. This generalization is essentially valid for command and control studies, online/offline com-parisons, and educational studies. It does not hold up as well in statistical modeling studies where operations research professionals have been prominent. The upshot is not at all surprising—in experiments involving human behavior, it is the social scientist who is better equipped to handle the vagaries of individual differences, creativity, motivation, learning, human error, and other attributes of human performance in an experi-mental setting. The computer specialist is currently not equipped, either by formal training, tradition, or by job skills, to deal with individual and social behavior.

As the information utility wends its way into diversified individual use, so will the services of psychologists be increasingly required. As com-puter utilities spread into public education and into other community services, so will skills of educators and sociologists be increasingly needed. As public information services make their impact on economic behavior (as in online telepurchasing) and on voting and polling behavior, so will the services of economists and political scientists become increasingly vital. Prudent planning recommends early and timely incorporation of a broad spectrum of social science skills to guide long-range development of the information utility. The research framework developed in the next chapter bears out this general recommendation.

Lest I be accused of scientific chauvinism, it is not my intention to pit one type of science against another. It cannot be too strongly emphasized that for the sake of the best possible research and development of computer utilities, research should utilize all the skills required, matched to the unique needs of the object problem. To the extent that such problems represent human problems, to that extent will social science support be warranted, and in public information services the warrant is writ large.

8

EXPERIMENTAL FRAMEWORK

AND

RESEARCH PRIORITIES

FROM THE PRECEDING review of the literature pertinent to the information utility, it becomes increasingly apparent that we need a radically new approach for effective introduction of mass information services to the general public. As we have seen, the human use of computers is neither humanistic nor scientific, and this cultural lag grows ominously wider as innovation outraces verification. The radical solution requires accelerated science and universalized humanism to harmonize the social effects of technological innovation.

In a nutshell, the proposed solution is large-scale, cooperative social experimentation to develop, implement, and operate computer utilities. Prototype information services need to be cooperatively developed on a sufficiently large scale so that major social variables may be systematically incorporated, tested, and evaluated for intelligent selection of the most socially desirable alternatives. Traditional laboratory techniques are too esoteric, too atomistic, and too far removed from the hurly-burly of the real world to offer scientific comfort for the massive impact of public information services. The experiment has to be in and of the real world, not a laboratory surrogate. The scientific leap is from the traditional laboratory to the real world, a leap that merits the name radical. The humanistic leap is equally radical, from independent development by isolated groups working largely under proprietary wraps to open and cooperative development at a total community level.

More bluntly, the public information utility is too big for government, industry, or the community to handle separately on its own—either they work together and achieve together in the framework of open social experimentation, or else the great social potential of the computer utility may become the most barren wasteland of them all. The proof is in the pudding. The study of the human use of computers, according to the testimony of existing trends, is a shambles. New forms of cooperative social experimentation, as I have repeatedly emphasized and will now attempt to demonstrate, are our best hope.

The general argument is as follows: the scope of designer-user-social problems is so enormous and fast-moving with the computer utility, that only large-scale experimental prototypes can uncover and ask the relevant questions and provide field-tested answers fast enough to solve these problems as they arise. In contrast, an independent investigator here, a university study there, a company project in another place, and pious breast-beating at annual conferences or at after-dinner speeches will not cut the mustard. A look at the vast complex of research and development problems for information utilities should convince even the most hardened misologist that research must be stepped up by at least an order of magnitude. To buttress this line of argument, the scope and range of some of these socio-economic-educational-behavioral research problems in implementing public information utilities are briefly surveyed.

Many of these problems were anticipated in the previous literature review. While conducting this review, lists of user problems were drawn up as they were encountered or suggested. The final list included over 200 items (many redundant) which were inspected, juggled, and classified along alternative lines by the author. Out of this exploratory sorting, four major groupings were finally derived for categorizing user problems: social effectiveness, methodological, normative, and behavioral. These are briefly sketched and key categories under each grouping are discussed in turn.

The social effectiveness category has a long-range orientation toward the emergence of the computer utility; it stems from the need to marshal and systematize verified user data to help meet the numerous problems that are likely to arise in serving the public interest. Methodological problems refer to concepts, tools, and techniques for experimental investigation of user performance in the computer utility setting. Normative issues, on their quantitative side, refer to statistics of the leading parameters of user performance, and on their qualitative side to empirical descriptions and classifications of user facilities, tasks, and behaviors. The normative category thus constitutes a kind of continuing census on the variety and number of information utilities and what users are doing at such facilities. The behavioral category goes beyond relatively straightforward normative description of user activity. It is concerned with critical experimental hypotheses and behavioral theories that attempt to explain and generalize performance effectiveness of users in their system context.

8.1 SOCIAL EFFECTIVENESS

Table 8.1 lists problem areas concerned with social effectiveness under two broad areas—user quality assurance and pooled social information. User quality assurance refers to the pursuit of excellence in the design, development, installation, and operation of user information services. This can assume many forms that are amenable to experimental test, and only several of the more important possibilities are shown in Table 8.1. The first item flies right in the face of current practice with user services. It says that only when user services are tried out with representative users working on representative tasks can we have any confidence as to whether the service delivers the goods as promised. This fundamental step for user quality assurance is not practiced today because it costs time and money, because relatively few information system designers are qualified to conduct experimental tests involving people, and because users are still apathetic to the need for normative and quality assurance testing. There are other factors, to be sure, but the above reasons provide some notion of the magnitude of the task to be accomplished.

Not only could representative users be included in developing information services, but continual user feedback in evaluating information services—evaluation occurring on-the-spot and online—could be incorporated as an integral feature of computer utilities. Ongoing user certification, coupled with initial user feedback during design and development, would ensure continual user validation of information services throughout their entire life-cycle—an essential requirement for the high order of reliability of service mandatory for a regulated public utility. This form of evolutionary user validation has not been formally applied to any existing time-sharing system.

It is not hard to see that considerable experimental work needs to be done to develop satisfactory means for obtaining responsible and balanced evaluations that permit objective assessment of user and system performance. Since user validation, broadly considered, will probably

Table 8.1. SOCIAL EFFECTIVENESS PROBLEMS

A. *User Quality Assurance*

1. Assessment of user performance for information services with respect to representative users and tasks prior to public dissemination.
2. Incorporation of online user feedback for continual public evaluation of information services.
3. Assessment of cost-benefit analyses of alternative approaches to user information services.
4. Development and establishment of minimal professional standards in social application and in human engineering of computer utilities for those who design, install, and maintain public information services.
5. Design of information services to accommodate large individual differences in the general population.
6. Competitive and cooperative prototype experimental information utilities dedicated to social benefit in serving the public.
7. Planning techniques and procedures for early warning of user problems and orderly growth of computer utilities.
8. Comparative analyses of computer utilities with other public utilities; reconstruction of public utility law.
9. Experimental advisory and appeal agencies for information consumers to provide checks and balances on potential misuse of personal or proprietary information and for voluntary arbitration of user/system grievances.

B. *Pooled Social Information*

1. Experimental development of concepts and resources for pooling social knowledge and making it openly available to all citizens.
2. Development of prototype agencies and centers for pooling, analyzing, and disseminating user experience with computer utilities.
3. Development of a national census of computer utilities to measure and assess equitable distribution of information services to the public.
4. Experimentation with alternative online voting procedures leading toward improved techniques for efficient and effective expression of public opinion.
5. Experimental investigation of personality changes associated with differential use of computer utilities in the general population.
6. Development of online social indicators in a national reporting system for local, state, and federal early warning and action.
7. Development of "checkless" credit, telepurchasing, and related services in key urban areas with adequate social safeguards.
8. Experimental exploration and integration of information utilities with mass media of communication for evaluating real-time user participation in public events.

represent a significant cost in designing and producing information services, special effort should be devoted toward cost-benefit studies, with "benefit" construed in terms of long-term social gains. In addition, professional standards will need to be worked out for those concerned with the design and development of information services to ensure that such services will meet minimum acceptable levels of social proficiency. One of the key criteria for social utility is the extent to which information services will accommodate large individual differences, to permit individuals to work at their own pace and within their capability.

The pioneering experimental time-sharing facilities that have been built to date have been oriented toward demonstrating the feasibility and versatility of the time-sharing concept. Now that the concept has become a working reality and is spreading rapidly throughout the United States, the large-scale, cooperative experimental facility needs to be implemented for prototype computer utilities. These experimental prototypes should be devoted to public information problems and dedicated to serving public needs. Many advantages would accrue from such experimental arrangements, as shown in Table 8.1. Such facilities are indispensable as experimental early warning systems, for anticipating public problems, and for developing alternative solutions to permit more effective planning, more intelligent selection among tested possibilities, and more orderly growth of computer utilities. Such experimental probes could provide a working basis for comparative studies of information utilities against other forms of public utilities. They could also serve as prototype advisory centers for users, as a focal point for voluntary arbitration and self-policing of user/system conflicts.

The Federal courts are loath to get involved in labor-management disputes and prefer voluntary arbitration by mutually acceptable third parties to settle such disputes. Similarly, disputes over the use and misuse of information services—an omnipresent problem for public and private information utilities—might be solved in large part by mutually satisfactory arbitration machinery. Experimental prototypes for public information services could make empirical inroads in defining and grappling with these and related problems.

To return to our central theme, the growing body of legislation and legal precedent in public communications highlights the necessity for cooperative, prototype computer utilities. The relations between the supplier of information services, the computer communications vendor, the CATV operator, the user, and the government regulatory agencies are extremely complex and largely unprecedented. Information is not a homogeneous product as is gas, electricity, or water. No one agency or no single interest, including the government, is wise enough to do the job alone. Large-scale voluntary social cooperation is required with each social interest appropriately represented. Competition can assume a new and higher form—each prototype information utility can compete with other experimental information utilities. The higher form is team competition, social teams that share their knowledge for the benefit of all while competing. So much new knowledge is needed and at such an accelerated rate that we can no longer afford the self-seeking luxury of independent proprietary development of all aspects of computer utilities by all comers.

The category of "pooled social information" is oriented toward the broad social goal of making a significant portion of the cultural store of useful information available to all citizens through computer utilities. This goal is indicated in the first entry. The pooling of social knowledge can be measured, its availability to the public can be determined, and its growth and use can be quantitatively followed to trace experimentally the social effectiveness of public information services. Prototype centers for collecting, pooling, analyzing, and disseminating user experience with computer utilities would facilitate this development and, with the proper instrumentation, could help chart more effective courses of evolutionary social growth. Ultimately a national census of information services would be necessary to determine whether equitable distribution of information services is being attained, within reasonable bounds, throughout the country.

The advent of large-scale computer utilities could ultimately lead to radical changes in social process. For example, voting could occur at the home terminal, verified perhaps by fingerprint, and it could alter democratic procedures toward more extensive public inquiry and more frequent voting over a much larger number of publicly contested issues. Various online polling procedures could be experimentally investigated to demonstrate new forms of voting that could lead to more effective participatory democracy at local, state, and national levels. The computer utility should be explored for more rational decision-making on the basis of more extensive and more easily available public information. New relations between the citizen and the state may emerge.

As information utilities spread wider and deeper into society, the impact of computerized services on personality and on human intelligence may become a matter of grave concern. Rather than wring our hands in despair or joyously chant that the millennium of the computer has finally arrived, we could pursue the more sober course of determining experimentally what man's use of the computer hath wrought on human personality and on effective social intelligence. This body of experimental data could be organized to permit real-time testing of systematic trends for objective social indicators. It could be especially helpful in planning extension of information services to other societies where our own experience would serve as a provisional prototype for others.

The last item in Table 8.1 refers to an eventual outgrowth of pooled social information—the integration of information utilities with mass media of communication to permit real-time public participation and enhanced democratic control of public affairs. This marriage could lead to a tyranny of the majority at one extreme (recall de Tocqueville's analysis of the excesses of democracy) or a tyranny of an elite at the other, depending on how it would be regulated. Needless to say, there should be extensive experimental field trials of competitive approaches before particular systems are chosen and implemented. This speculative stage in social development represents a conceivable transition from indirect and delayed participation, to more direct, more highly informed, and more timely participation in democratic endeavor—a transition that might be described as real-time democratic control of public affairs in the computer-serviced society of the future.

8.2 METHODOLOGICAL PROBLEMS

Table 8.2 lists methodological problem areas for user studies under three headings, conceptual, performance measures, and experimental techniques. The individual items are suggestive tags that can only hint at the area of concern, and hopefully, give some crude indication of the range and scope of associated problems.

The "conceptual" items point up a pragmatic approach to user test and evaluation. Experimental investigation of users presupposes specification and analysis of the user system. The emphasis is on live test of real user tasks, tapped directly from online behaviors. Many of these tests can be performed by users on their own operations and, as such, will require self-service testing resources. When the user-system is conceived from an evolutionary point of view, there will be many different types of tests conducted at different stages of the user's unique development to meet changing problems. A taxonomy of user-system testing

Table 8.2. METHODOLOGICAL PROBLEMS

A. *Conceptual*

1. User system analysis.
2. Real-world online testing.
3. User self-service resources.
4. Taxonomy of evolutionary testing.
5. System simulation and system exercising procedures.

B. *Performance Measures*

1. Response times for optimal, adequate and degraded performance.
2. Central system vs. individual user measures.
3. User efficiency indices.
4. User satisfaction ratings.
5. Ratio of learning to using time.
6. System capacity measures.
7. Team vs. individual measures.
8. Online opinion sampling.
9. Accuracy and error indices.
10. Standardized measures of effectiveness for typewriter, graphics, languages, and data systems.
11. Security/privacy box scores.

C. *Experimental Techniques*

1. Accelerated regenerative recording for the entire system and for individual users.
2. Semiautomated exploration of large user data bases via data management vehicles.
3. Online job analysis procedures.
4. Testing the limits throughout the range of effective system capacity.
5. Cost-effectiveness models of user performance.
6. Standardized user task accounting procedures.
7. Cross-system comparisons with standardized user profiles.
8. Multiple-facility studies.
9. Self-comparison techniques.
10. Cross-sectional vs. longitudinal studies.
11. Paper-and-pencil tests.
12. Opinion and questionnaire surveys.
13. Case histories of users.
14. Comparative historical studies of time-sharing users.
15. Sociological studies of computer utility development.

would provide a helpful framework, particularly if it is structured along evolutionary lines. A provisional taxonomy of system testing has been developed along such lines by the author (1967).

The Performance Measures listing in Table 8.2 suggests the diverse dimensions of user performance. These include individual user measures, central system measures, timing variables, user opinion and attitude indexes, system capacity, user accuracy and error levels, user learning time, and various efficiency indexes. An example of the latter is man-computer communication efficiency, which may be broadly defined as the ratio of useful messages to total messages. This listing is also concerned with standardization of performance measures for more effective cross-comparisons between different tasks, programs, and tools, and with a working classification of user performance measures.

The items under Experimental Techniques in Table 8.2 reflect a variety of procedures as diverse as the performance measures. These include manual as well as semiautomated and fully automated techniques, in the belief that all pertinent experimental approaches should be used, as appropriate, to obtain a more comprehensive picture of user performance, and to provide independent checks and balances on the findings derived from each technique. Case histories, longitudinal investigations, and historical studies are also listed to underscore the long-range evolutionary element in user systems. Standardized techniques permitting wider cross-user comparisons are mentioned, such as user task accounting, standardized user profiles, and paper-and-pencil tests. Some items are application-oriented, such as online job analysis. Other entries offer powerful potential for systematically exploring user behavior. One is the use of general-purpose data management tools which may be linked to a large data base of user characteristics for online exploration and analysis of user performance. Testing the limits is a powerful technique for determining effective system capacity, the usefulness of fallback procedures, and "graceful degradation" under emergency conditions.

Special attention is devoted to regenerative recording because of its unique potential for a major breakthrough in computer-aided experimental method. As mentioned earlier, regenerative recording refers to the recording of initial conditions and subsequent system inputs so that a later rerun will reconstruct initial conditions and execute all succeeding computer operations in the same sequence in which they originally occurred. In contrast to standard regenerative recording, accelerated regenerative recording refers to similar recording of initial conditions and subsequent system inputs, but with selective short-circuiting of large file transactions in a simulation mode so that a later rerun will result in a faithful reconstruction of system events in accelerated real time.

Regenerative recording can be viewed from the vantage point of the total system, requiring the recording of all system inputs for complete reconstruction of total system operations at a later time. This mode of total system recording is of prime interest to those concerned with central system operations, user accounting, and system maintenance and debugging. On the other extreme is selective regenerative recording for the individual user who is interested in capturing only his own interaction with the computer. In between these two extremes is selective recording of specified subsets of users, such as students using CAI, or members of the same design or research team. Ideally, regenerative recording in time-sharing should permit optional recording ranging from the complete system, to user subsets, to individual users. See Figure 8.1 for a comparison of standard and accelerated regenerative recording, and for experimental mutations of original computer utility events. In Figure 8.1 the first box represents initial recording, the second box is the playback rerun, and the third block describes the playback output. This figure should be compared with the previous diagram (Figure 7.2) for standard regenerative recording.

For projected computer utilities, the vast storage requirements of user data files, the great varieties of user programs, and the rapid rate

TIME-SHARING SYSTEM FLOW

REAL-TIME REPRODUCTION OF ORIGINAL COMPUTER EVENTS

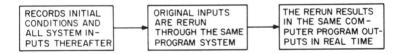

ACCELERATED REPRODUCTION OF COMPUTER EVENTS

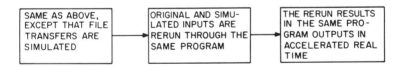

ACCELERATED MUTATIONS OF ORIGINAL DIGITAL EVENTS

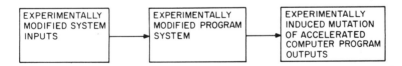

Figure 8.1. ACCELERATED REGENERATIVE RECORDING

of change of programs and data—all conspire to prohibit total recording of all computer system transactions. A preliminary examination of the cost-effectiveness of regenerative recording reveals that file transfers would have to be simulated (identified and time-tagged, and linked to the system response) to keep recording volume within manageable bounds and to minimize inadvertent disruption or destruction of user files. Further, the extent of simulated information transfers should be a flexible design feature to permit varying degrees of real-time acceleration appropriate to the user's needs.

Accelerated regenerative recording has been successfully developed and applied in a time-sharing context by Karush (1970). He has recommended further research and development, leading to useful variants of regenerative recording for both the user and the central system. A major research breakthrough may stem from a closer and more detailed look at user/system performance, perhaps comparable to the invention of the microscope to aid the naked eye.

8.3 NORMATIVE PROBLEMS

Table 8.3, which lists normative problem areas, includes three groupings—classification problems, individual differences, and performance norms. Normative studies are useful in drawing a statistical map of user and central system performance, describing leading parameters and their quantitative relationships, and in weaving a network of related findings that lead to critical performance hypotheses. One of the direct payoffs of normative studies is the development of empirical classification schemes for users, programs, and tasks as indicated in the Classification listing. As shown throughout the literature review, the lack of suitable empirical data on what constitutes representative tasks for representative users has made it virtually impossible to conduct general experimental comparisons of computer systems, languages, and terminals. We will have no basis for understanding the nature, size, and scope of task and user sampling problems until we get adequate data on user statistics derived from working practice.

The items under Individual Differences in Table 8.3 are largely self-explanatory. In many respects, the fundamental challenge of the computer utility is the challenge of matching information services to the vast range of individual differences in the general population. If early trends in the literature hold for new investigations, we may expect to find large

Table 8.3. NORMATIVE PROBLEMS

A. *Classification*

1. Classification and empirical frequency tabulations of users, programs, tasks, languages, information services, etc.
2. Specialied norms for separate application areas (e.g., business, engineering, education).

B. *Individual Differences*

1. Comparative speed, error, and accuracy scores for individuals.
2. Differential learning times for individuals and for key classes of users.
3. Biographical and experience data on users.
4. Empirical correlations between users, programs and tasks.
5. Comparative opinion polling of experienced users, new users, and nonusers for attitudes toward computer utilities.

C. *Performance Norms*

1. Empirical description of user and task response times.
2. Differential training times for various types of software tools and services for different classes of users.
3. Empirical compilations of authorized and unauthorized access to secured data.
4. Comparative use of man-computer languages by user and task.
5. Longitudinal use of information services vs. user experience.
6. Comparative user profiles for different classes of information services.
7. Comparative online vs. offline performance norms for similar tasks.
8. Measurement of user time spent on manual, offline, and online tasks.
9. Frequency tabulations of structured and open-end user evaluations, collected under online and offline conditions.

performance differences, even within stratified samples of users, in learning to master information services and in derived measures of speed, errors, and accuracy in utilizing such services. Biographical and experience data are necessary to establish sampling norms, and differential attitudes toward time-sharing may reflect important motivational factors in user performance. Empirical correlations between users, programs, and tasks are also listed as a preliminary, exploratory technique to work toward the structure and nature of individual differences for subsequent experimentation.

The largest part of Table 8.3 is devoted to the various facets of performance norms. These cover a variety of problem areas concerned with key measures of performance and different techniques for obtaining such measures. For example, performance measures include measurement of interactive response times, training time, frequency of unauthorized access to private data, and comparative usage frequencies of different languages and object programs. Diverse techniques for structuring performance norms are indicated by entries covering longitudinal user trends, by using standardized formats comparing online and offline activities, by accounting for all the user's time, and by tabulations of open-end evaluations.

8.4 BEHAVIORAL AREAS

Table 8.4 lists user behavioral areas under four distinguishable, but unavoidably overlapping headings. The first category, Learning, for example, cuts across all the other headings. The initial entry suggests that user learning effectiveness would probably benefit considerably by selectively adopting general techniques developed from computer-assisted instruction. From another direction, in formal psychological studies of learning, benefits may accrue from examining the experimental literature in such areas as massed vs. spaced learning, and whole vs. part learning, and adapting such findings to investigations in the computer utility context. The fourth item is oriented toward the differences in short-term learning with transactional tasks, such as looking up information, as compared to longer-term learning as in extended problem-solving. The fifth item, concerned with transfer of training and overlearning, could provide guidelines on the economy of user learning. The last item, representing a different approach—informal cross-sharing of user tools— is a new form of man-computer learning for computer utilities, a type of socially reinforced learning suggested particularly from Project MAC experience.

The items under "individual differences" in Table 8.4 indicate various approaches that may account for the nature and extent of observed variation in user effectiveness. One approach is to conduct detailed case histories of individual problem-solving. Another is to test for systematic effects in size and complexity of programs with increasing levels of user experience. The literature on man-computer communication indicates that many users, particularly the less sophisticated users, show very high error levels—the detection and analysis of error-prone individuals could be of considerable value. The analysis of user errors could be conducted in the framework of man-machine analysis with tests for the separate effects of user behavior, software and equipment features, and their interactions. Such studies could lead to better training for users and improved tools to service their needs. There may exist certain types of users who are out to "beat the system," and these might be detected by attempted frequency to gain unauthorized access to private programs and private files. Attitude studies may tap motivational factors related to individual differences in performance, frequency, and duration of time-sharing usage. These various analyses of individual differences may lead to paper-and-pencil tests of user readiness (analogous to "reading readiness" in educational practice) for selection, training, and assignment of prospective computer users.

One of the correlates of individual differences in man-computer communication that is suggested in the literature is the tendency for lower-echelon personnel to show higher computer usage rates than their supervisors. As mentioned earlier, the author has shown this in command and control studies (1967), and Dunlop has shown similar trends at IBM (1968). Comparisons gleaned from user statistics would indicate whether there is any recognizable trend from subordinates to superiors in the introduction and extension of computerized services. This and other trends could be traced by longitudinal studies of users, by tracking those who stick with it—the dropouts, the repeaters, the enthusiasts, and personal payoff.

The "real-time dynamics" grouping is primarily oriented toward matching the synchronization of computer service with the user's natural or optimal pace in working at his task. The striking consistency of the 10-second median value found in the literature for user interarrival time—the interval between the last computer output and the next human input—could be analyzed to determine whether there is a natural or spontaneous human conversational rate underlying this consistent finding. This analysis might break the interarrival interval into identifiable and perhaps additive components, such as response time for scanning the computer output, decision time for analyzing the output, formulation time for determining the next response, and input time for composing the next message for the computer. These crude steps could be partitioned further, as appropriate to the user task, and qualified by alternative stimulus-response sets. This general area could eventually become an important branch of human reaction time studies, benefitting from and contributing to the considerable psychological literature in this domain (for example, Woodworth and Schlosberg [1954]).

Many references were made in the previous literature review to the naive stereotype of "the faster the system, the better." This crude stereo-

Table 8.4. BEHAVIORAL PROBLEMS

A. *Learning*

1. Overlap with CAI for user training and self-tutoring.
2. Massed vs. spaced learning of user tools and procedures.
3. Dynamics of whole vs. part learning in man-computer communication.
4. Differences in learning patterns between transactional man-computer tasks (e.g., information retrieval) and problem-solving tasks.
5. Transfer of training and overlearning in related tasks.
6. Informal emergence of user sharing behaviors and associated group learning.

B. *Individual Differences*

1. Comparative case histories of user problem-solving.
2. Relation of size and complexity of object programs against skill and experience.
3. Detection and analysis of error-prone users, error-inducing software, and their interaction.
4. Random vs. systematic occurrence of authorized and unauthorized access to proprietary data.
5. Relations between user attitudes toward time-sharing, user software features, and user online activity levels.
6. Development and validation of paper-and-pencil tests of user readiness for selection, training and assignment of potential users.
7. Systematic man-computer communication differences between supervisors and subordinates, and between different occupational categories.
8. Longitudinal studies of user growth, dropouts and repeaters, and unusually creative individuals in computer utility settings.

---

type could be replaced by tackling the problem directly and determining optimal, adequate and breakdown response times by experimentally testing the limits. These tests could extend in both directions, fast as well as slow response times. With such experimental data, gross stereotypes would be replaced by empirically verified bands of response latencies within which the user and the system designer could choose acceptable levels of system variation.

It may turn out, as suggested by some of the literature on man-computer communication, that high variability in response time may be more unsettling for users than low variability; that is, greater objective variability in system response time may induce greater subjective uncertainty and discomfort in using the system. In this connection, it would be useful to determine "just noticeable difference" thresholds in user perception of system response time, an application of psychophysical meth-

C. *Real-Time Dynamics*

1. Universality of user "thinking" times in relation to spontaneous user pacing at his console.
2. Analysis of optimal, adequate, and breakdown computer response times for tasks and individuals.
3. Effects of differential variability of computer system response times on users.
4. Systematic modification of acceptable system response times via computer-produced expectation cues.
5. Investigation of forced user waiting periods after completed computer outputs.
6. The impact of cost-accounting techniques and computer charging algorithms on user behavior at terminals.

D. *Problem-Solving*

1. Studies of creativity: preparation, incubation, illumination, and verification—away from and at console.
2. Insight vs. trial and error in man-computer problem-solving.
3. Systematic differences in exploratory behaviors—online, offline, and away from computer.
4. Tests for Zeigarnik effect, or closure, in interactive vs. noninteractive problem-solving, and its effect on quality of work.
5. Comparison of introspection, man-to-man, and man-computer communication for higher- and lower-level problem formulation and solution.
6. Attitudinal and motivational differences between online and offline forms of man-computer communication.

---

ods to man-computer communication. Along related lines, it might be possible, by using the right kinds of cues for users—such as "OK" signals indicating legal user messages, or successive computer estimates as to when the output will appear—to extend system response time well beyond present latencies and still keep the user happy (and productive). We might find that the discrepancy between subjectively expected response time and objectively perceived response time may have much to do with user "satisfaction," and that the right kinds of expectancy cues from the computer might go a long way in helping the user to pace his own work at the terminal.

Item 6 raises the question of the relationships between real-time user behavior and economic constraints. We may expect systematic user differences in real-time man-computer communication patterns between "free" services vs. various forms of "paid" services, and, by the same token, between different types of changing algorithms. We may conceivably discover real-time behavioral profiles for "generous" and "stingy" users.

The last grouping in Table 8.4 is problem-solving. It is concerned, among other things, with the implications of enhanced human creativity. This area could be linked with psychological studies of creativity as indicated in the initial entry. Traditional paradigms of creativity, such as Wallas's classical preparation-incubation-illumination-verification model (1926) could be matched with activities at and away from the console. It would be interesting to determine the relative occurrence of operationally defined "insight" in problem-solving, at and away from the user terminal. As indicated by the literature review, some experimental evidence has accrued that interactive computer assistance can materially change the speed, range, and depth of user exploratory behaviors. Related experimental data has indicated that online man-computer communication lends itself more easily to psychological closure (a kind of "Zeigarnik" effect) in subjectively perceived subproblem steps, than in offline problem-solving procedures.

It is all too easy to become enamored with man-computer communication and to take a jaundiced view toward "manual" forms of communication, such as thinking to oneself or man-to-man communication. An experimental equivalent of time-and-motion studies in problem formulation and problem-solving could reveal the division of labor between manual and semiautomated forms of communication and, in so doing, provide us with clues as to where computer assistance is most effective in achieving user objectives. Finally, it would be desirable to investigate the nature and course of the online bandwagon effect that seems to have developed among users. Attitudinal differences between online and offline users may cast some light on underlying motivations causing users to take sides, and such analyses may lead to useful recommendations for cultivating and improving both types of computer services.

To recapitulate, the above survey highlights several key factors in the thesis put forth that only large-scale research in experimental prototype utilities can meet the urgent, practical needs for the introduction of mass computer utilities. First, the problems are so diverse and require so many interdisciplinary skills and experiences that no one agency or group can hope to encompass them on its own. Government-industry-community cooperation is an essential prerequisite. Second, it is apparent that the problem areas themselves will undergo rapid and complex change as technology improves; long-term, evolutionary research is needed. Third, regulatory procedures will be far more complex for information which is a heterogeneous product than it has been for electricity, water, and gas, which are homogeneous products. Fourth, no monolithic research theory or conceptual formulation can encompass the required research and development. Pluralistic, pragmatic approaches are required which use real-world prototype computer utilities as their own test bed. Finally, the humanistic stakes for enhancing social effectiveness are so great, that only the vision of continuing public experimentation, conducted in the open democratic tradition, can bring the best talents and wisdom to bear in constructing public computer utilities that will earn the grateful praise of posterity.

8.5 CONCLUSIONS AND RECOMMENDATIONS

This section has been aimed at a formulation of the problem of user research for public computer utilities and the establishment of guidelines that would lead to the most productive and useful types of research. Key conclusions and recommendations follow.

The Rapid Advent of the Public Information Utility. A consideration of technical and legal developments in the areas of computer communications, computer technology, and Community Antenna Television supports the contention that a cost-effective and probably highly profitable public computer utilities will appear "soon" and spread rapidly throughout the United States, with CATV probably providing the broadband communications highway into the American home.

Regulatory Problems of the Public Computer Utility. The history of public utility development in the United States revealed a socially responsive and plastic concept of the "public interest," a concept that is likely to assume new and challenging forms for an unprecedented public utility product—social information. It is predicted that mass information utilities will become so heavily "affected" with a public interest (for example, linked with public education and voting) that new forms of cooperative social experimentation would be required to arrive at fair and equitable public information services for vendors and consumers.

Traditional Neglect of the Human Use of Computers. The review of the historical development of computer science and technology revealed a pervasive and growing humanistic lag. The systematic and scientific study of the human use of computers has been blocked and thwarted by economic, sociological, professional, technological, and educational factors that are not likely to change rapidly, even under the growing stimulus of mass information utility developments.

Primitive Scientific Status of Man-Computer Communication. A survey of experimental work in man-computer communication uncovered a poverty-stricken domain. Suggestive studies were performed in early command and control systems, some interesting leads were gleaned from time-sharing user statistics, a small group of online/offline experiments have shed some light on the dynamics of man-computer problem-solving, but other areas, such as computer language comparisons, are utterly devoid of any respectable scientific work. The conclusion: computer science and technology is in the embarrassing position of entrenched institutionalized ignorance on user behavior and user performance as it prepares for a massive breakthrough in the rise and spread of computer utilities for all levels of society.

The Promise of Social Science. The relatively peripheral involvement of social science in the development of computer science and technology is protracting the humanistic development of public computer utilities. Although the current state of the art of man-computer communication is admittedly threadbare, the best studies were consistently produced by social scientists skilled in experimental work involving human subjects. To the extent that information utilities are concerned with people, to that extent should social scientists be involved in interdisciplinary teams dedicated to the progress of such utilities.

Research Framework for Mass Computer Utilities. The scope, range, and variety of needed research and development on the human use of mass computer utilities is staggering. Research needs run the gamut from online voting, to arbitration of consumer complaints, to the detection, diagnosis, and correction of error-prone users, to an empirical census of user tasks and data needs, to the development of a doctrine of privacy, and to analyses of the impact of computers on human creativity. Numerous areas of inquiry were delineated under the general headings of social effectiveness, scientific methodology, normative problems, and behavioral hypotheses. It was apparent that an increase in the scope and tempo of user research was essential, an increase of at least an order of magnitude to meet the massive experimental challenge of public information services.

Experimental Computer Utility Prototypes. The above conclusions represent the assessment of the problem of user research for the computer utilities. These conclusions and the supporting evidence converge into a single, fundamental recommendation, the recommendation raised at the outset and stressed throughout all parts of this book—the need for cooperative, experimental information utility prototypes to formulate the problems and gain the experience necessary for intelligent regulation and growth of this new social force. The cooperative interests require a sufficiently diversified consumer community, local government, the local regulatory agency, computer communications representatives, software and information service suppliers, CATV operators, and a scientific-administrative organization to manage the enterprise in accordance with chartered objectives. It is further recommended that more than one such experimental prototype be implemented so that competitive alternatives may be pursued, openly evaluated, and pluralistically resolved in a democratic manner in the public domain as the computer utility evolves.

Undesirable Alternatives. Failure to follow the above general recommendation would result in an extension of the inadequacies and the apparent bankruptcy of current practice to meet the vast needs of mass computer utilities. The current trickle of user research is too little and flows too late to exercise a significant impact on public information services. Anachronistic clinging to the doctrine of maximum effective laissez-faire (the least possible regulation is the best possible regulation) would probably lead to the ugly conflicts between public and private interests that have punctuated the history of earlier public utilities. The pulsating information arteries of the country embodied in emerging computer utilities may conceivably become the most vital artery of all, and will increasingly be affected by a growing public interest. Industrial leaders should help pioneer the way into this new utility, in the name of and for the sake of the public interest, rather than be dragged into it, kicking and screaming, by an irate public, later, after irretrievable investments had been made in the largest information market of them all. The problems of the computer utility are so vast that no one agency, industry or interests can span them without the continued cooperation of the other interests. And new problems are likely to arise so rapidly, that only the most powerful method available—scientific method on a broad social scale—can develop the social knowledge and techniques necessary to solve these problems.

The Next Steps. Assuming that the proposal for a prototype experimental computer utility is acceptable, there are several immediate steps that could be pursued. Three are singled out below.

One is to perform systems analyses of proposed computer utility prototypes in sufficient detail so that the basic working structure of such prototypes would be spelled out, leading to working estimates of system cost-effectiveness. This type of analysis, beyond the scope of this book, requires an appropriate interdisciplinary team to mesh all the parts.

A second step that needs to be taken is to try out leading concepts for an experimental computer utility on a small and easily manageable scale in a live setting. One approach is to use a laboratory to test information users in an online setting. Another approach is to instrument a working time-sharing system with appropriate recording, reduction, and analysis tools superimposed on normal operations to tap user behavior along lines most relevant to computer utility problems. Many of the hypotheses and questions raised in the suggested research framework could be systematically examined in either of these settings. Such experience would be invaluable in developing pilot methodology and supportive findings to be applied on a larger scale in the recommended social prototype.

A third and crucial step is to cultivate the interest and cooperation of other parties essential for extensive social experimentation with prototype computer utilities for one or more specific communities of users. This is an educational and motivational effort to effect the necessary social cooperation required to start working on a feasible community prototype. The goal of this step is to arrive at an authorized charter agreed upon by all cognizant interests to initiate the design and development of the initial prototype, and to develop the techniques for open social evaluation of the results of prototype experience. Initiative in this area today could act as a pacesetter, and would go a long way toward making the computer utility the hallmark of a more enlightened concept of public excellence for the computer-serviced society of tomorrow.

PART IV

OPTIONS FOR
SOCIAL RECONSTRUCTION

9

SOCIAL OPTIONS

THE CONCLUDING SECTION of this book is broadly oriented toward social planning to meet the challenge of mass information utilities for public excellence. Planning is conceived in its broadest sense—from critical assessment of fundamental social values to the delineation of social objectives, to possible strategies to approach such objectives, to tactical and operational measures required to arrive at them. The pursuit of social excellence in the introduction of mass information utilities involves social reconstruction along the lines of the more promising available alternatives. This chapter and the three that follow approach the problem of social planning for mass information utilities in an exploratory inductive manner.

The first chapter ranges through social options, the second explores individual options, the third investigates the method and theory of social planning, and the final chapter works toward an integrated philosophy to guide the long range evolution of mass information utilities.

In approaching the area of social options, we are fortunate in having available the deliberations of a conference on "The Information Utility and Social Choice" held in December 1969 at the University of Chicago. This chapter is largely concerned with a critical review of some of the main findings and recommendations of this conference from the viewpoint of social planning.

This conference was jointly sponsored by the University of Chicago, the American Federation of Information Processing Societies (AFIPS), and the *Encyclopaedia Britannica,* to help commemorate the 200th anniversary of the *Britannica.* Professor Norman Nie was co-chairman with the author, who was also the AFIPS delegate; Professor Nie represented the University of Chicago. Proceedings of this conference have been published (Sackman and Nie, 1970). The three key areas of the proceedings include introductory papers, general social directions, and political implications, and the review in this chapter proceeds along the same lines. The present review is highly selective and abbreviated for the purposes of this chapter. It cannot possibly do justice to the original articles, which should be consulted for further details.

9.1 SOCIO-TECHNOLOGICAL OPTIONS

Broadly speaking, conference participants were able to agree on the technological imminence of mass information utilities; they disagreed to a greater extent on social implications. More was known about the technological building blocks of computer utilities than their social use. This dilemma is apparent in the introductory papers.

Licklider's paper (1970), "Social Prospects of Information Utilities," is the keynote address. In a whirlwind tour of the computer world, he reveals that the necessary elements are already available in computer communications, and that only a cost-effective synthesis is needed to universalize mass information services. He envisions pluralistic information utilities as a "network of networks" with decentralized, competitive information services fueled by the energy of virtually unlimited technological advances in computer wares. Trillion-bit stores, low-cost plasma displays, interactive graphics, artificial intelligence, CATV, communication satellites, and microwave transmission are some of the kaleidoscopic elements cited for a technological world that has been witnessing a doubling of computer power and a halving of computer costs every three years. On the negative side, he points to persistent problems in programing large-scale systems, which may turn out to be a major bottleneck for information utilities. Stressing participatory feedback in mass information utilities for individuals, Licklider appeals for the redirection of this technology to serve human creativity and social cooperation, with appropriate safeguards for individual privacy in an "Information Bill of Rights."

In "The Emerging Technology of Information Utilities" Dunlop (1970) concentrates on the emergence of CATV as the broadband communications highway into the American home. He puts forth many arguments for CATV as the most cost-effective choice among the various alternatives for penetration of the mass market. First, basic CATV rates approach telephone rates for individuals. Second, the coaxial cable has an information-carrying capacity on the order of 100,000 times the capacity of voice-grade telephone lines. Third, FCC rulings have been consistently favorable in encouraging the growth and spread of diversified information services over CATV. Fourth, data processing technology for handling individualized information traffic over CATV lines has been solved by leading computer communications firms. Fifth, CATV is a rapidly growing and highly profitable industry that will probably dominate the TV market before the end of this decade, and as such, will serve as an ideal communications link into the American home (see Table 9.1). Dunlop predicts a multibillion dollar information utility industry via CATV before the end of this decade. Although the argument for CATV is far more complex than this quick account indicates, the above provides a preliminary sketch of the emerging economic battleground.

Table 9.1. GROWTH OF CATV (from Dunlop, 1970)

	1952	1960	1965	July 1968	Est. 1972	Est. 1975
Number of Operating Systems	70	640	1325	2100	3500	5000
Subscribers (millions)	.02	0.7	1.6	3.5	8.3	30.0
Percent of TV Homes	—	1.4	2.9	6	15	50
CATV Equipment Sales (millions of dollars)	1	10	30	50	120	500
CATV Operators' Revenue (millions of dollars)	1	39	96	210	500	1800

In the third introductory paper, "Information Utilities and Mass Communication," Parker (1970) explores the impact of public information services and CATV in the framework of mass media of communication. Parker agrees with Dunlop that CATV is the most likely avenue for initial penetration of mass information services. Starting from the premise that information is power, Parker raises the question of how we can design an equitable distribution of information power for all strata of society.

He brings to our attention a key social option in planning for mass information utilities. In the absence of any plan, Parker predicts that the initial content for computer utilities will be derived from materials previously prepared for other mass media such as newspapers, magazines, and TV. Only later will content specifically designed for information utilities appear. Thus, in the absence of social planning, a reasonable estimate is that information utilities will more or less repeat the dreary history of TV, following the path of maximum immediate profits aimed at the largest common denominator in the consumer market. Parker cites six key advantages of computer utilities that should deter us from following the laissez-faire example of TV.

- More information.
- Greater variety of information, ultimately individualized.
- Greater selectivity of information by user.
- More powerful information processing capability.
- Individualized user feedback to the system.
- Conversational permissiveness, encouraging exploration of information.

Parker concludes on an upbeat note (p. 70):

> The only hopeful alternative I see is to start immediately making the case for a new national information policy. A National Goal of equitable distribution of education and information to all members of the society may prove more beneficial to the society in the long run than a National Goal of putting a man on Mars. It is a goal in keeping with the democratic traditions of our society and one which can only strengthen our political system.
>
> My suggestion, therefore, is that we begin at once the task of spelling out in detail a technical, economic, and political plan for creation of public information utilities serving the interest of the entire public. Such detailed plans will be needed before we can successfully argue for the proportion of the federal budget that will be required. If we can prepare those plans soon enough, we may reach a major milestone in the history of the human species—the first time in which the distribution of a major technological change is planned and directed in the public interest with the likely social consequences taken into account. The alternative is to proceed the way we always have in the past—and be the unwitting victims of our own unplanned technological development.

In the panel on general social directions, Kestenbaum (1970) presented a paper on "The Regulatory Context of Information Utilities," drawing from his prior experience as head of policy planning in the antitrust division of the Department of Justice. This lucid, balanced paper may become a classic in its field. At the outset, Kestenbaum stresses the great flexibility of the current regulatory spectrum, with options ranging from comprehensive carrier regulation (as in telephone utilities), to partial regulation (as in broadcasting), to limited forms of government intervention through Federal expenditures and antitrust enforcement (as in computer manufacturing and data processing). Several interesting analogies are drawn between computer utilities and other types of mass media such as radio and TV broadcasting, and the press. These analogies are concerned with the relations between private and regulatory constraints and their impact on profits in the mass market. In effect, Kestenbaum indicates that neither government nor the vendors of mass media have solved problems with mass media to the satisfaction of the public and most observers, and that the introduction of computer utilities will be likely to exacerbate existing dissatisfaction.

Reviewing the regulatory history of computer utilities, communications carriers, and CATV, Kestenbaum indicates a slow-moving but consistently positive pragmatic attitude on the part of the FCC, intended to encourage and promote the growth of diversified public computer services. He closes on a warning note, echoing Parker's concern for intelligent long range planning. In essence, Kestenbaum points out that regulatory bodies such as the FCC have limited administrative roles that preclude policy formulation and comprehensive planning. If effective social planning is to occur, new roles must be developed in the executive branch with the power to develop policy, command appropriate budgets, implement plans, and evaluate the effectiveness of authorized programs in meeting the public interest.

> To conclude, the discussion of the regulatory context of information utilities does not lead to a conclusion, for there is no single formula or key to the various regulatory issues. In communications, the task is to define the proper scope of the existing common carrier system, and the roles of new systems and diverse suppliers; thus to consider the needs of information utilities within a long-term national communications policy. In cable television, the task is to resolve present broadcast controversy while laying the groundwork for a new service of broadband communications distribution. The operations of information utilities may call for direct regulation, to protect privacy and security and to achieve antitrust goals of moderating the exercise of economic power. Finally, the public interest in potential applications of information utility systems requires an affirmative exercise of government responsibility in developing and employing such systems, and the development of governmental institutions, now lacking, which are capable of carrying out this responsibility. Just as the information utility mixes computers and communications, so the regulatory context calls for mixtures of technical and economic expertise, private and government initiative, monopoly and competition, flexibility and farsighted planning, and rulemaking. (pp. 96-97)

Dunn's paper (1970) on "The Information Utility and the Idea of the Public Data Bank" strikes at shortcomings in popular stereotypes of computers and society. Putting forth an evolutionary approach to information utilities, Dunn emphasizes that there are many varieties and species of information services, and that it is misleading to create the impression of a monolithic, national information service. He makes a sharp distinction between routine and innovative information services, and he stresses the need to devote special effort to the enhancement of social learning with mass computer utilities. Here is another fundamental social option: to what extent do we wish to allocate resources to deliberately design mass information utilities to enhance social creativity?

Dunn is deeply concerned over the roadblocks and pitfalls generated by crude public stereotypes of computers, privacy, and data banks. He deplores the data bank enthusiast who believes that a computer-accessible data dump will make it possible to tackle and solve national information problems. He equally deplores the privacy advocate who insists on a priori, foolproof safeguards before any venture is made into national data systems. Dunn, one of the key figures in the original national data bank controversy, urges a rational evolutionary compromise between these two poles—develop experimental prototypes of national information systems so that we can gain the necessary experience and knowledge to "both improve the efficiency and humanize the work of a complex and changing society."

To accomplish this end, Dunn recommends, as did preceding participants, the establishment of a joint executive-legislative commission to study the need for a national information policy. He further urges a concerted effort on the part of social scientists of all callings to contribute urgently needed research on the impact of information and mass information utilities on society.

The last paper in this panel of the conference was presented by Borko (1970), on "Experimental Prototypes for International Information Utilities." Borko compares national developments in the United States and in the Soviet Union in scientific, technical, and educational information systems. Sharply contrasting with the national picture, international information utilities are shown to be still in the germinal stage. Borko reviews the status of UNISYST, a world science information system sponsored by the United Nations. He asserts that the long-range implications of this system could "stagger the imagination," and that "UNISYST provides an opportunity for the computing community to direct the application of data processing facilities to the solution of significant social problems and to further scientific progress." The fundamental social option raised by Borko is: to what extent do we wish to pursue the development of international information utilities for the benefit of world cooperation and world peace?

In a summary paper on this panel, "The Information Utility and Social Change," Bengelsdorf (1970) reviewed the contributions of the previous participants and some of the subsequent discussion that emerged from these papers. The ensuing commentary is summarized here.

One of the discussants, Melkanoff, urged serious consideration of the possibility of establishing a new cabinet-level post of Secretary of Information and Communication. He felt that the role of information and communications has become so crucial for the successful functioning of our complex and rapidly changing society, that nothing less than top-level federal planning and management would suffice to resolve the mounting issues springing from all sides. Many problems were raised in connection with this new cabinet post, which would require prior planning along the lines of a comprehensive national information policy suggested by previous speakers.

The author, building on other recommendations for cooperative, experimental prototypes of mass information utilities, pointed to the experience of the COMSAT Corporation for national communication satellite services, and INTELSAT for international services. He suggested that perhaps analogous quasi-public institutions be considered to facilitate the national and international development of mass information utilities.

Parker suggested the possibility of a national goal of an information utility in every home by 1985, Borko urged an accelerated commitment to UNISYST to help undeveloped nations who "do not have time to repeat the past," and the author suggested a goal of international computerized networks between all major urban centers on Earth by the year 2000.

Bengelsdorf concluded with the recurrent theme that haunted the participants of the conference: "In short, will mankind be wise enough to plan, *in advance,* to use information utilities for its future glorious benefit? Or will we plunge into still another further social crisis—the pollution and defilement of our national and international information resource?"

9.2 POLITICAL OPTIONS

The second panel of the Chicago conference, as mentioned earlier, was devoted to political implications of information utilities. Five papers were presented during the conference, and two were prepared later. The summary paper is reviewed first to set the background, followed by brief comments on the other four papers presented at the conference, concluding with the two post-conference papers. As in the previous section, only key points bearing on social options are emphasized for the purposes of this chapter; the original articles should be consulted for more detail and as a corrective to the author's bias.

The second panel consisted almost exclusively of political scientists from various universities in the United States. They selected facets of the impact of information utilities on politics bearing on citizens, representatives, interest groups, and opinion polling, among other topics. Prewitt (1970) delivered the summary address of this panel at the concluding session of the conference. His comments provide a backdrop of key points, and areas of agreement and disagreement delineated by the other papers.

A fundamental area of agreement, according to Prewitt, is the prediction that mass information utilities will exert an evolutionary rather than a revolutionary impact on politics. It will probably enter the political scene with gradual, piecemeal changes along established lines of power in the pluralistic, stratified, and fragmented society that characterizes the United States.

Prewitt admits that the panel was not able to penetrate into the socio-psychological consequences of information utilities, particularly as to whether such utilities will lead to more political activism or to greater apathy. For example, the entertainment potential of information utilities could lead to increased citizen privatization, and increased political apathy. Broad social consequences are equally uncertain at this early stage. In 1900, for example, could we have predicted the vast impact of automobiles on urbanization and mass production?

Some predictions are made on political consequences of mass information utilities. A leading consideration is that the uncertainty of politics will be reduced to some extent by instant, inexpensive mass polling. Other tentative forecasts include the following:

- No populist electronic "town meeting democracy" will emerge.
- Greater stratification and fragmentation of existing groups will probably occur.
- A new type of middleman or information broker will arise, a kind of political information specialist.
- More people will vote, and vote more frequently, especially if home computer utilities are free, easy to use, and provide direct help to the citizen.
- Rise of smaller groups organized around single issues and common data banks, more splinter groups, more multimodal opinion, possible fragmentation of the two-party system.
- New potential will be created for manipulating individualized persuasion.
- The representative process may gain by greater interaction between representatives and their constituencies, but such increased surveillance could limit the freedom and the effectiveness of the representative in legislative bargaining and negotiation.

A major impact on social science is forecast with the advent of on-line polling and automatic recording of user behaviors. Recommendations are cited by Prewitt for investigation of the politics of information and its regulation, for prototype experimentation with small communities (also recommended by the other panel), and for safeguards to protect the privileged nature of social science information from subpoena.

Marvick's paper (1970) was on "Some Potential Effects of the Information Utility on Citizen Participation." In attempting to assess the impact of information utilities, Marvick distinguishes between two main types of information services—entertainment utilities and organizational intelligence utilities. The entertainment utilities are predicted to encourage privatization, tending to insulate and remove individuals from the mainstream of political activity. On the other hand, the organizational intelligence utilities (for example, occupational, professional and other interest groups) are likely to encourage individual participation because of the possibilities of extensive feedback and meaningful interaction on the part of the user. Of the two types of utilities, Marvick believes that the "organizational intelligence" alternative holds greater promise for a "more salutary change in the vitality of American political life."

Bradburn (1970) addresses himself to "Survey Research in Public Opinion Polling with the Information Utility." Here the tone is less restrained as Bradburn sketches the potential revolutionary impact of mass information utilities on polling. Online polling will be much cheaper, faster, more automatic, and more accurate. Sampling could be more precise. Polling demands on individuals could be load-balanced by selecting adequate rather than maximum sample sizes from polling registries, by the use of sequential analysis techniques for minimum sampling, and by extensive cross-filing of population characteristics. More effective and comprehensive experimentation could be conducted by social scientists. Social indicators could be standardized, collected, and tabulated to trace broad or specialized measures of social change. Bradburn anticipates a new and probably more permissive doctrine of privacy than exists today to permit society to benefit from mutual sharing of opinion and knowledge possible with mass information utilities.

> Perhaps one of the impacts of movement into a world of greater electronic communications will be a decline in people's interest in privacy and confidentiality. I sometimes believe that I see signs that the world is more and more willing to conduct its affairs publicly and that things which were once thought to be extremely private are now talked about and done in public. Indeed the whole distinction between public and private might be considerably reduced and only the old-fashioned, the subversive, and the eccentric will have interests in privacy. (p. 286)

The next paper, by Eulau (1970), is concerned with "Some Potential Effects of the Information Utility on Political Decision-Makers and the Rule of the Representative." He states his bias in an opening salvo ". . . what I would anticipate is a participative nightmare rather than the good society . . . the prospect of the computerized democratic and equalitarian polity makes me shudder to my liberal bones."

Eulau fears that the representative will suffer from an information overload, that he will become too taken up by his own political information management system to discharge his responsibilities effectively in the legislature. He is concerned that legislative power will pass from the representative to the citizen's living room, which will become the new seat of government.

Eulau attacks the stereotype that sheer increase in the amount of information, coupled with sheer acceleration in the rate of transmission of information will, by itself, improve the political process. He is especially sensitive to the problems of information overload and information pollution. But in his concern over quantity of information, Eulau overlooks the technological possibilities of information utilities on quality and selectiveness of information. He does not explore the potential of information utilities for selective collection, organization, storage, retrieval, and analysis of political information for individualized exchange for both the representative and his constituency.

Eulau views the proper function of the representative as one of continuing negotiation and compromise among conflicting interests in political decision-making. He takes a dim view of an opposing interpretation in which the representative simply mirrors the preferences of his constituency. In that case, "one might as well replace the representative process with a computerized decisional apparatus, very much along the models of rational choice that need only be properly programed to be operative." He later asserts: "Not even the best information system in the world can generate political demands."

Eulau develops his position from the popular stereotype of the computer as a neutral, objective processor of facts and figures. On the contrary, if we look long and hard at the face of the computer, we see ourselves. Computer programs reflect the endless parade of prejudices and fallibilities of their creators, besides being unpredictably error-prone. It is not generally appreciated that computers could be used for adversary procedures, to sharpen and augment debate, to solicit contested opinion, to facilitate consensus or point to polarization of issues. For example, computers have already been used in Delphi forecasting techniques in which experts cast online opinions over controversial issues, receive feedback, and iterate until consensus or stalemate is reached.

Computers are soft plastic in our hands to use as we wish—the creature is constructed in the image of his creator. We can cast computers in the Hollywood role of the impeccably correct and factual man-servant for our "objective" needs or we can dress them in battle regalia to fight for one or both or many sides of controversial issues, perhaps in some advanced modification of courtroom procedure. Just around the corner is high-speed, electronic digital-aided debate, in which the human, not the computer, makes the decisions—for better or for worse. The representative, whether he likes it or not, will find himself in the center of the political ring with his supporters and his opponents. In view of this, I take issue with Eulau's conclusion that "the coming interactive information system will, in my judgment, have only limited bearing on the problematics of representation in a democracy."

Zeigler's paper (1970) is on "The Communications Revolution and the Future of Interest Groups." He feels that information utilities will increase the number and diversity of interest groups, and that this in turn, will reduce the influence of individual lobbyists and pressure groups. "The fewer the number of groups which come to the attention of a decision-maker, the greater the influence of any one group." A related consequence of information utilities, according to Zeigler, will be to compel organizational management to reflect the majority will of its members more faithfully. This may lead to fewer "liberal" organizations, but also to more flexible behavior on the part of interest groups.

Zeigler anticipates various changes in the role of the lobbyist, whose role as transmitter of political information may be substantially reduced. On the other hand "The job of hammering out specific provisions of bills and policy statements would still require the expertise of a lobbyist." But with the advent of online polling of specialized publics, both the lobbyist and the legislator will have fewer degrees of freedom and "less to bargain about."

The advent of online polling will make it possible for special interest groups to appear suddenly and organize themselves at unprecedented speed, particularly under the stimulus of a public policy debate on their core issue. Mass information utilities could spur more effective organization of the "forgotten man"—the consumer—which "might reshape the universe of interest group politics." Zeigler makes the interesting point that feedback to citizens is well-developed in the mass media—individuals can learn quickly of new developments via the press and TV—whereas feedback from individuals to the government is much slower since there is no equally rapid way for individuals to communicate to decision-makers. However, with mass information utilities, this response lag could essentially be eliminated. Zeigler suggests that the course of American policy in the Vietnam war might have been different had the antiwar groups been able to get earlier feedback to political leaders via information utilities. This new sounding board for real-time individual citizen expression could serve as a more effective form of early warning for decision makers, and, for judicious politicians, as a safety valve against the buildup of hostile antiadministration feeling. Zeigler closes on the note of information utilities as a potential expressive outlet for reducing the anxiety of excluded groups.

After the conference, Nie, the co-chairman of the conference, prepared a paper (1970) entitled "Future Developments in Mass Communications and Citizen Participation." Nie argues that direct democracy, in spite of its utopian appeal to some idealists, is undesirable and infeasible, even with mass information utilities. Too many cooks spoil the broth, and there must be a rational division of labor between the executive, legislature, judiciary, and the constituency. Although total participatory democracy is utopian, Nie believes that there will be a continuing useful role for information utilities in the form of citizen polling. He points out, however, that information utilities are most likely to enter the American home via CATV, and as such, political participation in citizen polling will be performed in the context of competition with entertainment and other features of the CATV-information utility. So Nie asks the pivotal question of his paper—will competition from nonpolitical features of information utilities divert time and attention away from political activity? Will information utilities turn the public toward politics or away from politics?

Since there are no available mass computer utilities to conduct empirical tests of this hypothesis, Nie suggests that we look at the history of TV, for which considerable data is available. In examining the data, Nie reports a characteristic curvilinear correlation between TV viewing time and level of individual political activity. That is, maximum political activity, as measured by a composite index, shows a peak for individuals who average about one hour of TV per day, with tapering off of level of political activity in both directions. The interpretation given to this curvilinear relationship is as follows. No TV or too little TV viewing leads to less awareness of political issues, which, in turn, leads to minimal activity. An optimal amount of TV, say one hour per day, is associated with higher rates of political involvement. Too much TV, on the other hand, deprives the individual of the necessary time needed for sustained political activity. Thus politics competes with TV for individual time and attention; with almost half of all families watching TV three or more hours a day, politics is a chronic loser. Nie points out that politics is not the only loser; with its massive grasp on the lion's share of American leisure, the same type of curvilinear correlation occurs with less participation in other interest areas such as reading, travel, and voluntary associations.

Nie develops his argument further by pointing out that socio-economic and educational levels have consistently been positively correlated with political activity; that is, the higher the socio-economic and/or educational levels, the more politically active the individual is likely to be. If this correlation is valid, then we should have expected more political activity with increasing income and more education since TV became prominent. Nie indicates that although the general population has moved to higher levels in socio-economic status and education during the ascendancy of TV, there has been no commensurate increase in political activity. He suggests that the increasing demands on individual leisure time made by the rise in TV viewing effectively neutralizes the increase in political activity that would otherwise occur with rising social status.

Extrapolating by analogy, Nie suggests that the home entertainment potential of CATV/information utilities, if sufficiently attractive, could offer improved programing that would result in a significant decline in political activism. He argues that with custom-tailored programing CATV could appeal to special interest groups. Thus the more educated groups who are consistently turned off by the mediocre fare of most TV programing, could be turned on by a greater variety of offerings directed to their tastes. Accordingly, Nie predicts that the CATV-information utility is likely to decrease political activism and increase privatization in American life.

Nie does not extend this prediction to cover voting, which he treats as a separate case apart from other political activities. Since home voting systems, if adopted, will be easier to use than present facilities and more accessible to individuals, voting will probably increase. Further, since politically active citizens have traditionally exerted significant checks and balances on the political process, a decrease in such activity will make selection of political leaders even more critical than it has been in the past.

Nie grants that his chain of thought, with its reliance on analogy, does not constitute a substantive proof for his allegation that information utilities will probably decrease the level of individual political activity. His paper has the merit of laying out a significant line of empirical research on explicit hypotheses associated with political activity in the United States with the introduction of mass information utilities.

MacRae's paper (1970), the last in this series, also written after the conference, is on "Some Political Choices in the Development of Communications Technology." The orientation of MacRae's paper is paced at the outset by a quote from Marx, "philosophers have only interpreted the world differently, the point is to change it." MacRae went on to insist that technological change inescapably involves ethical choice, and that social scientists should not shirk their responsibilities in contributing to an understanding and evaluation of the ethical alternatives. Thus the fundamental option of information utilities is ultimately a moral option posing a challenge to basic social values.

Like other contributors, MacRae stresses the importance of social experimentation "that will yield the necessary knowledge concerning system performance at minimum social cost." The statement of the problem, as MacRae sees it, is ". . . how to design a communication system (and implicitly a political-economic system) that will maximize the welfare of the citizens."

MacRae raises social options in the area of the distribution of information to various strata in society, options that are intimately linked with the economics of information utilities. "But insofar as an information utility . . . operates according to prices, it risks giving differential access and information to the wealthy." One suggested way to neutralize this inequity is government subsidy of such service so that key services are available to all at a low price, as in the postal system.

MacRae envisions the emergence of the information gatekeeper who "may be the interpreter, the screener of inputs, the censor, or the summarizer (as in survey analysis)." This new class will be especially pivotal because of the inability of the human consumer of information to sift, interpret, and assimilate vast amounts of information coming from all sides. The problem of information overload will arise as the citizen is exposed to a new barrage of stimulation for his time and attention. MacRae warns that it will become crucial to know which areas of information should be cut off or decoupled so that selective privacy can be maintained by individuals. With increasing variety of alternatives, it will become necessary to exercise the option of shutting out areas that clamor for attention to narrow down the field for selection of desired alternatives. MacRae touches upon a key variant of privacy likely to emerge with mass information utilities—privacy from unwanted information overload. Participatory democracy, he claims, is likely to be more effective if participation is selectively channelled.

9.3   AN APPRAISAL

The picture drawn by the conference participants was gloomy. Most felt that information utilities would go the way of TV. Short-term profits would nibble away at the edges until they reached the entrails of mass information utilities, where victory would be total and beyond redemption.

Individualized telepurchasing, educational, and library services would be fairly expensive at first, with the well-to-do initially subscribing to them, followed by successive incursions into lower socio-economic strata as the mass market proved itself. Many varieties of services would appear, compete, survive or perish, or merge into economic alliance with related services. The market would move inexorably from hundreds of millions, to billions, to tens of billions of dollars. Bitter battles would be fought over the CATV franchise and its regulation.

Most communities would get stale or warmed over fare (such as old TV movies from computer-accessible libraries) from the other mass media; some communities, a small number, would insist on a minimum of public interest and educational programing, which would probably compete unsuccessfully with money-making information services. The public would respond to low-cost, computer-retrievable entertainment libraries, subsidized by interactive commercials over the new media. A vast new branch of advertising would open up, with unprecedented opportunities for tuning and conditioning the masses—the interactive, sing-along, playalong, respondalong commercials. Polling would be conducted by private firms for private interests, utilizing private arrangements with privately owned information utility corporations. The consumer would quickly learn the rules of the game—if he didn't respond to the interactive commercial poll, he would not get the entertainment reward. Like Little Tommy Tucker, the masses would have to sing for their supper.

The information rich would grow richer, while the information poor would grow relatively poorer. Greater information power would lead to greater advantages in the marketplace, greater advantages in the polity, and greater advantages in general social status. The rift in class differences would grow wider and deeper along existing lines of burgeoning information power mediated by entrenched corporations through a new class of information middlemen.

With commercial information utilities, citizen polling would occur infrequently and only under grave or unusual conditions, accompanied by pious breast-beating by corporate information utility spokesmen, since the life-giving flow of profit-making services would be reduced with every second and every minute nonproductively dedicated to public affairs. We have seen this familiar pattern on TV, where it takes a national crisis to wrench programing from its commercial course. Economic relations, ties, agreements, jobs, services, arrangements, and habits would become cast in concrete; millions of people would become irretrievably enmeshed in mutual economic dependency in this vast new information industry, and nothing less than major social upheaval would be able to rearrange the genes and chromosomes of mass information utilities for the common weal. Information pollution would reach unprecedented heights, interactively reinforced by the lockstep cadence of its own victims.

Is this trip necessary? Most of the participants in the Chicago conference decried and denounced this perversion of a vast new resource, but admitted privately, in quiet desperation, that there seemed to be little that anyone could do about it. For every one of the small number of well-intentioned individuals from technical, professional, and political walks of life who can only devote a small fraction of their time to work toward social excellence in information utilities, there are at least one hundred or perhaps one thousand full-time employees of major and minor corporations dreaming, scheming, plotting, and planning on how to make a quick killing through the soft underbelly of the mass information market. Time is relentlessly and inexorably on the side of private commercial interests as mass information utilities, in the absence of any concerted social planning, are molded along the jumbled lines of greatest profit.

How can the gathering dam of information pollution be redirected toward social enlightenment? There are two basic steps that need to be taken. First, we need concerted long-range planning at all social levels—international, national, state, municipal, and local with interdisciplinary cooperation between public and private interests at each level. Second, within the framework of our freely competitive economy, we need a powerful, workable, economic base to pay for the growth and development of mass information utilities.

In regard to social planning, we already have the virtually unanimous recommendations of the conference participants that a top-level national information policy is urgently needed. State and local governments do not have to wait for national planning, they could pioneer on their own if they so choose.

There has been a burst of ideas on city planning to solve runaway urban problems. In the United States, for example, it has been estimated that a new city capable of sustaining one million inhabitants is needed every year up to and beyond the year 2000 just to keep pace with national population growth. All kinds of concepts have sprouted out of the woodwork as guiding designs and philosophies for such new cities. Although some have taken into account the concept of wired cities with direct cable information services, none have seriously pursued the possibilities of using social knowledge for creative individual and communal growth. The total urban complex may be viewed as a pluralistic information ecosystem, with mass information utilities as the central neural network for participatory urban evolution. We don't need final urban solutions because there aren't any. We do need continually adaptive urban complexes with well-developed evolutionary organs for participatory planning, cooperative implementation, citizen evaluation, and iterative reconstruction. Salvation does not reside in dazzling technological advances in the external artifacts of the urban complex, but in grasping the essence of the city as hypothesis.

Proceeding to the next step, I can foresee two pivotal public goals, foremost among others, emerging from planning efforts.

- *Participatory Democracy:* that mass information utilities be duly authorized and designed to permit home voting systems so that the government and the public may benefit from more consultation, feedback, polling, and voting from all citizens more frequently and on more issues as required by evolving legislation in response to changing social conditions.
- *Universal Lifelong Education:* that mass information utilities be duly authorized and designed to provide lifelong information and education for all citizens for computer-accessible knowledge in the public domain regardless of race, religion, or socio-economic status.

These two goals—participatory democracy and universal lifelong education—are nothing less than a direct social commitment to dedicate mass information utilities to the achievement of democratic and educational excellence in the computer-serviced society of the future. No pretense is made to spell out these goals in detail at this point, the aim is to put them right out up front in full view of everyone. Just about everyone will agree in principle. But in practice, who will bell the cat and pay the bill?

The answer, as I see it, could be disarmingly simple. In the Chicago conference, we spun close to it, but did not immerse ourselves in the problem long enough to get there. Mass information utilities, with their obvious capability of collecting, recording, and analyzing individualized responses of users quickly, efficiently, and cheaply—an order of magnitude cheaper as suggested by Bradburn—represent a stupendous new national economic resource. This vast public resource is nothing less than electronic accessibility to the opinion and the will of the people.

In its present scattered, relatively hard-to-get-at condition, public opinion is a highly expensive resource to tackle—witness the high price of mass advertising and polling. But with the public electronically linked together in wired cities, and with significant reduction in time and cost for accessibility, collection, recording, and analysis, public opinion looms up as a vast economic and political resource in its own right.

Now, who should be the prime beneficiaries of this great new resource? Juggle it, play with it, and look at it from all sides—the conclusion is inescapable. *The opinion of the people belongs to all the people, who should benefit first and foremost from its use before any other lesser or private interest.*

The economic solution for dedicating mass information utilities to the public could be plain and simple: public opinion is an extremely precious and valuable commodity, sufficiently valuable to pay for the major costs of installing, operating, maintaining, and improving information services in the public interest. Unfortunately, we did not have an opportunity to explore and test this allegation in any depth at the Chicago conference. As stated here, it exists in a crude and undeveloped form. However, the basic value-judgments underlying the proposed position are not fundamentally affected by differential dollar values placed on alternative ways and means to tap and use computer-accessible public opinion.

To make the present position clear, it is proposed that the political and educational functions of mass information utilities not only ought to, but can come first and have top priority over other uses. Entertainment, telepurchasing, and other services, while eminently useful and desirable, would be secondary. Thus, we would not have the disgraceful situation where time would be relinquished reluctantly by an information utility vendor only under a national crisis. Political and educational public interests would provide prime message traffic for mass information utilities, the economic value of public opinion would underwrite the major costs of such public services, and various forms of commercial information traffic would pay for additional costs, regulated profitable services, and upkeep and growth for privatized services. Although the economics are obviously far more complex than this capsule description, the above is a workable hypothesis as a starting point.

Who would own such mass information utilities? If the bedrock design of public information utilities is based on citizen feedback and on lifelong citizen education, then ownership would have to be fundamentally public. In practice many joint arrangements are possible in which the public is ultimately the basic owner in cooperation with a regulated consortium of private interests. As indicated in Chapter 2, we have considerable precedent in public utility history for public ownership, such as community cooperatives and municipal ownership of water and power utilities. We need new forms, perhaps radically new forms of joint public-private ownership in the public interest oriented toward information as a new type of commodity. As mentioned earlier, the quasi-public nature of

COMSAT Corporation at the national scale, and INTELSAT at the international level are suggestive examples of the new type of public-private consortium of interests that may be required. There are other possibilities, such as the community as a corporation, an evolutionary fusion of cooperatives and conglomerate corporations, suggested to me by H. Snowden Marshall. The community as a corporation is the community aggressively making profits on business conducted within and on community land, with such profits reinvested in the community for self-improvement. Information utilities may provide the economic core for the crystallization of such communities.

A related approach is that proposed by White (1968) in *Public Interest,* in which the community would organize a nonprofit corporation to manage community CATV on a self-paying basis, supported by a freely competitive commercial market. In White's scheme, CATV would open communication doors into the poorest homes, making all kinds of community services available (such as job and training information) in the living room. These nonprofit community organizations could be specially beneficial for depressed areas where low educational levels and functional illiteracy are widespread. White only had one-way CATV communication in mind when he published his proposal; the closed feedback loop from the resident back to central system with computer utilities could easily act as a multiplier for conceivable community services. Both suggestions—the community as a corporation or the community as the sponsor of a nonprofit corporation—are examples of possible community initiative in planning mass information utilities for grass roots community goals. Under the present proposal, wholly privately owned mass information utilities, without some form of public regulation, would infringe on the public prerogative of authorized home voting systems, universal political feedback, and universal lifelong education.

Private interests could subcontract with the publicly owned and managed mass information utilities for specialized services. For example, corporations would be able to get fast and inexpensive polling results on their own products or on proposed products to guide corporate planning. Information utility operators could select appropriate samples based on cross-filed user registries. Individual queries at the home console could be posted in a kind of electronic mailbox, with the user responding later at a time convenient for him. Responses could be automatically collected, reduced, and printed out for the corporate customer with, say, one-day turnaround.

With proper precautions, users would not be plagued by incessant polls if care were taken to employ adequate sample sizes for specified error levels, and if selection were random. The polling load would then be distributed more or less evenly over the entire consumer population. Cooperation from the public would be required which could probably be handled by minimal demands on individuals through poll load-balancing, and by an equitable accounting system of user participation. The public would be faced with the novel prospect of paying its own way into a free or nearly free public utility through the inherent value of its own feedback. It is conceivable and it may possibly be desirable that volunteers be paid for polling participation in excess of minimal public requirements.

A significant legal and educational effort would be required to spell out sanctions and penalties, citizen rights, obligations, and responsibilities, which would be no small task, particularly for those who would feel that a nosy national cable into their home constitutes an insufferable invasion of privacy. Recall Bradburn's prediction that mass information utilities are likely to liberalize our traditional views of privacy in the direction of more sharing and less hiding. This debate could assume major national proportions. Could you imagine how the two political parties might split on this issue, say, in the national presidential election of 1984?

The cost equation for the proposed mass information utilities may be interpreted various ways. Much will depend upon the number and types of requests made for citizen polling, and the variety and extent of private information services. Public information services could be free for all citizens, or they could require a flat low monthly cost for each family, or some low cost on a frequency-of-use basis, as in post office rates, for prime political and educational services. Metered costs could be applied for entertainment and commercial services over and above basic public services. Financial accounting would be virtually automatic with system computers. Details would have to progress beyond speculative armchair exercises into thorough systems analyses and prototype community experimentation, as indicated repeatedly throughout this book.

The presumption in this first pass is that regulated, authorized polling of citizen opinion would pay the lion's share of total costs, which would make it possible to pay for free or virtually free political and educational information services for all citizens. The economic value of computer-accessible public opinion is further held to subsidize costs for nonpolitical government queries, such as the census, authorized public research, and legally sanctioned social indicators. In addition, the economic value of public opinion could also reduce costs for commercial and private applications, with most of the savings passed along to the individual consumer.

This sketch of public-regulated information utilities should not be construed as an attack on corporate and private interests. There is no reason, in principle, why corporate and private information services cannot be developed, operated, and enjoyed side by side with public services, providing proper safeguards are employed. The plea here is for new ways of harnessing corporate energy and organizational inventiveness and releasing free competition in the public interest. There are many ways of developing quasi-public partnerships and consortia to permit a new and higher form of competition—the free and open competition of integrated social teams of public and private interests trying to solve similar social problems. We need every bit of expertise our society has to offer to make mass information utilities a great social success, and we can not afford to alienate or neutralize the creative intelligence of dedicated corporate effort. If we agree that we are all socially accountable, then there is no inherent contradiction between the profit motive and social effectiveness in corporate endeavor.

As of this writing, apparently no major corporations in the computer communications industry have come out with definitive proposals linking mass information utilities to social benefits. There are vast opportunities for profitable and challenging work in higher-order public-private teams in mass information utilities. If the current establishment won't take the lead, perhaps the newer generation of corporate managers will have the courage and the imagination to make the evolutionary leap from maximum laissez-faire to cooperative and aggressive planning and development of corporate goods and services in the public interest—not only for mass information utilities, but for all social problems where they can be effective.

There is no pretense of putting forth the above recommendations as a definitive plan for proceeding with mass information utilities. They constitute a core argument for leading social values, fundamental goals, and broad social direction.

Democratic practice in advanced industrial states has become entirely too complex to rely on postmortem voting every two or four years. The accelerating tempo of contemporary change and the growing pressure for greater and more meaningful citizen participation in the political process have made it manifest that mass information utilities may have come barely in time to meet overwhelming social problems. Not only do we need to vote more frequently on selected issues, but we also need citizen feedback of all kinds to provide social indicators, reliable and valid social indicators, to achieve early warning and authenticated feedback on the progress and effectiveness of our kaleidoscopic social programs. For example, a simplistic 10-year census is not merely a quaint fossil from 1790 America; it is a hopelessly slow, nonreal-time anachronism for tracing swift social change.

The case for dedicating mass information utilities to lifelong public information and education for all citizens is developed more fully in the next chapter. Suffice it to say at this point, that in a democracy, the people are the rulers, and the rulers must be wise. The best investment a democracy can make for long-term excellence lies in enhancing the wisdom of the people. What greater ideal could we aspire to in consecrating mass information utilities?

Information is the most vital utility of them all. Water, electricity, and gas cater to our material needs, but information serves our social, intellectual, emotional, moral, and ultimately our spiritual needs. With mass information utilities we have nothing less than a dazzling opportunity for a major evolutionary breakthrough for democracy and human intelligence, not only in the United States, but throughout the world. Should we follow the path of least resistance and greedily grasp at immediate gains, and bring upon ourselves the pollution of our senses and our minds, or should we be bold and strive to earn the undying praise of unborn generations?

10

INDIVIDUAL OPTIONS

THIS CHAPTER IS a plea for the dedication of mass information utilities to individual excellence. It picks up where the last chapter left off, shifting the focus from the group and the collective to the individual and the personal. The issues are problematic and controversial, bearing on central personal values.

To set the tone, the chapter starts with a blunt reminder that computer science and technology have been created and nurtured by massive public investments of many billions of dollars since World War II, and that the return on this vast underwriting is long overdue and payable to the public in the universally available form of mass information utilities. The fundamental defense of this position is developed next: mass information utilities probably embody the best ultimate means for preserving and advancing the human species—the enhancement of effective human intelligence at all levels of society to new creative heights. This is the central and essential human advance necessary to solve the mounting complexity of social problems within the democratic framework.

Linked to this theme is the belief that each individual should have access to a lifelong education—free and unrestricted access to timely social knowledge in the public domain, guaranteed by an explicit human right to enjoy the cultural heritage of his forebears. The argument then shows how this view of free social knowledge collides with various current interpretations of individual privacy, and how working concepts of privacy can be reconstructed along new experimental lines. The ramifications of changes in human intelligence, computer-catalyzed lifelong learning, and new forms of privacy are assessed in the final section with an eye to their impact on the democratic renaissance which seems to be occurring throughout the world.

10.1 SQUARING THE PUBLIC ACCOUNT

The public treasury, in this country and abroad, has long subsidized the development of computer science and technology. Pascal, who developed the first digital adder, applied his device to relieve the tedium of accounting chores in the administration of Rouen, a post granted to Pascal's father by Cardinal Richelieu. Babbage, the godfather of large digital computers, was subsidized by 17,000 pounds from the English treasury for his "analytic engine"—an insufficient sum for a machine that was a century ahead of its time. The first electrical tabulating machines in the United States were given a major economic impetus from the 1890 census for a data base of 62 million Americans, where they cut data-handling time down to one-third that required for the 1880 census. Between the two World Wars, the United States subsidized the development of analog computers such as the Differential Analyzer developed by Vannevar Bush, which progressed from mechanical to electromechanical devices using vacuum tubes.

World War II spawned the modern digital computer. Analog fire-control computers were used in land-based, anti-aircraft installations and on ships. Public funds supported the creation of the first electro-mechanical digital computer, the Mark I, and the first electronic digital computer, the ENIAC, in the United States.

Continued military support led to stored-program computers after the war, and to digital transmission of data. The detonation of its first atomic device by the Soviet Union in 1949 spurred the fateful development of the first large-scale real-time computer network in the form of the SAGE air defense system. Following suit in the 1950's, other large-scale command and control systems were developed, with breathtaking advances in computer technology in a golden age of massive public support for the computer world running into billions of dollars. Distributed real-time command and control systems were developed for the Army, Navy, Air Force, joint commands, and, of course, for the NASA manned space-flight program.

In the 1960's the era of vast public expenditures for extremely expensive pioneering systems tapered off from billions to hundreds of millions. Dedicated real-time systems evolved into time-sharing systems, the precursors of mass use of central computer facilities. Time-sharing developments were underwritten with tens of millions of dollars by such agencies in the Department of Defense as the Advanced Research Projects Agency. In the 1970's, massive government support of computer developments shows a slowing trend as the 10-billion dollar a year computing industry gathers momentum to soar into higher orbits to become the largest industry of them all in the 1980's.

It is no secret that the government has been the owner of the largest number of computers, and remains as the largest consumer of computer goods and services in the world. American government is easily the most highly computerized government in the world, and the end is nowhere in view. Government fiscal policies concerning computers exert an enormous economic effect on the direction and growth of the computer market. But the government represents the people, and government expenditures are public expenditures. The public has a right to know whether its vast and continuing investment in computers has paid off—a total, cumulative investment which will soon approach the 100 billion dollar level for military and nonmilitary computer goods and services.

What has the public received in return for supporting the birth, growing pains, and turbulent adolescence of this vast industrial colossus? Has there been any long-range social plan directed by the government for the benefit of the public? Generally speaking, the computer-related military-industrial establishment has benefited immensely from the rise and growth of computers. The military services—with all their computer aches and pains—are still the envy of military establishments throughout the world, on both sides of the Iron Curtain. In all fairness, the defense of the United States has been kept ahead of the competition in no small part because of sophisticated computerization.

Needless to say, the American computer industry has moved from millions to billions in gross sales, and has evolved through spectacular technological advances in hardware developments, less so in software developments, and, as I have pointed out throughout this book, hardly at all in matching computers to human needs and individual behavior. This industry, despite its dominance by IBM and a small number of lesser giants, has been highly competitive, although this too may change in the current computer recession.

The federal government has profited enormously from computers. The NASA manned spaceflight program could never have gotten started without sophisticated real-time control systems based on massive injections of computer power in system design and development. All major federal agencies find computers indispensable for bookkeeping, accounting, information storage and retrieval, statistical services, and research and development. Americans can be justifiably proud of the remarkable diversity of computerized services in running the government, also the envy of the rest of the world.

The pattern of the record can now be seen in outline. The military-industrial complex has benefited most by vast public expenditures for computers. The most sophisticated and advanced planning in the computer world has been and is taking place in computerized military commands and in the board rooms of computer-related corporations. Civilian government has to struggle harder for the computer dollar; thus its planning is second best, often down at the level of fighting for computer budgets from one year to the next.

Now, how about the ordinary individual who will stumble upon his first significant encounter with computers when it comes in the form of mass information utilities? Sad to say, $100 billion later we find almost a total vacuum in responsible social planning to pass the benefits of computers along to the man in the street. Shocking? Scandalous? Draw your own conclusions.

We have fought and paid dearly for a whole generation to make computers safe for bureaucracy; now it is time to fight to make computers safe for democracy. The government and industry owe it, and owe it many times over, to dedicate mass information utilities to our highest democratic ideals. This may be an especially painful decision for the computer communications industry since they would have to deny themselves free rein over the mass computer utility market, a denial that they can refuse only at their peril and ours.

Two sides of the economic argument have been presented so far. In the last chapter it was pointed out that public opinion is a major national resource of vast economic value that can be harnessed to mass information utilities to pay major costs for development and operation for the twin public goals of citizen feedback and universal education, with commercial usage secondary. In this chapter, the argument has been put forth that the public has paid dearly to become a member of the computer club, and that responsible social planning must treat public needs first to meet the long-overdue return on the public investment on the eve of mass information utilities. Perhaps the greatest public need lies in the potential of mass information utilities for stimulating human intelligence, the key to public wisdom and social excellence.

10.2 COMPUTERS AND HUMAN INTELLIGENCE

In an invited address to the Society for the Psychological Study of Social Issues, Martin Luther King, Jr. (1967) quoted a theme from Victor Hugo which is the burden of this phase of argument: "If a soul is left in darkness, sins will be committed. The guilty one is not he who commits the sin, but he who causes the darkness." If mass information utilities can cast the light of informed intelligence and dispel the darkness of ignorance for Everyman, then the guilty ones are those who would sacrifice the intelligence of the many at the altar of the few.

If effective human intelligence—the application of knowledge to action—can be substantially elevated for the entire population with mass information utilities, then the payoff for the human species is so overwhelming that we dare not deny it to the public, not in this country nor any other country. On the other hand, although mass information utilities may increase the amount of information and will speed up the flow of information to and from individuals, it does not necessarily follow that it will fundamentally influence the quality or level of effective human intelligence. In that case, we would be less inclined to sink major national resources into its development for all of society.

It is beyond the scope of this chapter to enter into the intricate details of the technical literature on the nature, theory, test, and measurement of human intelligence. Instead, the main argument of the present position will be sketched, with an indication of various counterarguments. In essence, the present position is that mass information utilities, over the long run, will revolutionize the range and depth of all levels of effective human intelligence, above and beyond the restrictive and hazardous changes possible with genetic engineering.

Our present conception of human intelligence historically has been determined by conditions that antedated computers. These conceptions, in turn, are being and will be revolutionized by computers. These historical conditions have led to a series of stereotyped ideas on the nature and future of human intelligence. One is that intelligence is a relatively fixed and stable attribute, progressing through a predetermined developmental pattern throughout the life span of the individual. Another is that intelligence is primarily genetically determined and only secondarily influenced by the total socio-technological environment. A third, and crucial methodological stereotype, is that intelligence is what intelligence tests measure (especially paper-and-pencil tests). A fourth stereotype is that the development of intelligence is of special concern during youth, and that little or nothing can be done to influence intelligence during adult years, particularly in old age. These and related stereotypes have painted a kind of fatalistic picture of fixed human intelligence, tightly bound by the available variation in the genetic pool of the species.

Intelligence tests are strong on vocabulary, arithmetic, analogies, and factual symbolic data that lend themselves to inexpensive paper and pencil format. Intelligence tests are weak in measuring cooperative skills, sympathy, empathy, humor, the ability to communicate with others, and most personality traits that may be reasonably related to intelligence. These embarrassing methodological limitations are summarily excommunicated from "true" intelligence by labeling them as nonintellectual traits. As a result, psychologists have unwittingly foisted upon the public an unworthy ideal of human intelligence, one cast in the stunted image of what paper-and-pencil tests measure. Instead of pointing to the severe limitations of abstract surrogates of human intelligence, such as paper-and-pencil tests, psychologists have given tacit approval to wholesale application of paper intelligence to social affairs.

Unfortunately, the paper-and-pencil testing movement directed much of the energies of a whole generation of psychologists (largely between the two world wars) away from live human behaviors in real-world settings, and toward secondary areas of measurement methodology and the hypothetical structure of abstract traits and skills. It is to be hoped that the tunnel vision that only aspires to paper intelligence will give way to broader and deeper forms of behavioral intelligence tested in the real world on the whole man. Computers, particularly mass information utilities, are bound to play a significant role in the new version of effective, working intelligence.

My view of human intelligence is that within the variable bounds of the physiological phenotype, it is historically and culturally conditioned, environmentally cumulative, situationally open-ended, and eternally plastic in principle if not in practice. As we approach the era of mass use of computers, we should be aware of the distinction made by John Dewey, who said: ". . . in all ages, man has made discoveries, but it has been reserved for this age to discover the process of discovery." As we unravel the enigmas of human creativity and social innovation, our growing advances in the conditions of creativity will continue to rub off on individuals and groups to the benefit of all. Teilhard de Chardin (1964), in developing his concept of the "noosphere," the emerging composite intelligence of the human race, emphasized the driving force of science and technology in "planetizing and commingling" minds to ever-higher levels. "Humanity is building its composite brain beneath our eyes."

In a scholarly review of the technical literature on experience and intelligence, Hunt (1961) concluded that we can find better ways to design encounters with the environment so that children can "achieve a substantially faster rate of intellectual development and a substantially higher adult level of intellectual capacity." He further believed that maximizing each person's potential for intellectual development would increase individual differences as measured by available testing techniques. Concerned with the growing complexity of society, Hunt urged (p. 363) that we strive toward "an ever larger proportion of the population with intellectual capacity at the higher levels . . . for intellectual giants to solve the problems that become increasingly complex. The fact that it is reasonable to hope to find ways of raising the level of intellectual capacity in a majority of the population makes it a challenge to do the necessary research. It is one of the major challenges of our times."

Much of the semantic mischief over the stereotypes of intelligence is attributable to the platonic cast of thought in our culture; that is, we tend to think of intelligence as an independent archetype, as an abstract entity having an eternal existence of its own together with other luminous essences in Plato's heaven of pure forms. There is a long-standing philosophical dispute over this issue that need not be repeated at this point except for its bearing on our attitudes toward intelligence.

From a scientific point of view, we can never measure pure intelligence as such. We must operationally define intelligence with respect to controlled conditions in a standardized working situation for the individual—in effect, we can only deal with operationally defined *effective intelligence*. Effective intelligence refers to the capability to adapt to changing conditions and to solve problems as they arise, including the broader capability to understand and exercise directive control over the course of events in accordance with long-range objectives. Once the transition is made from abstract, quintessential intelligence to effective intelligence, we are free of the semantic trap. Further, we are better able to appreciate the difference between the genotype (the hereditary structure latent in the fertilized egg) and the phenotype (the developing individual throughout his life cycle). It then becomes apparent that we can only scientifically measure the effective intelligence of the individual in his capacity as a living, evolving phenotype.

Man does not live in a vacuum, nor does his intelligence operate in the abstract. Effective intelligence implies real-time individual transactions with the environment. We are prone to forget that we are pygmies standing on the shoulders of a three-billion-year evolutionary colossus on Earth. We take our current level of effective intelligence for granted. Studies of feral man, human beings reared without the benefit of any human contact, show us the vast advances in effective human intelligence made possible by community living and spoken language. Only in this century has most of the human world passed from preliterate to literate populations. Printing, reading, and writing are technical cultural inventions, and it is unnecessary to belabor their impact on effective human intelligence. The next massive evolutionary breakthrough in multiplying effective human intelligence is the transition of the human species from computer illiterates to computer literates, the transition finding its technological embodiment in mass information utilities. Just as the illiterate citizen is no match for the literate citizen in total potential, so will functional computer illiterates be no match for the effective computer literates in the computer-catalyzed world of the near future.

There are deep resistances to facing up to computer literacy as the next major evolutionary breakthrough in the effective level of civilized intelligence. Perhaps Wyndham Lewis (1928) touched the raw nerve at its root when he saw that scientific and technological advance would make past and current humanity look like "barbarous and foul creatures" to posterity, and that we would be "inferior fatally to all the future." We have only recently learned that we cannot have an unlimited expansion of population, nor an ever-expanding economy, but we have not yet learned that the most precious expansion, the plastic expansion of the human mind and spirit, is within our reach and freely available for all if we choose to make it so.

The skeptic may be amused by the sweeping vision of computer-catalyzed human intelligence that has been put forth, but he may remain convinced that the millennium has not yet arrived, particularly since no scientific proof has been offered to back up the glittering claims. Such proof is difficult since only fragmentary experimental evidence is available on man-computer problem-solving, as indicated in Part III, and since much of the argument must remain speculative. The appropriate scientific response is to empirically test operational hypotheses of the purported gains in effective intelligence. The proposed research program for man-computer problem-solving in Chapter 8 is a step in this direction. In the meantime, we have to lean on the meager available evidence and extrapolate as best we can.

10.3   HUMAN CREATIVITY IN MAN-COMPUTER PROBLEM-SOLVING

In this section, an interpretive review of available experimental data on human creativity is offered to support the general assertion that man-computer problem-solving is likely to substantially enhance effective human intelligence. The individual studies cited in Part III, and additional material covered in the author's text on man-computer problem-solving (Sackman, 1970) form the basis for the generalizations and suggestions that follow. At this early point, and in the absence of far more research, the argument is suggestive rather than conclusive.

The most significant findings in the experimental literature lie in the structure of individual differences and the dynamics of human problem-solving. Some of the leading findings are briefly mentioned. Time-sharing, the online precursor of mass information utilities, embodies the creative advantages of massed learning, whereas batch benefits from the advantages of spaced or distributed learning. For example, massed learning is better for more complex and innovative tasks, requires less warmup time, is better for short tasks learned directly to completion, facilitates extensive exploration, and involves less forgetting between successive work sessions. Spaced learning, which occurs more often in offline problem-solving, minimizes fatigue and boredom, works better for long routine tasks, involves fewer interference effects and mental ruts, requires fewer trials or less effort to reach the performance criterion, and places more dependence on long term as opposed to short-term memory.

A related area is part vs. whole learning. Behavioral studies have generally shown that optimal learning occurs when subjects attack the largest piece of the problem that they can handle and progressively work up to the total problem. The online mode tends to have the edge over the offline mode in this respect since it is easier for an online user to split the problem up into manageable pieces and work up to the entire problem. This is particularly crucial for the marginal performer who must start with small portions of the overall problem. An online mistake is easily recoverable at the console. An offline mistake can abort the entire computer run and force the user to wait the full turnaround time for the next pass at the computer.

Another major area in man-computer problem-solving lies in the distinction between trial-and-error learning and insightful learning. Both types of learning occur under online and offline conditions. Insight was found by most subjects to occur when they concentrated intensively upon their problem, particularly when they were alone. The online mode favored greater creativity and insight for open-end tasks, providing the terminal was accessible and the service satisfactory. Under such conditions, the online mode permitted subjects to explore their problems more extensively, try out more hypotheses, and generally build a richer internal data base to work toward the critical apperceptive mass that led to reported insight.

The fundamental stages of man-computer problem-solving were essentially the same as the classical problem-solving stages observed without computers.

The four stages posed by Wallas (1926) still remain as the basic paradigm for creativity: preparation, incubation, illumination, and verification. While there is some doubt over the nature and conditions of the incubation stage, the other stages are experimentally well established. A key stumbling block in all the problem-solving literature, with or without computers, is a reliable and valid taxonomy of problems, linked to the dynamics of problem-solving. For example, lower-order tasks such as rote memorization, nonsense syllables, mazes, and conditioning situations seem to be better interpreted by trial-and-error classical learning theories espoused by behaviorists and associationists; more novel situations and more creative tasks, for man and animal, seem to be characterized by insightful learning as depicted in gestalt and functionalist theories. The author has demonstrated a combination of trial-and-error and insight learning in solving computer programing tasks in which insight corresponds to improvements in logical solutions, with trial and error characterizing lower-order syntactical solutions in the debugging process. A working taxonomy of human problems still remains as a general theoretical challenge in the literature on creativity and problem-solving.

Another fundamental methodological problem in the general area of human creativity with computers lies in the distinction between problem formulation and problem solution. The online/offline literature and most of the behavioral literature is primarily concerned with solutions for well-defined problems. Except for case histories and biographical studies, we have not made much experimental headway into the analysis of creativity in the formulation of significant problems. Mackworth (1965) has stated the general case for problem finding as opposed to problem-solving. In the computer milieu, except for sporadic anecdotal reports, we have not done significant work on the potential impact of computers in enhancing the exploratory behaviors that enter into the creation of significant new problems.

Turning now to individual differences, the intent is to portray available evidence in man-computer problem-solving in a coherent conceptual framework. Factor analysis has been a leading tool in behavior studies concerned with the structure of the intellect, personality, and various skills. Major controversies have developed over the last few decades over competing theories of intelligence, personality, and occupational skill and trait structures. As computers enter the scene in force, they are bound to modify such theories. For example, the virtually exclusive reliance on paper-and-pencil testing will give way to online performance measurement not only in standard test situations, but more significantly for comprehensive real-time performance measurement in computer-aided tasks. In computer-assisted instruction, formal testing is superfluous at the end of the lesson or lesson series if testing has been occurring continuously with every new frame.

The author has developed a hypothesis, a Progressive Differentiation Hypothesis, which offers some advantages in explaining the initial results on individual differences in man-computer problem-solving. This hypothesis was motivated by several considerations. First, computers, viewed as an extension of the human intellect, or as an aid to effective human intelligence, almost seem to magnify individual differences. There is no need to enlarge on the ubiquitous presence of very large individual differences in man-computer effectiveness; it is everywhere in the available literature. The proposed hypothesis, as we shall see, goes a step further and asserts that computer developments are likely to continue to enhance effective human intelligence, perhaps almost indefinitely, and that these advances will probably continue to amplify individual differences over a growing spectrum of human capabilities.

A second motivation lies in the apparently limitless number and diversity of problems to which computers can be applied in mass information utilities. This virtually unlimited diversity requires a pluralistic conceptual framework to allow elbow room for new and perhaps radically different computer applications that could arise in the future. Here is one potential solution to the taxonomy problem mentioned earlier—a pluralistic, open-end, evolutionary framework changing with the changing ecology of human needs, skills, and technology.

A third motivation lies in the need to systematically chart the genetic growth of computer knowledge and skills in individuals from their first encounter with computers through the most advanced stages of computer skill and expertise.

A fourth motivation lies in the need for more effective teaching of computer knowledge and skills, and in systematic test and measurement of such attributes in a practical manner.

A fifth motivation lies in the desirability of channeling the computer-related skills into the mainstream of behavioral experimentation on the structure and dynamics of skills and traits in intellectual, personality, and occupational areas of inquiry.

With these various considerations in mind, the Progressive Differentiation Hypothesis is defined in two parts, as follows:

1. Advancing computer tools and information services tend to amplify the range of individual differences in man-computer performance, and such advances will continue to expand effective human differences in a freely competitive and open environment.

2. The pattern of expanding individual differences assumes the following general form: when individuals are first exposed to and indoctrinated in the use of computers, either a general factor, or a small number of well-defined group factors in man-computer communication proficiency, or a combination of both, are held to account for a substantial portion of observed individual differences; however, with the advent of diversified tasks and increasing experience, this relatively small set of general proficiency factors for beginners tend to progressively differentiate into numerous separate and independent factors associated with increasing specialized experience.

The pattern of progressive differentiation of man-computer skills was suggested to the author from long-established factor findings in the literature on intelligence testing (Garrett, 1946). In essence, at early ages a general verbal factor was found in scores of children on various ostensibly different tests, whereas at later ages, particularly at the college level, the factor structure progressively changed to differential, specialized skills that were relatively independent of each other, such as numerical, spatial, and logical skills. The analogy in the computer milieu, is that computers are becoming a powerful force in helping to shape effective human intelligence, and that computer services tend to elevate the average performance level and also accentuate the differentiation of human skills in man-computer tasks.

The fundamental justification for online creativity, according to the experimental literature, lies in the quality of the problem-solving experience and the excellence of the solution. Several demonstrable elements help online systems to contribute to a more satisfying and more effective problem-solving experience. Online systems are apparently more universally preferred by users. For various reasons, the interactive mode is generally more enjoyable, more challenging, more permissive, and more responsive. In view of the long and sorrowful history of prototype computer services that failed, it is crucial to have positive user preference working with proposed systems, and the online system represents an attitudinal evolutionary mutation toward greater user acceptance.

In addition, the online mode is more effective for situations requiring massed learning, easy movement from whole to part learning, insightful learning, individualized problem-solving styles, and immediate knowledge of results. Stating the case in a nutshell, the interactive mode, which is the online precursor of mass information utilities, is the method of choice for exploratory problems requiring intensive, highly individualized human efforts aimed at creative insight in open-end environments. Such problem situations are more likely to enhance the quality of the online problem-solving experience, and they are more conducive to the achievement of excellence in solution. If we design mass information utilities to capitalize on these leads and other advantages yet to be discovered by new research, we are bound to reach greater heights in human creativity, individually and collectively.

10.4 LIFELONG LEARNING

Lifelong learning is undergoing a profound metamorphosis from slogan to reality. The educational investment in corporations for in-house and on-the-job training, the professional outlay for meetings and symposia, the proliferation of university extension courses, and the growth of educational TV, among many other manifestations, point to the increasing concern of the adult population to forestall personal obsolescence in a swiftly changing world. It is almost commonplace to look forward to four or five different careers over the working life span. With the irrepressible growth of the knowledge industry—a conglomerate that might be very broadly defined as information goods and services, with education as its largest segment—we are rapidly becoming a learning society. And as we become more and more a learning society, we are beginning to gain working insight into the basic continuity between education and experience, a key concept espoused by John Dewey at the turn of this century.

Once we accept the idea of the learning society, we may be startled by some of the conclusions to which it leads. At the heart of this concept lies the ever-intriguing possibility of the elevation of the effective intelligence of individuals and society as a whole. If the learning society is upon us, the creative society cannot be far behind. We urgently need to switch from education as an activity historically and arbitrarily confined to childhood and early adulthood, and divorced from action, to education as continuous with life and linked directly to social action. Then the intellectual tunnel vision of the single skill is transformed to the limitless horizon of multiple and interdisciplinary skills. Diversity of education leads to new combinations of ideas, to offbeat creative possibilities, the hallmark of genius and a higher order of intelligence. With mass information utilities dedicated to lifelong learning, the door may open for new renaissance men, for men of all seasons.

Once we break loose from classical, rusty age brackets for education, we can seek educational possibilities in younger and older directions until such possibilities become coextensive with the total life-span. Then we can start helping many afflicted minorities in our society with the aid that Maimonides described in his "Guide to the Perplexed" as the most charitable and humane help of all—self help.

It is almost scandalous that the lion's share of educational resources is universally allocated to older students at higher rungs in the educational ladder when the vast weight of scientific evidence indicates that the greatest possibilities for influencing the formation of intellectual, emotional, and social behavior patterns occurs at the earliest ages. The middle and upper classes have instinctively understood this developmental correlation, and have traditionally sent their preschool children to various nursery schools. Project Head Start is a belated and token effort to provide positive preschool experience for underprivileged children in preparation for elementary school. Mass information utilities, backed up by tested libraries of diversified instructional sequences (yet to be developed), could make a massive impact on home and nursery school training of the very young. We know from studies with orphanages, institutional child care, and deprived homes, that children reared in stimulus-starved surroundings in their earliest years are intellectually crippled and socially stunted for life before they ever reach kindergarten. Mass information utilities, dedicated to universal lifelong learning, including the voiceless minority of the very young, could make democratic equality of opportunity more a reality and less a pious wish. If we do not speak up for the very young, who will?

By the same token, mass information utilities, with the infinite patience possible only in tireless machines, could revolutionize the education of millions who are mentally retarded and the more numerous millions of borderline cases, early in life and throughout life, to become more productive citizens and well-rounded human beings. When we talk about the possibility of uplifting the level of individual intelligence, we must think of the entire distribution of intelligence in both directions. For those at the low end of the scale, even modest gains could make a vast difference in personal achievement and social adjustment. Many now institutionalized could be helped to reduce their heavy burden on society and lead the independent lives so necessary for mutual and self-respect. If we do not speak up for the mentally handicapped, who will?

If we view education in its broadest sense, as applying to the whole man, we should be able to help the emotionally defective as well as the mentally defective. Preliminary work with interactive, computer-aided psychotherapy with autistic children and with psychotic patients—admittedly too early to warrant major generalizations—shows promise for bringing many of these individuals back into the social mainstream. The permissive computer program, tolerating high error levels and irregular progress, could offer a variety of machine personalities likely to open up channels of communication with those withdrawn from social contact. Studies in interactive man-computer communication have indicated that users inevitably tend to project a "personality" onto the computer, whether the program designers intended it or not (Sackman, 1967). Much of this projected personality devolves around the detection and handling of humman errors. We know virtually nothing about desirable and undesirable computer personalities and their effects on users.

The social potential of low-cost, machine-aided psychotherapy for regulated out-patient treatment at the home, could conceivably reduce the crushing need for bed space and soaring hospital and personnel costs at our overcrowded institutions for the mentally ill. Such computer-aided individualized psychotherapy could be judiciously combined with advanced and inexpensive forms of neighborhood group therapy, supplanted by computer-accessible group therapy videotapes. If we don't speak for the mentally ill, who will?

In our culture, by an almost unconscious code of common consent, elderly people are relegated to the human scrap heap. Much of this unfortunate stereotype is reinforced by the paralyzing adage, in young and old alike, that "you cannot teach an old dog new tricks." The middle-aged group, coasting along on the momentum of earlier successes, is also inclined to lose interest in further educational effort except when forced to it by circumstances. The downhill trend in "learning readiness" in the general population can probably be traced back to the day formal education was completed. If we take the concept of lifelong learning seriously, and if means are continually available for easy access to needed information, as in home educational services with mass information utilities, then the stupendous and pointless waste of talent in our "senior" citizens could be channeled into new areas of social creativity for the benefit of all. Some will see a new threat in this renaissance of the old from retreaded oldsters who will want to hold on to positions and power longer, making it harder for young blood to move up. Although the problems of a rejuvenated gerontocracy are not to be lightly dismissed, such fears pale before the liberating prospect that the human species may witness more productive wisdom and less self-imposed senility from every individual throughout his total life span. The fabled fountain of youth issues from the eternally creative springs of the human mind.

If we push the concept of lifelong learning and the learning society, all of society, to its limits, we arrive at a fundamental human right— the right of free access to open social knowledge. This is not a new human right; it has been proclaimed by the United Nations (1967) and by UNESCO, in particular, as a basic right. It was easy for the United Nations to enunciate these rights in principle since no one was significantly affected in practice. However, with the advent of mass information utilities, and with order of magnitude reductions in the cost of dissemination of individually requested information, this sleeper in the pantheon of human rights becomes a monumental issue for the entire human species.

We are now led full circle to Victor Hugo's moral option; shall we condone darkness and ignorant sinfulness or shall we strive for knowledge and enlightenment? We have the technological equivalent of the Biblical dilemma of Adam and Eve with the Tree of Knowledge. More knowledge creates greater capacity for good and evil; and as God passed along the gift of knowledge to man, so can we pass along our gift of shared social knowledge to posterity—a gift, this time, given with our blessings, not in anger or with vengeance.

The right to know springs from existing democratic doctrine and United Nations' principles. It could form the springboard for leaping over the stale arguments dividing nations to the higher plane of universal sharing and exchanging of all cultures. The arguments of old were rarely resolved on their own terms, they grew stale as they gathered dust and became irrelevant.

In its "Declaration of the Principles of International Cultural Cooperation," UNESCO proclaims the universal human right, to "enable everyone to have access to knowledge, to enjoy the arts and literature of all peoples, to share in advances made in science in all parts of the world and in the resulting benefits. . . . Cultural cooperation is a right and a duty for all peoples and all nations, which should share with one another their knowledge and skills. . . . Broad dissemination of ideas and knowledge, based on the freest exchange and discussion, is essential to creative activity, the pursuit of truth and the development of the personality" (p. 93).

While few would disagree with the basic human right to share and enjoy global knowledge, most would probably reject the idea as hopelessly utopian. After uttering some pious platitude, the average citizen would lack the courage to pursue the matter in a serious practical vein. However, if the technological predictions of experts are brought into account, it becomes obvious that the capability for achieving this seemingly utopian pipe dream is indeed close at hand—so close that we are already hard-pressed for the necessary time for intelligent social planning, or worse yet, it may already be too late for sufficient lead time.

By way of illustration, consider Figures 10.1 and 10.2, which depict systematic expert opinion of expected advances in computer technology. These opinions were collected in a study employing the "Delphi" technique (Parsons and Williams, 1968), named after the celebrated oracle of ancient Greece. In this technique expert opinion is solicited, compared, fed back to anonymous and distributed participants, and iterated until consensus or a point of diminishing returns is met. Figure 10.1 shows expected advances in computer developments, derived from Parsons and Williams in 1968 from a sample of approximately 100 experts. Figure 10.2 portrays expected advances in computer applications from the same study. In each case, the median for the given item is shown by the high point, and the interquartile range is shown by the low and high cutoff points. That is, 50 percent of all experts predicted the realization of each item in the indicated time frame.

These results show some interesting properties. Results are listed in rank order of median expectations. Note that the variability of predictions tends to increase as the estimated date is projected further in the future;

that is, the boxes in these two figures tend to get wider as you go down the list from earliest to latest predictions.

No brief is made for the reliability or validity of these predictions. It is obvious that the experts show considerable disagreement among themselves. Illustration of the total range of responses for all these items would underscore the disagreement more heavily. Use your own judgment or the judgment of your own set of experts to gain some appreciation of the speculation involved. After all these qualifications and provisos are made, it is nevertheless manifest that computer power will rapidly become far cheaper than it is today, and that the manifest destiny of computer services is to spread into every organization and home and to reach every individual in the United States, probably before the end of this century.

The time and rank ordering of computer advances and computer applications may vary significantly from these predictions, but barring major social catastrophe, universal computer services will be available for the general population, including computer network linkages between many or most major urban centers on Earth, by the year 2000. The checklist of techniques and applications in these three figures is only crudely indicative of the range, power, versatility, and ubiquitous presence of expected computer services.

To return to the earlier theme, is it too early or too late to initiate large-scale social planning for this stupendous set of changes in human communication and social control? The human right of universal access to open global knowledge is not a utopian pipe dream, it is a far-reaching social problem here and now that we neglect only at our own peril. And before fleeing from this raw confrontation into the reality of endless implications and complications, ask yourself where you stand on this human right, not just for today, but for the unborn generations who have no advocate in the "now" generation.

10.5 PRIVACY VERSUS THE RIGHT TO KNOW

A latent form of national paranoia has appeared in the United States under the militant banner of "invasion of privacy." Conduct a free-association test. Ask anyone to respond with the first words that pop into consciousness when you mention computers and society. "Invasion of privacy" is bound to be high on the list, combined in various forms with

1) Flexible internal storage, i.e. easily increased or decreased in size and at will with use of plugging units

2) Majority of software built into the hardware, i.e. small packages of integrated circuits to be attached to the computer

3) Briefcase computers ("advanced slide rules" with large memory)

4) Oral input to the computer

5) Laser memory

6) Transmission of data by laser signals

7) Cards and paper tapes no longer used as a communication medium

8) One million byte memory small enough to be included in an independent desk computer

9) Pocket-size computers ("advanced slide rules" with large memory)

10) Computers learning from their experience

11) Computer price decreased with a factor of 100

Figure 10.1. PREDICTIONS OF COMPUTER DEVELOPMENTS
(from Parsons and Williams, 1968)

"dehumanization" and "depersonalization." Instead of being welcomed for their vast potential to uplift humanity, computers are being attacked as the nemesis of humanity with privacy as the rallying point on the battleground. Opportunistic politicians have helped to fan the sparks into

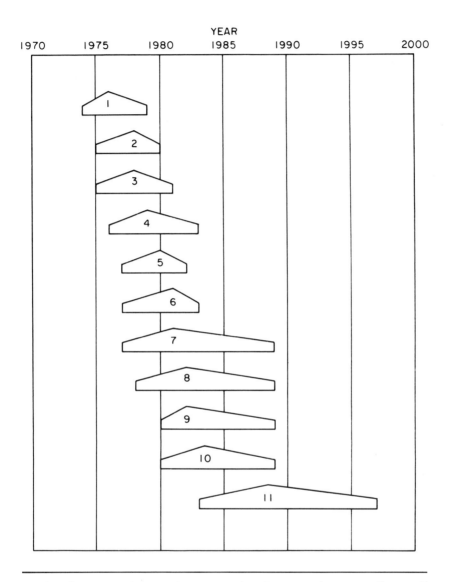

YEAR

roaring flames as they outdo one another in presenting an endless trail of bills purporting to protect individual privacy from the encroachment of computers. Privacy has joined God, motherhood, and country as one of the sacred untouchables, and in the stampede to protect privacy, society's right to know is being trampled in the dust.

Whether we like it or not, privacy has been riveted into the public mind with iron bolts, and any realistic attempt to use computers to

1. Increase by a factor of 10 in capital investment in computers for automated process control

2. Air traffic control — positive and predictive track on all aircraft

3. Direct link from stores to banks to check credit and to record transactions

4. Widespread use of simple teaching machines

5. Automation of office work and services, leading to displacement of 25 percent of current work force

6. Education becoming a respectable leisure pastime

7. Widespread use of sophisticated teaching machines

8. Automatic libraries looking up and reproducing copy

9. Automated looking up of legal information

10. Automatic language translater — correct grammar

11. Automated rapid transit

12. Widespread use of automatic decision making at management level for planning

13. Electronic prosthesis (radar for the blind, servomechanical limbs)

14. Automated interpretation of medical symptoms

15. Construction on a production line of computers with motivation by "education"

16. Widespread use of robot services

17. Widespread use of computers in tax collection

18. Availability of a machine which "comprehends" standard I Q tests and scores above 150

19. Evolution of a universal language from automated communication

20. Automated voting, in the sense of legislating through automated plebiscite

21. Automated highways and adaptive automobile autopilots

22. Remote facsimile newspapers and magazines printed at home

23. Direct electromechanical interaction between man and computer

24. International agreements which guarantee certain economic minima to the world's population as a result of high production from automation

25. Centralized (possibly random) wiretapping

TECHNICAL PROGRESS in automation as predicted by a panel of experts has been obtained by investigators at the RAND Corporation using the Delphi technique. The length of each bar represents various estimates put forward by the "middle half" of the panel. In each case one quarter — the "lower quartile" — proposed dates earlier than that at which the bar begins and another quarter — the "upper quartile" — give dates beyond that marking the end of the bar. Each bar has a peak value which represents the median date estimated

Figure 10.2. PREDICTIONS OF COMPUTER APPLICATIONS
(adapted from Parsons and Williams, 1968)

accelerate the flow and transmission of human knowledge has to take this misological stereotype into account. And what could possibly represent a greater threat to personal privacy than a Big Brother computer terminal in every American home? If a national data bank to improve

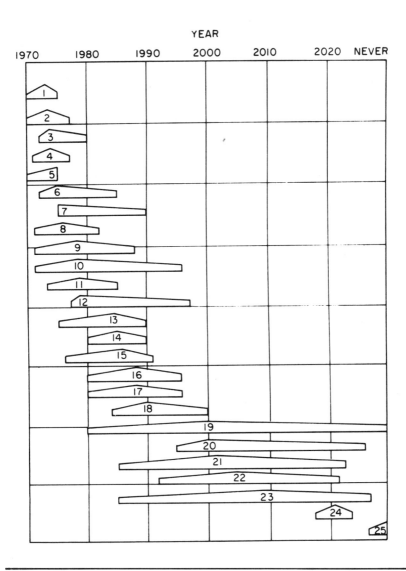

YEAR

1970   1980   1990   2000   2010   2020   NEVER

statistical government services can become the whipping boy for the purveyors of privacy, just imagine the political capital that can be amassed with public information utilities.

Computers may become the universal scapegoat of the twentieth century. Like all good scapegoats, computers are powerless; they cannot talk back; the thought of their mysterious, mind-like machinations inspires anxiety, and their arcane activities divert attention from true villains and real problems. If current stereotypes are unchecked, clever demogogues may convince growing numbers of gullible people that attacking and destroying computers can cleanse the soul and heal the mind.

Privacy has been reified and has taken its place in the platonic pantheon of archetypes with the good, the true, and the beautiful. The definitions of privacy put forth by the experts are sufficiently vague and amorphous to allow anyone to project exaggerated fear without limit. And amorphous privacy serves up a feast for the paranoid palate.

Take, for example, Westin's (1967) definition of privacy (p. 7):

> Privacy is the claim of individuals, groups, or institutions to determine for themselves when, how, and to what extent information about them is communicated to others.

This definition emphasizes the role of the individual or group to serve as gatekeeper for self-information. Westin adds:

> Viewed in terms of the relation of the individual to social participation, privacy is the voluntary and temporary withdrawal of a person from the general society through physical or psychological means, either in a state of solitude or small-group intimacy or, when among larger groups, in a condition of anonymity or reserve.

This second part of his definition stresses the right to be left alone.

Now, if anyone takes these and similar definitions literally, then individuals, groups, and institutions would register, track, and control all communicable information related to them, and decide whether they wanted to hold or release such information. If we incurred lawsuits over every alleged invasion of everyone's right to withhold information and their right to be alone, the legal profession would take over the world. All the time and resources of humanity from now till eternity would not stem the ocean of confusion that would follow.

Justice Black, expounding his philosophy in a series of lectures at Columbia University (1968), put forth a balanced interpretation that runs counter to the current apotheosis of privacy. He has refused to stand against such threats as electronic eavesdropping on the grounds that if the framers of the Constitution said nothing about it, they did not specifically intend to protect it. "Even though I like my privacy as well as the next person, I am nevertheless compelled to admit that the states have a right to invade it unless prohibited by some specific constitutional provision."

Justice Black expressed but one opinion. In an earlier opinion, Justice Brandeis (1928) extolled the inviolate nature of privacy, and linked it to the Fourth Amendment of the Constitution (p. 780):

> The makers of our Constitution undertook to secure conditions favorable to the pursuit of happiness. . . . They sought to protect Americans in their beliefs, their thoughts, their emotions and their sensations. They conferred, as against the Government, the right to be let alone—the most comprehensive of rights and the right most valued by civilized men. To protect that right, every unjustifiable intrusion by the Government upon the privacy of the individual, whatever the means employed, must be deemed a violation of the Fourth Amendment.

Sweeping subjective definitions of privacy, subjective in the sense that everyone decides for himself what is and what is not his cup of privacy, fall prey to vast and changing individual differences in taste, habit, and style of life. Between people there are vast differences along one major dimension of behavioral privacy, the introversion-extroversion continuum; and within each individual, as Freud pointed out to us, there are large unconscious domains that are kept removed and private from self-awareness by powerful motivational forces. We know pitifully little about the psychology, sociology, and economics of "privacy" and we would be foolhardy to impose lockstep, uniform standards on everyone whenever privacy is "threatened." In a one-sided crusade to defend privacy against all possible enemies we can greatly increase the protection of criminals, including the protection of the new robber barons who chart our future and are accountable only to themselves; we can cover up the suffering of the voiceless, aid and abet the child-battering parent, insulate and isolate the mentally disturbed, and, in the long run, maximize ignorance.

Westin chose to link privacy with freedom in the title of his classic, and I applaud the need to highlight and make public the new dangers to freedom inherent in the potential of technological intrusion on privacy. However, I also believe that an equal and opposite study of privacy and tyranny, particularly the privacy of the powerful, would balance the scales and point to the more rational wisdom of the golden mean.

In many respects, privacy is a new mask for an old and largely discredited philosophy—the philosophy of laissez-faire, a term that means to leave alone. Laissez-faire, invoked at the time of the industrial revolution also under the banner of freedom, enabled the powerful to exploit the weak. The new obsession with privacy draws its strength from the old laissez-faire, which, rejuvenated and rearmed, threatens to turn the clock back.

As long as privacy is deified and hypostatized we will be caught in a vicious circle to defend it at all costs. If we follow the example of scientific method, and reconstruct "privacy" into exact operational definitions for concrete situations, then the monolithic paranoid problem is transformed into separate, manageable problems that can be studied in their own right and resolved on their own merits under the test of controlled experience. To change the situation from maximum security hysteria to responsible social checks and balances, we need to crack the back of the privacy scare.

The above argument should not be construed in any sense as a defense of the position that all information should be public and none private. The boundaries and the shades of gray between public and private are continually in dynamic equilibrium, changing with new technology, new social forces, and new personal needs. The abuses of inaccurate and misleading data, random errors, unauthorized use, the new methods of physical and psychological surveillance, and the potential of computerized systems to obtain more personal data at much lower costs are well known and have been extensively documented. But, those who have dealt with secure and restricted information over many years, as in defense and aerospace industries, are fully aware that information security is invariably inexpensive and never truly foolproof. New standards and procedures are required within reasonable commitments and available resources to meet specified levels of protection under the law. And such standards and procedures need to keep up with changing technology, including computer technology.

For example, many have pointed out that derogatory files on individuals, as in credit records and employment dossiers, pose a major threat to individual freedom and mobility. We have become accustomed to the uncontested file. Adversary procedures need to be built into record keeping for evaluative files, not merely after the fact when the individual may be irretrievably harmed, but into the record-keeping process itself when information is first input to the system and throughout the life history of potentially controversial information. We know almost nothing about adversary information systems for evaluative data, and it is apparent that semicomputerized advocates of both sides of contested issues need to be developed for a balanced and open approach to controversial data. The next chapter outlines one early form of adversary information systems for social planning.

Many have pointed out that the law acts too slowly and responds too late to provide adequate safeguards for the public in a rapidly changing society. Miller (1968), for example, points out that law derives from a prescientific age. Law is based on authority and precedent, and, as Justice Holmes commented, "it is revolting not to have any better reason than history to justify a decision."

Miller makes recommendations for improving social relevance and providing more effective early warning in law. He proposes stronger development of public as opposed to private law. (Ralph Nader has long urged a new breed of advocates for the public to counterbalance the dominance of corporate advocates.) Miller feels that "law is too important to be left to the lawyers" and that all citizens should receive a fundamental grounding in legal concepts in high schools and colleges. He recommends a variety of reforms in law schools to bring them "screaming and bucking into the twentieth century." He urges lawyers to be active in systematic exploration and debate of public policy issues and in extended use of technical experts. In drawing his indictment, Miller does not respond to his leadoff issue—to make law responsive to social issues in real time rather than after the fact.

There is a curious carryover from ancient times that pervades the legal process today, a carryover that permeates the debate on computers and privacy. This is the form of wishful thinking that believes in the magic of instant social change by authoritative fiat. Passing a law makes it so; this stems from the ancient belief identifying rulers and authority with divinity and omnipotence. We suffer under the delusion that legislation for a War on Poverty automatically eliminates poverty, that Medicaid and Medicare sweep away medical problems for the aged, that legislation on freedom of information will make knowledgeable citizens, that anti-segregation laws resolve racism, and that proposed laws on auditing and contesting personal files will secure individual privacy. Neither individual wishing nor collective wishing incanted by the most august assemblies can make it so. The missing link in law is the acid test of verified experience—experimental formulation and empirical validation. Faith in fiat is no match for faith in empirical verification.

In the last chapter, Dunn's (1970) proposal for experimental prototypes for national data banks was cited as a basic recommendation for social experimentation. In previous chapters experimental information utilities have been consistently put forth as the method of choice to gain the social knowledge and experience necessary for mass use. This requirement is especially urgent in the area of legal safeguards establishing the proper balance between public knowledge and individual privacy. Experimental prototypes could serve as a test bed for legal alternatives. Following Brandeis's prophetic recommendation for experimental public utilities in the Great Depression, community prototypes would make it possible to get hard facts and figures on operationally specified infractions of provisional laws instead of condemning future users to the legal prejudice of well-intentioned but uninformed legislators and courts. The nub of the argument is that laws are hypotheses, not eternal principles, and the sooner we develop experimental institutions for testing legal hypotheses in the light of verified experience, the sooner will we bridge the gap from impotent fiat to empirically validated law. The metamorphosis to experimental law through institutionalized social experimentation would mark the liberation of legal process from the dormant cocoon stage to free flight.

In experimental tests of "privacy" a prototype system facility is required to record, reduce, and analyze user behaviors. These capabilities essentially amount to computerized tools for experimental recording and analysis of user performance. Further, successful policing of user requests subsequently requires the accumulation of large and continually updated samples of user statistics to maximize detections of unauthorized access and minimize false identification of authorized access (Type I and Type II statistical errors). This is, in fact, a problem in user quality control with formidable sampling difficulties stemming from low probability expectations for unauthorized access. Careful system design will be helpful in getting object systems off to a good start through "best" estimates of initial safeguards, particularly against inadvertent and accidental access of sensitive information to unauthorized users. But it is also essential to recognize that the changing nature of user behavior is a key variable in the privacy equation, and only through continuing empirical studies of human performance in the total system context will it be possible to keep up with changing user requirements for information security. Further, no lawmakers, system designers, managers, or users will be so prescient as to unerringly pick the best of all possible designs among competing design alternatives for information security. The changing alternatives will continually need to be experimentally tested and evaluated for evolutionary cost and effectiveness. The privacy problem calls for interdisciplinary design and test effort based on continuing experimental evaluation.

While experimental prototypes constitute a necessary condition for developing effective and humane doctrine in the balance between the need to know and the need to withhold, they are not sufficient. A philosophical confrontation on basic principles is required, one that goes beyond a single-track approach to protect privacy against all intruders. Privacy is close cousin to secrecy, and excessive use of secrecy is inimical to the free growth and development of a learning society. In appraising the balance between withholding and disclosing information, the Committee on Science in the Promotion of Human Welfare, sponsored by the American Association for the Advancement of Science (1969), concluded (pp. 787-90):

> Protective measures against the extension of regulations limiting disclosure are necessary, but they are not enough. It is equally essential to develop methods of dissemination and critical appraisal appropriate to the exponential growth of science and technology. Our task is to define, protect, and institutionalize the processes of science and technology so that they will contribute to the well-being of the whole of mankind.

For many, the emotional appeal of privacy is linked to the preservation of individuality and personal freedom. The thinking goes something like this: the more others know about me, the more vulnerable will I become, and the more harm they can inflict on me. Anonymity is equated with freedom. But the argument cuts both ways. The more an individual knows, the more options he has, the richer his individuality, and the greater his chances for creative growth. Greater sharing of knowledge is here equated with richer social communion and greater creative freedom. Although these stereotypes grossly oversimplify the issues, they point to some of the emotional stances that color personal philosophy and individual preference in the social design of mass information services. It is apparent that mass information utilities will transform individualism as we know it today. What directions can this transformation take?

10.6 INDIVIDUALISM AND THE DEMOCRATIC RENAISSANCE

Is there a connection, a common link, between worldwide student rebellion, the growing rift between the young and the old, the black and colored revolutions, the spread of industrial democracy, and the rising expectations of undeveloped nations? These are global trends, transcending national differences and penetrating into the heart of the most powerful of all forms of government, the family and the individual. The cause may be attributable to the progressive rise of effective human intelligence all over the world, fueled from new experience and diverse educational sources, expressing itself in greater demands for self-determination and self-government in the family, at business, in schools, in government, between nations, and in international movements. The gathering storm of rising human intelligence is blowing democratic winds into every nook and cranny of human experience, driving out authoritarian pollution, and creating a global democratic renaissance.

It is an irrepressible human trait that intelligence aware of itself seeks more choices, greater freedom, and wider participation. The learning society is social intelligence aware of itself, creating new avenues of group experience and cooperative accomplishment. The old authoritarian idols of the tribe are being overthrown and new idols are being substituted. Some are turning to offbeat religions, others to drugs, others to nihilism and anarchy, some are just dropping out, while others are tenaciously clinging to traditional patterns. Each individual is attempting to work out his own salvation as the leading creeds struggle for men's minds.

Heretofore, the struggle for men's minds has been framed in terms of the content of competing sets of beliefs rather than the method used to establish such beliefs. Thus, wars have occurred between religions, between nations, and between political systems. But with growing global expectations, a more fundamental conflict is occurring between competing methods, methods of perceiving and ordering the world, methods of conceiving and dealing with individual and social problems. The apocalyptic confrontation is between authority and science, between dogma and hypothesis, between fiat and experimental method.

In a world of accelerating social change, authoritarian method becomes less and less relevant as it increasingly fails to solve social problems. William James pointed out that people operate on conceptual credit, that they test their beliefs only when forced to it by adverse circumstances. The credit of authoritarian methods is running short, and the pressure of puzzling new problems forces creative search and novel solutions in ever-increasing tempo. The concomitant shift in internal values is from comfortable, established stereotypes to the precarious world of hypotheses. Paradoxically, we are being forced into a new life style where we must deliberately make more errors than ever before, systematic errors under controlled conditions, to attain new insight and better solutions. Forged in the crucible of necessity, the experimental ethos is reshaping human thought and reconstructing human relations.

The experimental ethos is being modulated and amplified by the media of mass communications. The first stage has been the information explosion, marked by vast quantities of information spewed over the airwaves on radio and TV, and over the press, indiscriminately spewed to all in the form of broadcast. The second stage is the personalized information implosion, where each individual receives concentrated information which he personally selects, and interactively modifies to suit his own needs. The information implosion is the online transition to mass information utilities. Social experimentation, sooner or later, must travel over the real-time communication arteries of society, and these arteries will increasingly become embodied in mass information utilities. This new medium will alter the structure of social messages and reconstruct the perceptions, judgments, and feelings of all who use it. And from the new form of social communications, new forms of individuality will arise.

New varieties of individualism stem ultimately from the creative growth of effective human intelligence. This creative growth, however, hinges on the reciprocal maturation of science and democracy—the democratization of science is necessary to release scientific method from the bondage of scientific aristocracies to make it available to all citizens, eventually culminating in citizen scientists in spirit and outlook. Experimentation with democracy is necessary to elevate democracy from its levelling tendency toward mediocrity, which Alexis de Tocqueville (1835) viewed as the principal shortcoming of democracy, toward the creative standards of individual excellence and cooperative social experimentation.

There are and will be great obstacles and pitfalls in the path of the democratization of science and the experimentalization of democracy. Many scientists, remote in their medieval exclusiveness, will continue to insist that only properly trained elites can practice science. But the scientific cloisters will crumble with massive intrusions of scientific method at the earliest ages in schools and at home.

Individuals such as Dewey (1939) and Piaget (1970), and organizations such as the American Association for the Advancement of Science (Gagné, 1966), have long clamored for early scientific training. Scientific method can be introduced earlier, taught more comprehensively, and followed up more intensively throughout multiple careers in lifelong learning. Waiting until college, as we do today, before significant scientific skills are imparted, results in too little too late. Eventually, it will become commonplace to encounter individuals with multiple Ph.D's in pursuit of overriding social problems, such as world ecology and population control, that do not respect artificial disciplinary boundaries. It may already be too late—elementary school children today will be in their prime in the world of 2000, when they will need every resource of scientific awareness they can command. Mass information utilities should make it possible for the public to pick the best knowledge, the best examples and the finest recorded thoughts of social and scientific leaders in developing new skills and talents.

The experimentalization of democracy will also be resisted on many sides from many quarters. Washington, Adams, and Jefferson had no illusions about democracy as an experiment; in their inaugural addresses they urged their countrymen to pursue the American experiment vigorously. In his first inaugural address, George Washington warned his countrymen to preserve "the sacred fire of liberty . . . as deeply, as finally, staked on the experiment intrusted to the hands of the American people."

Unfortunately, democracy arose more from avoidance reactions than from positive considerations during an era when the authoritarian ethos held undisputed sway over all civilization. In the United States the key consideration was the protection of the individual against the encroachment of the British government, generalized afterwards to all government. More emphasis was placed on negative constraints than on positive conditions for life, liberty, and the pursuit of happiness. Rugged individualism was extolled over fraternity, equality of opportunity, and the elusive responsibility for the well-being of others. Within the tall walls of personal privacy we have long forgotten that we are each our brother's keeper.

But democracy is founded on the constructive framework of real-time social experimentation, in which all continually contribute to the conduct and direction of the entire society. As science is universally based on empirical feedback, so is democracy based on empirical individual feedback—the fundamental experimental paradigm is there, in nascent form, waiting to be tapped. As science builds cumulatively upon the work of relevant findings, so does the citizen need to build upon accumulated social knowledge. The citizen-scientist of the future will require free access to available social knowledge so that his efforts can lead to creative extensions which, at the same time, conserve the best of the past. The mass information utility is the obvious real-time repository of open social knowledge, and the vehicle for systematic, individualized citizen feedback. And as such, the mass information utility is the prime technological catalyst for the experimental ethos and the democratic renaissance.

If democracy is ever to have a religious core, that core, as prophesied by Walt Whitman in *Democratic Vistas* (1871), will be founded on brotherhood. Egocentric democracy will be transmuted into allocentric democracy dedicated to social concern for individual growth. In allocentric democracy, it will be realized that individuality can only be attained by authentic concern—perhaps even religious concern—for the individuality of others. The ovens of Buchenwald and the ashes of Auschwitz bear mute testimony to the brutalization and the extinction of individuality.

All individuals are unique by virtue of nonreplicable genetic makeup and nonreplicable experience. Democracy in all walks of life enhances individuality, while authoritarianism demeans and flattens individuality. Each person is a living experiment in individuality. The human right to free access to available social knowledge enriches the personal experiment—a right that can become a reality with mass information utilities dedicated to lifelong learning and to uplifting all human intelligence. Individuality can then streak to new heights in creative profusion. If mankind hungers for an endlessly challenging frontier, only the frontier of new knowledge has the power to forever create new frontiers within itself.

Mankind is haunted by a dream—a dream that can materialize only if we so wish it—that the ultimate destiny of computers is to transform and enhance effective human intelligence. Not just technical intelligence, but moral and social intelligence. Not just for evanescent elites, but for all of humanity. Not just for present generations, but as long as the human species survives. We are in dire need of advocates for posterity, not only for the outer world of terrestrial ecology, but even more for the unlimited inner world of every human mind.

11

ONLINE SOCIAL PLANNING

MASS INFORMATION UTILITIES may revolutionize social planning as we understand it today. The revolution may be expected along the lines of greatly increased participatory planning in social affairs. People will want to contribute to basic decisions in the design of their future in democratized social planning.

This chapter is an initial, exploratory effort concerned with the problem of research and development in the virgin field of online social planning. To help cast the problem in perspective, the status of planning is reviewed for useful leads. Planning is seen to be in an early predisciplinary stage, undergoing rapid change and remarkable growth.

Planning theory is reviewed and found wanting. A provisional definition and theory of planning are developed to make planning more amenable to scientific method. The crux of the proposed approach is to conceive of plans as operationally defined hypotheses subject to empirical test and evaluation. Building upon individual and group expectation theory and findings in the social science literature, a mutual expectation theory is suggested. This theory is derived from an analysis of conditions that lead to a working consensus of cognizant individuals in object plans. The theory is aimed at democratized social planning.

Suggestions for Participatory Online Planning are outlined, stemming from initial considerations of mutual expectation theory for planning. In essence, participatory online planning refers to online implementation of problem-solving, tutorial, and adversary processes among planning alternatives that culminates in consensus, particularly among dispersed participants. Mass information utilities are examined for their potential in contributing to participatory social planning in a democratic context.

11.1 RETROSPECT AND PROSPECT IN PLANNING

11.1.1 The Predisciplinary Status of Planning

The general literature on planning reveals some noteworthy trends. Although most of the literature is of the anecdotal, case-history variety, full of platitudes and maxims on how to plan, there is, nevertheless, a growing awareness of the need for establishing an applied scientific discipline in planning. The United Nations has well-established standing committees on national and international planning; The Institute of Management Science (TIMS) conducts an ongoing College on Planning; the federal government continues to endorse the Planning-Programming-Budgeting concept originally developed in the Department of Defense under McNamara's aegis (Novick, 1965); voluntary international leagues for advancing the techniques of socio-economic planning are being formed by private groups, such as "Futuribles," (De Jouvenel, 1967), and a growing number of universities are recognizing planning as a unique discipline and are offering graduate programs in planning (Branch, 1966). In 1967, the World Future Society was formed, with over 1000 members from 18 countries. The Office of Education and the Department of Defense in the United States have funded a growing number of future-oriented research centers. The American Academy of Arts and Sciences appointed a Commission on the Year 2000 (American Academy of Arts & Sciences, Summer 1967). The Third International Conference on Science and Society, held in Yugoslavia in 1969, focused on scientific planning and "futurology." These quickening trends in planning for the economy, government, education, and international affairs are being matched by increased corporate and group planning, a trend that is extending rapidly to all levels of society. Mass information utilities may provide the ultimate vehicle for citizen participation in social planning.

The general literature on planning is useful in the present context for the light it casts on the method of planning, as distinguished from the content of the planning, which already has a vast literature in business, government, and social science. Branch is one of the leaders in this field; the following comments are derived from his text on planning (1966), which is oriented toward establishing planning as an interdisciplinary, applied science. He points out that the first significantly organized approach to planning occurred in 1909 in the United States to meet the needs of city planning. While city planning has the longest tradition and has become highly specialized, the more recent outgrowth of planning in the federal government has shown the most sophisticated developments, particularly in military contingency planning. He specially singles out cost-effectiveness techniques such as PERT programing and contingency modeling as indicative of qualitative and empirical trends in planning. Branch stresses psychological factors in planning and how little we know of such factors. His goal is that of "comprehensive planning," which he views as a distinct discipline in its own right, drawing freely from pure and applied sciences, and aimed at securing greater human control over changes in the physical and social world. Branch's claim for the scientific status of planning requires greater emphasis on empirical verification and corrective feedback. While he recognizes the need for checking predictions against outcomes, he does not formalize the verification of planning to the extent possible with modern experimental procedure. This criticism applies generally to the field of planning—planning will not become an applied science until plans are viewed as evolving hypotheses, subject to iterative formulation, test, and verification in the course of changing conditions.

De Jouvenel (1965 and 1967) disputes the claim that planning can become an applied science. He believes that planning is not concerned with "true or false" but with the "realm of the possible." His approach is to use "reasoned conjecture" by pooling the best techniques through organizations devoted exclusively to planning, through "look-out institutions." A major objection to De Jouvenel's approach is that he views the present largely intuitive status of planning as a permanent condition of planning. In this respect he seems to echo Henri Bergson's intuitive philosophy of "creative evolution." De Jouvenel espouses a planning aristocracy to handle human planning rather than a more democratic interpretation which holds that planning, in its broadest aspects, is everybody's business. De Jouvenel does capture the contemporary mood of planning, however, when he insists that the increasing tempo of change implies a decreasing life expectancy of present knowledge, which, in turn, requires more intensive planning at more frequent intervals. Increased planning can compensate, at least in part, for growing uncertainty.

Helmer (1966) stresses the value of structured expert opinion in planning and has attempted to formalize rating procedures in forecasting scientific and technological events. He describes an iterative rating scheme in which the experts do not interact directly, which he calls the "Delphi" technique. The original rating procedures were rather crude by modern standards in the construction and analysis of rating forms. Helmer originally applied such standardized techniques to a large and impressive panel of experts. A significant literature on Delphi studies has subsequently emerged, nationally and internationally, based on variations of Helmer's original techniques.

In connection with the possibility of evolving toward online Delphi, Helmer (1967) states:

> As for automating part of the Delphi process, I may mention that we have begun to experiment with the use of JOSS on-line computer consoles. By having each participating expert in a Delphi inquiry give his responses on a JOSS console, we can process a group's responses automatically and immediately feed back the information and instructions that make up the next questionnaire. Thus an effort which might otherwise take weeks or months can be carried through in an hour or less. Moreover, once the interaction among the respondents is via machine, it would be relatively easy to enrich the process by providing on demand automated access to existing data banks and eventually even to banks of mathematical models that might aid the expert in the analysis of the situation under consideration. Once this process has been perfected, it is easy to imagine that for important decisions simultaneous consultation with experts in geographically distinct locations via a nationwide or even a worldwide computer network may become a matter of routine.

Emery (1965) is among the theorists in the field who has attempted to formalize the planning process and relate such formalizations to computer models. Emery operates from a management context in virtually identifying planning with management.

Emery's central notion of hierarchical planning is essentially isomorphic with the organizational hierarchy; that is, broad planning policy is generated at the top, more detailed policy at middle-management levels, with fine details worked out and implemented at the operational levels. In his hierarchical model Emery poses a means/ends nesting of tasks within tasks where higher-level planning imposes constraints on lower-level planning.

Emery views planning as "deciding in advance what is to be done." He distinguishes between formal and informal planning but does not follow up on the implications of this useful distinction. The key steps in the planning process, according to Emery, are assembling data, constructing a model, developing alternative plans; evaluating consequences of the alternatives; selecting the best plan; implementing the plan; and controlling the plan in operation. Although Emery sees the educational potential of planning, he pays virtually no attention to the contribution of human elements, such as problem formulation, consensus, creativity, and problem-solving, or negotiation and compromise.

In describing computer-aided planning, Emery cites potential advantages of computers:

- Cut planning costs.
- Decrease planning time.
- Explore a wider variety of planning alternatives.
- Generate more comprehensive plans.
- Standardize planning procedures and planning control.
- Generate detailed consequences of planning alternatives.
- Provide more rapid convergence toward the few best alternatives.

In his recent text on forecasting and planning, Ayres (1969) does not list computers in the appendix nor does he treat computer-aided planning (let alone online planning) as a methodology in its own right. To take another example, while Kahn and Wiener (1967) expatiate on the impact of computers on society in *The Year 2000,* they do not pursue the impact of computers in their own domain of methodology in planning and forecasting.

A potentially revolutionary trend in planning is the involvement of an ever-increasing circle of individuals in planning, both qualitatively, in terms of diversity of contributing disciplines, and quantitatively, in terms of sheer numbers of planning participants. Jungk (1969) has epitomized the democratization of planning:

> The democratization of future research will really have to start at school level. Lessons devoted to the probable, possible and desirable futures should gain at least as much importance as the teaching of past history.
>
> A democratization of forecasting, future studies and future research will probably have to contend with the reproach that it will be time consuming. In fact, fast decision making is easier in autocratic types of societies. But in the next phase of humanity, there will be even less people willing to accept orders and directions coming "from above." They will want to participate actively in the shaping of their future destiny. The future belongs to all of us, not just a small elite of ruling experts and decision makers.

Fromm (1968) also foresees a democratization of planning along humanistic guidelines (p. 101).

This means that the knowledge of man, his nature, and the real possibilities of its manifestations must become one of the basic data for any social planning.

On the level of government planning, the personal interests of the politicians often interfere with their integrity and hence with their capacity for humanist planning. This danger can be reduced only by a much more active participation of the citizen in the decision-making process, and by finding ways and methods by which government planning is controlled by those for whom the planning is done.

The trend toward democratization of planning is occurring in the midst of growing dissatisfaction with the methods and effectiveness of planning at all social levels. The United Nations finds national planning, particularly for developing countries, in a state of disarray. Political instability, poorly trained planners, unrealistic goals, inadequate resources, lack of planning controls, and indifference to planning plague many countries. National planning has been criticized as aimless, misanthropic, and destructive of cultural values in advanced countries on both sides of the Iron Curtain. Corporate planning is under continuing attack by planners who claim that management has yet to understand the scope and role of planning, and the disciplined support it needs. Individuals find personal planning increasingly unstable as the rate of social change spirals upward, and as personal obsolescence is accelerated. Problems are mounting faster than they can be solved, and some, such as Platt (1969), claim that "Every problem may escalate because those involved no longer have time to think straight." There is a gloomy cloud of impatience and impotence hanging over contemporary planning as the circle of participants widens.

11.1.2 Alternative Methods in Planning

Although the planning literature is immense, spilling over into almost every imaginable field of social endeavor, the literature on planning methodology, as indicated above, is conspicuous by its absence. One reason is the newness of planning as a discipline. In a recent review of the theory and practice of planning, Mockler (1970) points out that there were virtually no books on planning prior to 1960, but 25 book-length studies in the 1960's. Perhaps the key reason for this embarrassing state of affairs is that planning hypotheses have not been tied to experimentally controlled empirical verification of such hypotheses. There are many factors contributing to this unfortunate situation. A leading factor is the lack of a tradition of real-world experimentation; experimental method is still confined primarily to the laboratory, while planning must prove itself in the crucible of the real world. A show of scientism is put on by many practitioners through the use of esoteric mathematical, statistical, and logical techniques; but without the acid test of empirical verification in a credible experimental setting, the most elaborate mathematical and verbal posturing on the planning stage, while full of sound and fury, does not signify science.

Failure of planning to achieve scientific status is related to human culpability. Freewheeling armchair speculation is safer, faster, easier, and, for many, more fun than careful experimentation. Esoteric models of planning provide excellent insulation from the outside world against invasions of the modeler's privacy. And neither do managers like their planning estimates and predictions to be compared with actual outcomes —a gentlemen's agreement not to seriously pursue such comparisons seems to be an article of faith in the planning management establishment for mutual privacy, protection, and security.

Finally, there is a lack of scientifically based planning theory to guide research. Tools, models, and techniques are not theories, no matter how elaborate they may be; simplistic or fanciful analogies are not theories unless they are systematically linked to experimental method. Later in this chapter, an attempt is made to develop a theory of planning amenable to experimental test and evaluation for online planning, and ultimately, for mass information utilities.

The immediate goal of this section is to present an introduction to the variety and scope of planning techniques, and to some preliminary comparisons among them. We are fortunate that this task has been initiated by Rosove (1967) in a project concerned with educational planning. Building upon techniques described by Bell (1964) and others, Rosove lists 21 planning and forecasting methods, to which I have added 5 additional categories: dialectical planning (Mason, 1969), PERT/CPM, PPB (Bureau of the Budget, 1965), normative planning (Ayers, 1969), and confrontation techniques. The 26 "methods," adapted from Rosove, are briefly described below.

DEFINITIONS

1. *Brainstorming.* A form of group dynamics designed to encourage creative and imaginative thinking about the future via an uninhibited exchange of ideas.

2. *Delphi Technique.* A procedure for systematically soliciting and collating the opinions of experts on the future of a preselected subject by sequential individual interrogations, usually by questionnaires. An effort is made to achieve consensus or convergence of opinion by the feedback of results to the participants.

3. *Expert Opinion.* The opinions of qualified specialists about the future of the phenomena within the field in which they have renown or the recognition of their peers.

4. *Literary Fiction.* Novels or other forms of literature which imaginatively or creatively construct future social systems or conditions.

5. *Scenarios.* The imaginative construction into the future of a logical sequence of events based upon specified assumptions and initial conditions in a given problem area.

6. *Historical Analogy.* Inference of the similarity between attributes or processes of two or more different historical developments, social conditions, or societies, on the basis of other presumed similarities.

7. *Historical Sequences.* Formulations of the independent recurrence of similar sequential social, economic, and cultural processes and conditions in different societies or nations; or the treatment of socio-cultural phenomena, in general, in terms of logico-historical sequential phases or stages of development.

8. *Content Analysis.* Abstracting from content—speeches, novels, art forms—generalizations or trends pertaining to a wide range of phenomena such as public attitudes, values, political ideology, national style.

9. *Social Accounting.* An effort to conjecture about the future of a nation, social system, or institution by determining the "sum" of a series of independent factors, a, b, c, . . . n which comprise it at time t, resulting in profile A, and then progressing to series a', b', c', . . . n' at time t', resulting in profile B.

10. *Primary Determinant.* The interpretation of socio-cultural events, conditions, and processes in the past, present, and future in terms of the consequences of a single major factor or primary determinant such as Marx's mode of production or McLuhan's media.

11. *Time-Series Extrapolation.* The extension of a series of measurements of a variable over a period of time from the past into the future.

12. *Contextual Mapping.* The extrapolation in graphic form of the interrelationships of functionally related developments. A "map" shows logical and causal interdependencies.

13. *Morphological Analysis.* A systematic procedure for exploring the totality of all possible solutions to a given large-scale problem; for example, all possible ways of propelling rockets. The definition of the problem provides an initial set of parameters, and the full range of possible answers to the problems inherent in each initial parameter represent another set of parameters, and this set is then explored, and so on, until all the parameters have been exhausted. A possible solution to the problem of propelling rockets may then be any combination of the dependent parameters within the sets of parameters at different levels of the analysis.

14. *Relevance Trees.* A procedure for determining the objective means or techniques required to implement an explicit qualitative goal, for example, to permit all students to proceed through educational programs at their own pace. Each branch point of the tree, moving downward from the stated objective, represents a potential decision to follow a particular implementation direction. Either qualitative or quantitative criteria, or both, may be used to aid the selection process. Each subsequent branch level is considered, in turn, as a possible set of alternative goals and each alternative is analyzed to determine the objective means required to implement it.

15. *Decision Matrices.* A method for allocating resources, determining priorities, or selecting goals by graphically displaying the relationships or multiple interdependent variables in two or three dimensions. For example, one dimension of a decision matrix in education might be available funds while the other dimension might be faculty and administrators' salaries, maintenance costs, or library costs.

16. *Deterministic Models.* A deterministic model is a mathematical abstraction of real-world phenomena. It is a set of relationships among quantitative elements of the following types: parameters, variable inputs, and variable outputs. The development of computer technology has made possible the implementation of models which are too complex for noncomputerized solutions.

17. *Probabilistic Models.* A probabilistic model is a mathematical representation of the interactions among a number of variables in which the value of at least one variable is assigned by a random process. The numerical results of repeated exercises of the model will yield different numerical values. The values of variables may be based on estimates of

future conditions. A computer facilitates running many exercises with the model.

18. *Gaming.* (Not to be confused with game theory.) Provides a simulated operational present or future environment which makes possible multiple simultaneous interactions among competing or cooperating players. Games may be entirely manual in nature, or a computer may be used in some types of games to provide simulated inputs to the players, and to record and analyze their performances.

19. *Operational Simulation.* The exercising of operators of a system in their actual environment by the use of selected simulated inputs to provide education and training to the system's operators and/or to facilitate analysis and understanding of the system's operations for evolutionary design and development. The inputs may represent the world of the future.

20. *Benefit-Cost Analysis.* A quantitative method designed to assist decision-makers to make the most efficient tradeoffs between financial resources and competing programs. The total cost of each program, both direct and indirect, is estimated and the programs may be evaluated in terms of the advantages, outputs, or results (benefits), both short-run and long-run, which each is estimated to have. These estimates are expressed quantitatively. Since both program costs and their benefits have specific values, several alternative courses of action may be systematically compared and evaluated.

21. *Input/Output Tables.* Models of an economy which is disaggregated into sectors and in which explicit account is taken of sales and purchases between sectors. One set of parameters which is common to all such models is technical coefficients; the technical coefficients of an industry are the numbers of units of input of each industry which are required in order to produce one unit of output of the given industry.

22. *Dialectical Planning.* Generation of an opposing set of "best" plans representing conflicting values and views, followed by structured debate using the same data base until the data bank is exhausted, performed by opposing advocates for management.

23. *PERT/CPM.* Program Evaluation and Review Technique using Critical Path Method analyses; the analytic portrayal of costs, manpower, and schedules in graphic form in terms of activities and milestones for an object system to achieve planning objectives within specified resource levels.

24. *PPB.* Planning, Programing, and Budgeting; technique intro-

duced by the Department of Defense and used extensively in other government agencies since 1965; requires systems analyses of agency objectives, definition of a five-year plan, cost-effectiveness analyses of proposed programs, with annual updating of plans and budgets for the five-year projection, and continuing assessment of programs.

25. *Normative Planning.* Also referred to as teleological planning; deliberate and critical examination of the fundamental value judgments underlying planning goals, prior to and distinguished from strategic planning for working toward specified goals, and tactical planning to achieve defined goals.

26. *Confrontation Techniques.* This category includes a broad class of techniques involving some element of involuntary external coercion of individuals or groups to change individual traits, group policies, or plans by some form of social confrontation—for example, psychodrama, T-groups, sensitivity training, Synanon game, intervention in professional meetings, marches, strikes, and "sit-ins."

11.1.3 Classification of Planning Techniques

As an aid to determine where research needs in social planning are greatest, Figure 11.1 portrays a classification of the planning techniques mentioned earlier. The context incorporates planning stages (*x*-axis) and system development (*y*-axis). Planning stages, from earliest to final stages, as shown in Figure 11.1, are Normative, Strategic, Tactical, and Operational. The system development steps are self-explanatory. Both scales show a time dimension from the present as the origin reference point, to the future, in rank-order of stages in planning and system development. The planning/system development space has a significant property, probably not obvious at first glance. In essence, it indicates that all levels of planning occur at all points throughout the system development process. That is, normative, strategic, tactical, and operational planning occur not only when the system is still a gleam in someone's eye, but also throughout the definition, design, operation, and obsolescence of the system. This portrayal thus emphasizes both the gestalt nature of planning and its evolutionary thrust. It also provides a backdrop for scientific test and evaluation of planning in a systems context.

Note that planning techniques are distributed in the system development/planning stage space in Figure 11.1 in six groups. Starting from earliest planning and earliest system development stages, the first group of techniques consists of brainstorming, Delphi, expert opinion, scenarios,

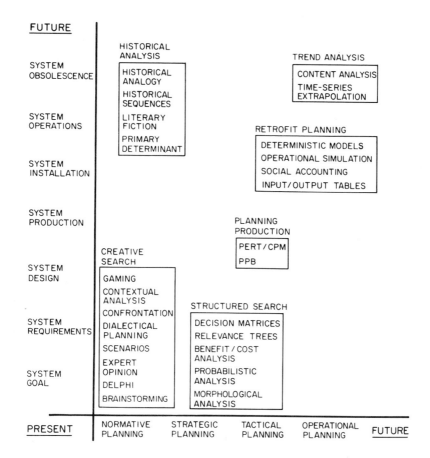

Figure 11.1. DISTRIBUTION OF PLANNING TECHNIQUES IN
SYSTEM PLANNING AND SYSTEM DEVELOPMENT

dialectical planning, confrontation, gaming, and contextual analysis. This group of techniques represents the earliest, most creative, most controversial, and most open-end aspects of planning and system development; they may be characterized as creative search techniques. These techniques represent the more formative aspcts of planning where, probably, the least research has been accomplished, the greatest need exists, and the greatest research breakthroughs might be expected to occur.

The Structured Search grouping in Figure 11.1 includes decision matrices, relevance trees, benefit-cost analysis, probabilistic analysis, and morphological analysis. These techniques are characteristically employed further down the line in planning and system development—in early system design and at the junction of strategic and tactical planning where the end in view is well structured and where the problem is to determine the most effective means to achieve the desired ends. Although this area is fairly well researched, there are still many leads open for planning development.

Closely related to the Structured Search techniques are the two listed Planning Production methods, PPB and PERT/CPM. Although these techniques cut across the entire planning cycle, they generally focus on system implementation, when the planning problem is well-structured and when most of the searching for alternative means has been completed. Detailed budgeting and scheduling at this level are indicative of the planning production process. Although this area has been extensively researched, much work remains to be done.

The next category, Retrofit Planning, refers to ongoing evolutionary modifications of relatively well-established plans based on feedback from deterministic models, operational simulation, social accounting, and input/output tables. These techniques typically occur further down the planning and system development pipeline. Although much research has been done in some of these areas, a vast area is opening up in newer applications such as social accounting.

The Trend Analysis techniques occur last in the planning/system development cycle since they require historical perspective to demonstrate trends, as in content analysis and time-series extrapolation. This area has been heavily researched; significant improvements could occur in the development of more accurate and more powerful techniques for data collection and analysis leading to more effective trend determination.

The last category is designated as historical analysis. In this category we find historical analogy, historical sequence, literary fiction, and primary determinant approaches to planning. Note that these techniques are located at the normative stage of planning and at the obsolescence point in system development in Figure 11.1. The reason for this juxtaposition is that historical techniques provide one of the most powerful methods available for evaluating the normative assumptions in planning. Historical perspective is probably the broadest perspective of all, but under current conditions, it suffers from entering into planning too late with too little. What is needed is a real-time acceleration of historical data collection and analysis so that credible historical evaluations can be more timely and more relevant. The discipline of the history of science and technology is still very new; we still do not know how to design useful data collection and reduction techniques for effective historical analyses in the fast-moving technological arena. There are many unprecedented opportunities for planning research in this area that have hardly been tapped.

11.2 TOWARD A THEORY OF PLANNING

11.2.1 The Vacuum in Planning Theory

Advanced research in online planning presupposes a theoretical framework for planning. One looks in vain for a substantive planning theory in the literature. For example, Branch (1966) speaks about a "comprehensive planning process," but not a planning theory. Ayres (1969) discusses the "epistemology of forecasting," but does not come up with any theory of planning. Emery (1965) describes a "formalization of the planning process," but does not venture into planning theory. The record of the Commission on the Year 2000 (American Academy of Arts and Sciences, Summer 1967) does not lead to any planning theories among its numerous articles.

LeBreton and Henning (1961) wrote a book entitled *Planning Theory.* Their "theory" turns out to be an amalgam of activities and disciplines that contribute to the planning process, consisting of seven subtheories: theory of need determination, theory of choice, theory of data collection and processing, testing theory, theory of organizing for planning, communication theory in planning, and persuasion theory. What LeBreton and Henning put forth is not a theory, but a description of planning, arguing that all and any disciplines that contribute to such activities are part of planning theory. Their effort at theorizing is valuable in highlighting the eclectic and pluralistic nature of planning.

In an extensive and thoughtful compendium on management planning, Steiner (1969) puts forth fundamental requirements for a theory of planning (p. 715).

This is an aggregate body of theory that has a number of characteristics. First, it should have a set of principles and laws with broad applicability. Second, these should have predictive value. Third, the detailed theories should be tested and found to be valid. Fourth, the theory must explain and describe the phenomenon of planning in total and in its parts. Fifth, it must be useful in actual practice. Sixth, the theory must organize effectively and classify properly the relevant knowledge and experience. Finally, it should give direction to research and teaching of the subject.

In his assessment of the status of planning, Steiner asserts that planning theory is rapidly approaching maturity, but has not yet arrived. He bases his overall conclusion on several generalizations: a variety of planning models have been tested and found to be usefully valid; description and classification of planning are advanced in important areas (e.g., the system development cycle is well understood); prescriptive statements—such as the proposition that top-management involvement and support is essential for successful planning—have been generally validated, even though such statements are scientifically imprecise; and quantitative methods and tools in planning reflect a high degree of precision, sophistication, and diversification.

Steiner has demonstrated, by and large, that an eclectic methodology has been recruited from many disciplines and has been pressed into service for planning, and that fragmented findings are scattered unevenly in the planning arena. His assertion that planning theory is approaching maturity may itself be criticized as premature. Although, like Branch, Steiner speaks of comprehensive planning as a framework for planning theory, nowhere can a theory of comprehensive planning be found in his book in the sense and spirit of his own criteria quoted above. Although all of us would like to wish otherwise, planning theory is not premature, it is immature.

The planning literature presents a problematic pyramidal structure. At the bottom is a vast literature on planning applications for almost every endeavor known to man. The massive five-year plans of the USSR are a case in point. In the middle is a much smaller and more limited literature on planning methodology (e.g., the 25 books on planning techniques produced in the 1960's, as mentioned by Mockler [1970]). At the apex is the virtual nonexistence of any substantive literature on planning theory. What are some of the reasons for this state of affairs?

Some have already been discussed. Planning is in a fast-moving predisciplinary stage. Planning is everywhere at individual, group, national, and international levels. Planning begs, borrows, and steals from all disciplines and is applied to virtually every social endeavor. In its broadest sense, planning spreads over almost every area of human behavior, which invariably contains an anticipatory element. Planning is like a vast, amorphous inkblot into which one can project any type of human or social behavior that can be linked to some aspect of the future. As such, mass information utilities are bound to become increasingly identified with numerous activities related to the spectrum of planning.

11.2.2 Current Definitions of Planning

The definitions of planning are legion. Illustrative examples are shown, leading toward a definition suitable for a scientific discipline of planning.

At a general level, Meyerson and Banfield (1955) define *planning* as "a method for delineating goals and ways of achieving them"; and they define a *plan* as "a course of action which can be carried into effect, which can be expected to lead to the attainment of ends sought, and which someone intends to carry into effect."

At the individual level, Miller, Galanter, and Pribram (1960) define a plan as "any hierarchical process in the organism that can control the order in which a sequence of operations is to be performed."

Steiner defines planning as a process coextensive with management in its broad sense. "Planning is a process which begins with objectives; defines strategies, policies, and detailed plans to achieve them; which establishes an organization to implement decisions; and includes a review of performance and feedback to introduce a new planning cycle."

In economics, Clay (1950) defines planning as "the opposite of reliance on a market economy." In a more positive vein, Florence (1953) defines national planning as the "intention to promote the public interests by the more or less visible hand of the state."

For Mannheim (1940) planning is "a mode of thought which not only changes individual links in the causal chain and adds new ones, but also tries to grasp the whole complex of events from the *key position* which exists in every situation."

In another attempt to reach at the essence of planning, Millet (1947) says "the job of planning, reduced perhaps to its most elementary aspect, is the constant task of defining and sharpening the objectives."

Along similar lines, Bell emphasizes that "The true function of the planning process is not to designate the most appropriate means for given ends, but to predict the possible consequences to explicate the values of a society and make people aware of the costs of achieving these." In the same paper, Bell also states that "the function of prediction is not, as often stated, to aid social control, but to widen the spheres of moral choice." Bell's concern anticipates some of the requirements of democratic planning for mass information utilities.

Ayres does not offer any general definition of planning, but distinguishes between three main types: policy planning, strategic planning and tactical planning.

- *Policy Planning:* Formulation of alternative goal patterns or functional objectives for the future—based on alternative future environments or scenarios—in a (continuous) comparison, selection, and feedback process.
- *Strategic Planning:* Formulation of a set of alternative routes or options for achieving the chosen set of goals, together with a procedure for systematic comparison and assessment.
- *Tactical Planning:* Delineating the sequence of actions necessary to implement a particular strategy. The technological aspects of tactical planning would be concerned with reaching well-defined technological (as opposed to functional) objectives generally in terms of specified systems or subsystems.

In anticipation of the definition of planning linked to scientific method that is developed later, note the approach of Nadel (1951), which points to the analogy between means and ends in relation to cause and effect: "we can readily visualize the double relationship of means-and-ends and cause-and-effect as a gradual process in which, step by step, one becomes adjusted to the other; that is, an end is anticipated, however vaguely; causal effects are observed which suggest a suitable means, until the means has been fully tested and fitted to the desired end."

The above definitions underscore the diffuse, predisciplinary status of planning, and the need for a rigorous approach more amenable to scientific method. The following approach to planning is offered as an initial step toward a scientific theory of planning. The proposed approach is an outgrowth of ideas on experimentally regulated system development found in the author's book (1967).

11.2.3 Prolegomena to a Theory of Planning

The foundation stone is disarmingly simple, but crucial: plans may be conceived as hypotheses, subject to empirical test and evaluation in a scientific manner. Given certain conditions, hypotheses predict consequences in accordance with specified relations among operationally defined variables. Why shouldn't we construct plans in the form of hypotheses so that we can rigorously test plans and the planning process?

Hypotheses are included in the context of an overarching theory. How can theory be linked with plans? The necessary step is to include plans in the context of an object system such that the system serves as an operational definition of a plan in a concrete working context. Thus, plans could be working hypotheses concerning system performance subject to continual test and evaluation throughout the life-cycle of the object system. The plan is essentially a blueprint of evolving hypotheses concerning system performance, and system development is the embodiment or actualization of the plan, which permits empirical measurement of the validity and internal reliability of the plan. An overriding advantage of the proposed approach is that the real-world system serves as the source of its own planning hypotheses, and also provides the means for testing such hypotheses.

The scientific confrontation between general abstractions and concrete systems is a new version of the age-old controversy of pure vs. applied science. This controversy is taking on a significant new twist with the advent of formally planned systems, particularly with computer-aided systems. In the past, scientific man-machine experimentation was conducted in a laboratory setting in which dependent and independent variables in object system behaviors were relatively isolated, while other factors were controlled or held constant, in an idealized and simplified model or representation of the system. This approach may be described as experimental idealism. At present, particularly in computer-serviced systems, it is becoming increasingly possible to tap real-world and real-time system behavior in a credible test setting involving an adequately representative complex of the elements of the object system and its environment, with results that have useful predictive value in extrapolating and assessing system performance. This approach may be described as experimental realism in contrast to experimental idealism. To state the case bluntly, why test abstract surrogates when we can test the real thing? Why plan with laboratory esoterica when we can go where the action is?

The basic starting point is that system plans and derived system design can be viewed as a set of evolving hypotheses concerning system performance—hypotheses that are continually subject to system test, evaluation, and reformulation in the light of new findings and changing conditions. Therefore, planning objectives, planning requirements, system design, and system specifications should be conceived and written as operationally defined procedures subject to empirical testing. It also means that resources and facilities for system test and evaluation have to be anticipated in early planning at the system definition phase.

When planned system development is viewed as a scientific activity, a number of far-reaching differences from traditional scientific endeavor can be seen. One of the most striking is that there are as many applied sciences as there are concrete systems. The planned system spells out its own framework of hypotheses concerning its development and performance, with respect to its own resources and objectives. As plans for systems are plastic creations of men and are virtually unlimited in the imagination of men, so is the domain of planned system sciences also unlimited. Whereas traditional sciences tend to be compartmentalized into classical Aristotelian subject areas, such as the mathematical, physical, biological, and social sciences, planned system sciences, in contrast, are freely interdisciplinary as required for the accomplishment of system goals.

Traditional science has as many competitive sets of theories for a given subject area as there are recognized experts in the field who can attract a following. In the proposed approach to scientific planned systems, there is usually just one set of authorized, official plans and system specifications that describe the system and its leading performance hypotheses. In traditional science, the logical classification of subject matter is relatively abstract, whereas in systems, the detailed plans, including the men, machines, and communications of an object system, provide a tangible, coherent framework for operational performance hypotheses that does not exist in generalized scientific domains. In particular, real-world experimentation lends itself naturally to a concrete systems setting, whereas generalized scientific models are designed to be temporally and situationally invariant.

There are basic behavioral differences between conventional science and planned systems science in the proposed approach. In the systems approach, those significantly involved in system development and operations—such as planners, managers, designers, analysts, users, operators, and technicians—constitute the potential planning community of the object system. The associated technical literature, including evolving system plans, design specifications, and published test findings, can serve as the equivalent of a public forum for this community, open to criticism from peers and subject to continual reformulation in response to changing conditions. The system community can thus provide many of the checks and balances on method and findings in system planning that are provided by the scientific community in its own specialties in scientific matters.

In this view, experimental method is not restricted to the scientific elite who have been professionally trained in a specialized subject area. It is widely dispersed to all who can participate and contribute significantly to system planning and associated system development, with experimental techniques and aids designed specifically for the role and skill level of the user. With this approach, experimental method could evolve into more humanized and approachable forms that would facilitate user planning and user self-service from grass roots to managerial levels. If planned systems are conceived as forms of applied science, each unique to the object system, what sort of science will this constitute? Systematic eclecticism, a term suggested by Allport (1963) in another context, seems well suited to characterize, at the same time, the diversity and unity of the proposed approach. As plastic human plans, each system extracts what is useful from available science and technology. Planning is eclectic and justification is pragmatic—will the planned pieces fit together and do the job? This kind of planned eclecticism is not arbitrary or capricious; it must prove its worth in successful system operations.

The proposed philosophy of scientifically planned system development is admittedly sketchy and incomplete. The limitations stem from the youthful status of planning and system science. Fundamentally, this philosophy is an appeal for excellence in system planning through the extension of experimental method in system development.

11.2.4 Definition of Planning

In accordance with the above philosophy of planning, the following definition of planning is offered.

> *Planning refers to plastic evolving hypotheses concerning system objectives and system performance in specified environments, including embedding ecosystems, to achieve operationally defined effectiveness levels, within stated resources, throughout the life-cycle of the object system and successor systems.*

The above definition is not easy to digest when swallowed for the first time. But a closer examination will reveal that it meets key criteria for the philosophy of planning outlined above.

- It states that plans are hypotheses.
- It places planning in an evolutionary system context.
- It requires that plans be operationally defined so that they can be tested in the system setting.
- The environment of the object system also includes the ecosystem in which it is embedded.

- It emphasizes that plans are plastic human creations of desired futures within time and resource constraints.
- Plans are placed squarely in the middle of the real world.
- The definition underscores the fallibility of the "best laid plans of mice and men" by insisting on the need for accountability through continual testing in an uncertain world.

Other definitions of planning have anticipated various aspects of the proposed definition, as indicated earlier, but apparently none have encompassed all of the above attributes in a single definition that uncompromisingly weds planning to scientific method.

There are further implications of the above definition of planning, the proposed theory of planning, and the intersection of the above approach to planning with online problem-solving. These are treated next in working toward a recommendation for research and development in online planning, and by extension, to pluralistic social planning in mass information utilities.

11.3   PARTICIPATORY ONLINE PLANNING

In this section, previous considerations on planning are joined with additional considerations and constraints not mentioned earlier—leading to suggestions for research and development in online social planning. The first step is to develop the theoretical backdrop for participatory planning.

11.3.1   Rudiments of a Mutual Expectation Theory of Planning

Earlier discussion of a theory of planning was primarily concerned with the application of scientific method to planning. The emphasis in this context is more on an interpretation of problem-solving dynamics in planning. An early statement of a mutual expectation theory of planning is presented at this point to identify a crucial research area in social planning and to provide additional theoretical support for the proposal for online planing that follows in the next section.

Planning may be viewed as the institutionalization of meaningful social change for individuals and groups. As such, planning is the vehicle for directed social change. The accelerating tempo of contemporary change, and the growing complexity and ecological interdependence of social problems—and this assertion is central to the proposed theory—require an increasingly broad social consensus, qualitatively and quantitatively, to create a working mandate for viable plans. That is, plans are born contingent upon a prior mandate from cognizant social interests. The political process and the corporate process, to cite only two examples, have well-established channels for the institutionalization of change in the form of authorized plans. Accordingly, plans are the overt embodiment of the mutual expectations of concerned individuals and groups. The genetic structure of embryonic plans is embedded in such mutual expectations.

The general hypothesis put forth is that the planning process—viewed as authorized and directed social change—is initially triggered and sustained by an effective consensus in the concerned community which is shaped by mutual expectations concerning social values, goals, resources, alternative courses of action, and priorities. This hypothesis further states that such consensus is increasingly reaching into more diverse levels of society and to more individuals as social problems grow in size, scope, and urgency, leading to increasing need for participatory planning in all walks of life—mass planning that would eventually require the cost-effective public resources of mass information utilities.

The proposed mutual expectation theory of planning holds that the initial stage of planning—normative consensus—is undergoing a profound process of democratization, by evolutionary and revolutionary methods of social participation throughout the world. Perhaps the most crucial challenge to research in planning lies in systematic and rational extension of participatory planning, particularly in the earliest stages of planning.

The mutual expectation theory of planning does not maintain the untenable position that everyone and his brother could or should participate in all stages of planning; this would undermine the rational division of labor in planning and lead to chaos. The proposed theory applies primarily to the germination stage of planning, the point at which social sanction occurs in some form of consensus. As such, it is put forth as a partial rather than a comprehensive theory of planning. Subsequent to the initial mandate, the design and implementation of a plan follows the characteristic division of labor in the system development process. The planning mandate, which is the point at which a plan is overtly institutionalized, increasingly involves a broader set of individuals than those engaged in the immediate design and implementation of the plan, a consensus set that might be called a planning community or a planning public. It is this planning community that is the object population in the proposed mutual expectation theory.

Expectation theory is not something new under the sun. Stogdill (1959) provided a useful, early review of group expectation theory. Although still a loosely aggregated body of theory and experimentation, expectation concepts have a long and fairly extensive history in the social Roethlisberger and Dickson (1941). These authors have posited expectation as a basic dimension of group behavior and they have variously suggested that: stable expectations render predictable behavior; socialized individuals are those who act in accordance with the expectations of others; and systematic changes in expectations are correlated with systematic changes in group performance. Learning theorists such as Tolman (1932), Mowrer (1950), MacCorquodale and Meehl (1953), and Rotter (1954), have accumulated substantial experimental data demonstrating systematic relationships between the reinforcement of expectations and the rate of learning. Kelly (1955) based his theory of personality on the fundamental premise that "a person's processes are psychologically channelized by the ways in which he anticipates events."

Stogdill believed that expectation theory is the most promising avenue in learning theory to unravel the problems of social learning. He developed expectation theory as one of the keystones of his theory of group achievement. Expectation is defined as "readiness for reinforcement, a function of drive, the estimated probability of occurrence of a possible outcome, and the estimated desirability of the outcome."

Although an extensive review of expectation research is beyond the scope of this chapter, a few illustrative findings may help to suggest the value of expectation theory for understanding the dynamics of planning. As a starter, Stogdill puts forth the general hypothesis that much of what is known of reinforcement theory in learning can be transferred to the reinforcement of expectation.

- Some studies have shown that prediction of social events may be strongly influenced by the desirability of alternative outcomes, and that attitudes toward events tend to dominate predictions when little information is available on such events.
- Unrealistic expectations tend to be more highly generalized in predicting events than realistic expectations; that is, unrealistic expectations exhibit a more extensive "halo effect" in predictions of related classes of events.

- Individuals tend to shift their expectations to conform with overt group norms, particularly in cohesive groups.
- Expectations are systematically linked to individual value systems in a manner that tends toward selective perception to reinforce well-established values.
- Deviant individuals tend to demonstrate greater certainty in their value systems and greater rigidity in their expectations.
- Group and individual expectations vary with the perceived effectiveness of the group.
- Individuals with similar expectations tend to seek each other out and to reinforce mutual values.
- Public expression of expectations tends to be more powerful in changing expectations than private expression.
- Under certain conditions, anonymous feedback of individual expectations is more accurate and more efficient than face-to-face confrontation.

As mentioned in the title of this section, only the rudiments of a mutual expectation theory of planning are presented. Beyond this introductory and cursory treatment, the reader is left to his own devices in assessing the value of the proposed mutual expectation framework for social planning, and ultimately, for democratized planning.

11.3.2   Initial Framework for Participatory Online Planning

Participatory planning refers to mutual expectations in social creation of a plan—the attitudes, beliefs, values, goals, priorities, judgments, and supporting rationalizations that enter into social consensus for defining and initiating an authorized plan. Research in participatory online planning refers to systematic experimentation in the creation of plans as expressed in planning consensus in an online computing environment.

What do these general statements imply for a program of research in participatory online planning? First, the emphasis is not evenly distributed over the entire planning process from the gleam in someone's eye to the completed final plan. The focus is primarily on the early normative stage of planning—the creation of a concurred and accepted mandate for planning in a specified planning community. Thus, the planning techniques for the earliest stages of planning (normative planning) and the earliest stages of system development (system goals), as shown earlier in Figure 11.1, are the starting point for participatory online planning. It was previously seen that these earlier and more creative stages in planning were most in need of research and development and probably represented the best possibilities for planning breakthroughs. They include gaming, brainstorming, dialectical planning, Delphi, expert opinion, scenarios, contextual analysis, and confrontation techniques.

The heart of the required evolutionary mutation to an online configuration lies in adaptive generalization in man-computer communication. Adaptive generalization refers to an evolutionary advance that enables the organism to cope with and adapt to a wider range of problems and situations. The human brain is the ultimate example of adaptive generalization. The four major evolutionary steps are the advent of natural input/output, or natural language I/O, the development of adversary information systems, the inclusion of educational features, and the application of teleconference procedures for remote planning. Although these steps represent second and third generation features for mass information utilities, they are feasible for initial research and development now, and they provide a notion of the power for social planning possible with advanced mass information utilities.

Natural I/O refers to the use of natural language as it is spontaneously written, spoken, or otherwise expressively used in man-to-man communication, transferred to an online setting as in typewriter, voice, graphic, pointing, or pushbutton input. The advantages of natural I/O are obvious, and significant breakthroughs in this area would lead toward adaptive generalization.

The adversary information system is a newer and less well understood concept. Adversary information systems refer to the organization of information on opposing sides of contested issues such that reasons for and against each position are solicited, stored, and tracked in a real-time transaction that converges toward an operationally defined resolution. Statistical hypothesis-testing is one objective form of simple adversary decision in the sense that a hypothesis, such as the null hypothesis on the significance of the difference between two means, is accepted or rejected by a precise quantitative test.

The proposed concept of adversary information systems goes further than isolated hypothesis testing in also including reasons for and against the position taken on contested issues. In matters of opinion, the proposed adversary information system would not only poll participants but would also record and organize the reasons put forth for the positions taken. This process of querying participants generates a dialectical data base. As the dialectical data base grows and changes in real time in an online context, an adversary dialogue develops in which participants can exchange views, take sides, and follow the course of consensus, deadlock, or polarization.

The adversary information system has several notable properties not found in conventional information systems and data bases. The conventional data base is comprehensively organized a priori to encompass all queries of users in the data domain. It is encyclopedic and deductive and may be described as Aristotelian. The dialectical data base, after the originator of dialectics, is organized along Socratic lines. There is always a point or issue that is being contested. Statements are oriented for or against specified positions. The dialectical data base starts virtually from scratch, develops inductively as the argument progresses, and is completed when the argument is terminated by some specified criterion or reaches a point of diminishing returns.

Dialectical data bases need to be tied to natural language to encourage active participation, credibility, and high motivation on the part of the user. They should be concise and highly relevant data bases that can be easily generated and easily disposed as the overriding inquiry takes new turns. The ideal dialectical data base is a boiled-down, agreed-upon list of key reasons for and against a contested issue with such reasons ranked in order of rated importance. Throwaway data bases, or easy-come, easy-go data bases, are needed to permit the adversary information system to adapt in real time to online users.

The proposed adversary information system combines available advances of natural I/O with the requirements of searching mutual expectations in initial planning. Primitive forms of adversary information systems are possible now within the current state of the art, such as online opinion-polling, accompanied by one-word or one-phrase reasons or justifications in English. The aim of such systems would be interactive convergence toward rationalized consensus in planning.

The third evolutionary feature may be described as online education. Among other characteristics, planning is largely an educational experience. The planner emerges from the planning process better informed and hopefully wiser in the trials and tribulations of his planning problem and in planning skills. If planning is in fact a type of learning experience, it should be explicitly supported and designed as an educational tool. Accordingly, online planning systems should have an online facility available to support interactive construction of plans and selective presentation of textual material, and to provide tutorial capability and real-time tracking and measurement of planning performance against specified criteria. The educational aspects of planning should be systematically exploited to improve planning skills and the quality of end-item plans.

An interactive educational computer language such as PLANIT (Feingold, 1967) would meet the above general requirements. PLANIT (Programing Language for Interaction and Teaching), or an equivalent tool, could be used for the design of any instructional, questionnaire, or itemized planning sequence that can be broken down into frames, for rating or classifying user responses, for tracking the course of consensus, for tutorial branching, and for measurement of man-computer performance.

There has been no tradition in the planning literature to define, measure, and track the proficiency of planners in the performance of their task. An educational vehicle for online planning could make such experimentation possible, and open up a new area of study in real-time planning effectiveness.

The fourth evolutionary feature is to work with planning communities in which individuals and groups are physically remote from each other—teleconference planning. Since more and more planning problems require more diverse skills and more extensive opinions, it becomes virtually impossible to get all concerned individuals together to work out a common approach for a planning mandate. In public issues large numbers of people may be involved. The far-reaching problems of large organizations such as the Department of Defense often involve many people and require a great variety of experts from different disciplines. Computer networks such as the ARPA prototype, with approximately 20 "host" computers throughout the United States, are needed to distribute such issues to "planning publics," to collect and organize responses, and to mediate rationalized consensus in planning. Thus, mass information utilities may be advocated as a plausible approach to dispersed community participation in developing rationalized consensus for planning.

Computerization of planning consensus, as described above, offers several fundamental advantages for social planning. First, it is an ideal way to very rapidly collect and disseminate diverse opinions and the rationale behind such opinions to and from individuals in different locations. Second, there is a distributed arrangement of participants as opposed to face-to-face groups, which become unwieldy in large numbers. Helmer (1966) and Dalkey (1969) have presented extensive experimental evidence in connection with Delphi studies to the effect that more accurate and more useful consensus can often be achieved in distributed groups, under certain conditions, as compared to face-to-face groups for many types of problems. In fact, the proposed scheme for online planning can pick up where Delphi and related techniques have left off. Third, research now will permit an extensively tested technique for polling, adversary presentation, and consensus to be available for use later when extensive computer networks and mass information utilities become commonplace. Fourth, adversary information systems, as sketched above, represent a powerful vehicle for exploiting the vast potential of natural language I/O for social solutions to a virtually unlimited number of decision-making applications. Fifth, the relatively simple and straightforward requirements of polling and examining both sides of a contested issue in natural language make the proposed technique an eminently painless and attractive way to introduce a vast user audience to online information services—a popularizing breakthrough that no computer service or application has achieved to date. Finally, participatory online planning could exploit the great educational potential of planning, objectively testing for improved planning skills and better plans.

The fundamental problem is a basic problem in society; face-to-face communication is inadequate to resolve numerous multifaceted issues involving dispersed individuals and groups. Computer utilities can help in catalyzing man-to-man communication to clarify issues and resolve differences to the point where working consensus may be reached, or at least to the point where polarizing issues are explicitly identified and understood. Planning can be designed to catalyze social consensus via computers.

11.4 SUMMARY AND CONCLUSIONS

Statement of the Problem. How can improvements in social planning be scientifically advanced within the framework of online computing systems today and mass information utilities tomorrow?

Growth of Planning. Formal and informal efforts in planning are growing by leaps and bounds in national and international affairs and in education and industry at state and local levels, and are spreading to virtually all walks of life.

Predisciplinary Status of Planning. Although planning borrows liberally from many fields and operates as an eclectic enterprise, and although the applications literature in planning is immense, there is surprisingly little work on the theory and methodology of planning, and virtually no scientific work in this field.

Varieties of Planning and Forecasting Techniques. Some 26 methods used in planning and forecasting were extracted from the literature, covering a broad spectrum of approaches, ranging from operations research techniques, to accounting practice, to expert opinion, to statistical trend analysis, to historical and fictional approaches. These were later aggregated into five functional areas: creative search, structured search, planning production, retrofit planning, trend analysis, and historical analysis.

Scientific Planning Theory. In working toward a scientific theory of planning, it was maintained that plans should be conceived as hypotheses subject to empirical test and evaluation in an operationally defined environment. It was argued that plans may be interpreted as a set of evolving hypotheses concerning system performance throughout the life cycle of object systems. According to this view, the theory of planning is the theory of correspondence between hypothesized system planning and actualized system development.

Definition of Planning. Planning refers to plastic, evolving hypotheses concerning system objectives and system performance in specified environments, including embedding ecosystems, to achieve the desired levels of operationally defined effectiveness, within stated resources, throughout the life cycle of the object system and successor systems.

The Mutual-Expectation Theory of Planning. The mutual-expectation theory maintains that the planning process is initially triggered and created by an effective consensus in the concerned community, a consensus which is shaped by mutual expectations concerning social values, group goals, resources, and priorities. The planning mandate, which is the point at which a plan is overtly institutionalized, involves a broader set of individuals than those normally engaged in design and implementation of a plan. This broader "consensus" set might be called a planning community or planning public, and it is this planning community that is the primary population in the proposed mutual-expectation theory. According to this theory, the crux for advanced research in planning lies in systematic and rational extension of participatory planning. Expectation theory should build upon related experimental knowledge in the areas of human learning and group dynamics.

Participatory Online Planning. Participatory planning refers to mutual human expectations that enter into the consensus that leads to social creation of a plan. Research in participatory online planning refers to systematic experimentation in the creation of plans in the form of planning consensus in an online computing environment. The research focus is primarily, although not necessarily, at the early, normative stage of planning—the creation of a concurred and accepted mandate for planning in a specified planning community. The research objective is to develop a new generation of online planning capability to advance and catalyze rational planning consensus, particularly in a dispersed planning community for eventual application to democratized social planning in mass information utilities.

Computerized Design Features. There are four novel design features of the suggested planning vehicle in the online computing environment. One is the inclusion of natural I/O, primarily typewriter, voice, and graphic communication.

The second is the development of adversary information systems. Such systems refer to the organization of information on opposing sides of contested issues such that reasons for and against each position are solicited, stored in a "dialectical" data base, and tracked in a real-time man-computer transaction that converges toward an operationally defined resolution.

Third, the online planning system is envisaged as a vehicle for distributed planning communities in which individuals and groups who are physically remote from each other work toward common planning goals, particularly for planning problems requiring diverse skills and extensive opinion to arrive at a planning mandate. Large-scale time-sharing systems and distributed computer networks could provide the appropriate setting for initial development of participatory online planning.

Fourth, planning is conceived, in large part, as an educational process. Planning is fundamentally a problem-solving, learning experience. Educational design features are mandatory for accommodating large individual differences, human error, self-tutoring, differential reinforcement, and performance evaluation. All four features—natural I/O, adversary information systems, distributed computer services, and educational monitoring—require extensive new development for eventual application to social planning in mass information utilities.

12

A PUBLIC PHILOSOPHY

FOR

REAL-TIME INFORMATION SYSTEMS

THE ADVENT OF mass information utilities transforms the role of the public from spectator to participant in real-time social information systems. This transformation requires the development of a public philosophy that is consistent with democratic development of social information power, which is growing at an unprecedented rate. The elements of such a philosophy, derived from basic theoretical concepts concerned with real-time events, real-time information systems, and the extension of experimental method to social affairs, are outlined in this chapter. To deal with mounting social problems in time to solve them, emphasis is placed on human mastery over real-world events, particularly through the planning, design, and implementation of pluralistic mass information utilities and real-time information systems in the public domain. The case is presented for an extension of the legacy of American Pragmatism—particularly the work of Peirce, James, and Dewey—to meet the growing need of a public philosophy for real-time information systems.

12.1 THE NEED FOR A PUBLIC PHILOSOPHY

As mentioned in various contexts throughout this book, science is on trial. Amid all the conflicting loyalties, dogmas, religions, and value systems that have issued from human history, the one world that all nations strive toward is the scientific world. Of all the fads, fashions, and foibles that have been generated by evolving human cultures, only science has consistently progressed toward wider and deeper universal knowledge. Science and its applied offspring, technology, have been the most powerful revolutionary forces at work throughout the world, relentlessly undermining the mores and folkways of cultures everywhere. While we entrust science with the task of reconstructing the physical artifacts of society, we have not yet developed compensatory techniques for scientific reconstruction of the working values of society. Science is on trial to reconstruct directive human values as it reshapes the physical world, and the fate of humanity may hang in the balance. Science without conscience, without human goals, without an ethic—except for a mindless pursuit of "truth" wherever it may lead—is a schizophrenic discipline, a severance of means from ends, a disembodiment of intelligence from action.

John Dewey (1939) warned us of the bitter fruits of this moral renunciation (p. 154):

> Science through its physical technological consequences is now determining the relations which human beings, severally and in groups, sustain to one another. If it is incapable of developing moral techniques which will also determine these relations, the split in modern culture goes so deep that not only democracy but all civilized values are doomed. Such at least is the problem. A culture which permits science to destroy traditional values but which distrusts its power to create new ones is a culture which is destroying itself.

Weinberg (1970) has asked that we "construct an axiology of science" to answer the ever-recurring question: what is scientific value? He believes science must justify its social relevance, not merely for the perpetuation of science, but because "in our arduously built scientific-technological tradition lies our best chance of ultimate survival."

Freud put forth a similar warning: "Science is no illusion. But it would be an illusion to suppose that we could get anywhere else what it cannot give us."

Compton (1938) reminds us: "In recent times, modern science has developed to give mankind, for the first time in the history of the human race, a way of securing a more abundant life which does not simply consist in taking away from someone else. . . . The advent of modern science is the most important social event in history."

Will and Ariel Durant (1968) also see science on trial: "If another great war should devastate Western civilization, the resultant destruction of cities, the dissemination of poverty, and the disgrace of science may leave the Church, as in A.D. 476, the sole hope and guide of those who survive the cataclysm."

Contemporary science, while potentially providing a presumably better model than authority, religion, nationalism, anarchism, and other creeds for a higher order of effective human intelligence, suffers from many defects as currently practiced. It needs to be reconstructed along lines of greater humanization, a greater relevance to human values and social affairs, and greater accessibility in spirit and method to all of mankind. In particular, scientists have a new imperative to provide early warning to society for joint exploration of social consequences of new knowledge and new technology, for contributing to constructive social design of the fruits of science, and for scientific testing and evaluation of the human use of new technology. Information utilities can play a significant role in universalizing a democratized version of an experimental ethos.

The computer scientist was initially able to take refuge in the once-respectable, but now largely discredited notion that philosophy and human values lie in a transcendental subjective domain far removed from the objective operations of science. On the social side, the experience of the atomic scientists in World War II has underscored the social accountability of all scientists in radioactive human debris. On the psychological side, the analysis of scientific problem-solving—in the real world, not the paper world—has shown the all too human behavior of scientists. Human values and scientific method are passengers in the same boat, traversing the same stormy sea, sharing a common destiny.

The refusal to think problems through and to take a stand is itself a philosophical position—a position of passivity, drift, solipsism, nihilism, or agnosticism—depending on one's temperament. The admission of the need to start thinking problems through and basing action on rational, tested belief is admission of the need for a philosophical quest, for a public philosophy of real-time information systems.

The diverse needs for a public philosophy on the use of computers for planning, regulation, and control of social affairs stem from many cultural roots. Perhaps the most fundamental source is the accelerating tempo of social change spurred by the advance of science and technology. Situations and events seem to be moving faster than we can recognize them, let alone cope with them. Social solutions which once had a useful half-life spanning decades now have useful total lives over much shorter periods, and they have to be constantly revised and updated along the way to keep pace with swiftly changing conditions.

The concept of the real-time information system—a system that monitors events in a specified environment and controls the outcome of such events in a desired direction—is a leading technical concept that is being increasingly applied to control fast-moving changes in many walks of life. The power of computerized real-time information systems to meet rapidly changing problems and situations has been garnered from over 15 years of experience in computer-assisted command and control. The technique is well-known: continual surveillance over the object environment to permit early warning of critical situations; identification of problems; corrective regulation and control in accordance with established standards of system performance; and evolutionary adaptation of system design and operations to meet changing conditions.

The real-time information system is a new class of social institution, a more radically powerful and rapidly responsive social form to recognize, meet, and deal with specified problems at the time they occur and in time to modify their outcome. If we neglect to formulate desirable social consequences for these new systems, we neglect them at our own peril, and at public peril.

Information power is a new dilemma for modern society. Social control of information power is a focal problem for a public philosophy of real-time information systems. Prior to the advent of real-time computing systems, information was collected and stored in a manner that tended to separate knowledge from action, as in books and films. Radio and television allowed more timely collection and dissemination of information, but these mass media were still not linked to direct social action. In real-time computing systems, however, the collection, organization, and storage of information leads directly to action, to integrated surveillance and control over the object environment. This dynamic marriage of information and control in real-time systems is a fusion of knowledge and action, and, through directed action in real time, information is expressed as power.

In many respects, mass information utilities may become the ultimate embodiment of real-time social control. Mass information utilities represent the socially generalized form of real-time information systems. In political life, we can envision their potential as the fastest and most efficient way of registering the will of the people. Fundamentally, the national economy may be viewed as a real-time information system; with increasing telepurchasing and other financial transactions the computerized flow of money will dominate economic life. We have already described the vast potential of mass information utilities for lifelong education for all citizens. Many examples from other major social areas may be added to this list. Suffice it to say that mass information utilities are likely to provide the technological embodiment of real-time social control in politics, economics, education, law, and in institutional and organizational life broadly considered.

As more and more social knowledge becomes computer-accessible, so will more extensive, interlocking, and more powerful real-time systems come into being. As surely as the night follows the day—or the day follows the night, depending on your outlook—so will computer-accessible information be followed by real-time control. In a democracy, the public is the ultimate source of social power, and information power, accordingly, is ultimately a public trust. A public philosophy of information power needs to account for new democratic forms and procedures bearing on the organization and equitable distribution of social information.

Philosophical challenges are encountered in diverse areas such as meeting the tempo of contemporary change and coping with the institutionalization of information power, and in problems of social implementation. A workable philosophical position should provide guidelines for social method, for putting principles into practice. While many agree on broad principles, consensus often vanishes when details of implementation are hammered out.

A public philosophy for real-time information systems is, in many respects, unprecedented and extremely complex, at general levels, in details, and in implementation. At the same time, the need for such a philosophy is vital and long overdue. The next section is an inquiry into key elements of a public philosophy of real-time information systems, including the special case of mass information utilities. This inquiry then leads to a synthesis of these elements into an initial philosophical framework.

12.2 ELEMENTS OF A PUBLIC PHILOSOPHY

The desiderata of a public philosophy are developed in three stages, starting from definitions of the area of inquiry, proceeding to scientific and technical aspects, and culminating with social considerations. Each stage builds upon and incorporates the preceding stage. The focus is on the broader class of real-time information systems generally considered, rather than the special case or subclass of information utilities.

A philosophy of real-time information systems presupposes some definition of the concept of "real time." Historical interpretations of time, and by extension, "real time," have assumed the varied forms of the conceptual containers into which notions of time, like a liquid, have been poured. These interpretations range from the ceaseless flux of Heraclitus, to the flickering unreality of Platonic change, to Newton's geometrization of time, to Einstein's space-time, to probabilistic and indeterminate temporal constructions in quantum physics, to ecological statistical trends in evolutionary time. While probabilistic and contingent interpretations of time seem to be gaining increasing ground in the physical, biological, and social sciences, controversy has been and still is the rule.

For present purposes, three aspects of real time are distinguished: real-time events, real-time information systems, and real-time science. Each is defined and discussed in turn.

Real time essentially refers to events—their appearance and duration, their passage and succession, and the hypothesized interrelations of events as empirically tested and demonstrated in any referent system and its environment. Real time is thus our perceptions of the way events happen, our description of how they happen, and our best interpretations of why they happen as they do. This definition also implies that warranted interpretations are those empirically certified by experimental method in a systems context.

Real-time information systems refer to systems that 1) continually sense and respond to selected changes in an object environment 2) in a manner and in time to enable regulation and control over some ongoing events in the system and its environment while they occur, 3) within the bounds of minimal or acceptable levels of system performance as determined by continual test and evaluation of feedback from system events.

As mentioned earlier, the central feature of real-time information systems is direction and control over selected system events while they take place; and in order to exert such cognizance it is necessary to maintain constant surveillance, identification (decision-making), and control to modify the environment as required. Note that the definition does not mention computers. It essentially states that any system that is organized to sense and respond to an object environment according to some criterion of effectiveness is, in principle, a real-time information system. The crux of this definition is that real-time systems are not merely passive spectators of their own events; they are active creators of desirable outcomes, that they are directive agencies which mold a partially plastic environment in accordance with a preconceived image.

The next definition—real-time science—moves into the second, and also more controversial, stage, toward a public philosophy: the technical and scientific stage.

Real-time science deals with temporally and situationally contingent events amenable to experimental method, and it results in an extension of human mastery in planning, creating, and controlling such events; it is broadly eclectic, borrowing freely from the methods and findings of the pure and applied sciences, and from any mix of interscience and new science as required and needed to understand and control real-world events.

As we enter the era of computer-catalyzed real-time information systems, we need a scientific discipline to develop the theory and practice of real-time systems, and the suggested discipline is real-time science as defined above. This definition is different from conventional concepts of science in several leading respects, and here is where the greatest controversy is likely to arise. First, it explicitly fuses knowledge and action together as a single entity; no pretense is made for the pursuit of antecedent, abstract knowledge for its own sake. Second, the pursuit of knowledge is for human purposes, for improving social and individual effectiveness. Third, the proper object of real-time science is real-world events—real-time science belongs where the action is. Laboratory events and abstract constructions are not excluded, but they are preparatory rather than consummatory, in the sense that they contribute toward the ultimate objective of understanding, shaping, and controlling real-world events for human ends. Fourth, real-time science is guided at all points by evolving human values, wherein such values are themselves hypotheses, subject to continuing reformulation, test, and evaluation.

The eclecticism of real-time science is a restless, fast-moving, aggressive eclecticism, itself changing in real time with new methods and findings. Real-time science borrows freely from any established or new experimental discipline that contributes to improved real-time system performance. Anyone who has worked in the design and development of real-time information systems is acutely aware of the creatively eclectic and pluralistic nature of such systems, of the requirement to optimize interdisciplinary teamwork, of the necessity to adopt new science and technology into system design and operations, of the need to be open-ended, to improvise, jazz-like, against residual uncertainty, of the requirement to continually test and modify system configurations throughout the entire life cycle of the system.

The relation of real-time science to traditional forms of science is that real-time science borrows experimental method and findings wherever and whenever they are useful for understanding and directing real-world events. The common denominator is experimental method. With the advent of computer-serviced societies we may expect a flowering of new species of computer-catalyzed experimental method, particularly in real-time information systems embedded in real-world happenings—the emergence of real-world experimentation.

A criticism that may be leveled against the foregoing definitions of real-time events, real-time information systems, and real-time science is that they seem to be so broad and all-encompassing as to become meaningless; little is left out. The antidote to indiscriminate universalization of real-time concepts lies in its distinction from nonreal-time concepts. There are two basic senses in which nonreal-time events, systems, and science may be construed: as entities in their own right, and as examples of failure of a real-time system.

In the first sense, a nonreal-time information system is one that does not continually sense and respond to selected changes in the object environment in a manner permitting control over events at the time they occur. Analyses of past events and planning for future events fall into the nonreal-time category. In computer systems, batch processing is generally conducted in nonreal time, and abstract simulations or temporally telescoped computerized simulations are nonreal-time operations.

The results of analyses of the past, of planning for possible futures, or batch information processing and of nonreal-time simulations may eventually be applied to a real-time systems context, and as such, nonreal-time behavior may be interpreted as propaedeutic to real-time behavior. Nonreal-time behavior may even have its own characteristic real-time pace (as in accelerated real-time simulation), but, insofar as no immediate control is exerted over online events, such behavior is interpreted as nonreal time for concurrent events. From a practical point of view, the heart of the distinction between nonreal time and real time is the distinction between knowledge disembodied from immediate and concurrent action and knowledge expressed in action.

The second sense of nonreal time is failure of a real-time system to meet some specified standard of performance in controlling the system environment. Thus, in computerized real-time systems—if SAGE does not destroy a hostile bomber before it reaches its target; if the Apollo spacecraft is not being picked up by the ground tracking system; if SABRE airline reservations are swamped with erroneous manual inputs; if the executive program of a time-sharing system has to handle too many users at one time—to that extent the object real-time information system deteriorates in performance and regresses to a nonresponsive or nonreal-time mode of operations.

What does social effectiveness mean when applied to real-time information systems? It was mentioned earlier that real-time systems represent the most advanced means available for regulation and control of social change, and that in a democracy information power ultimately resides in the public. Social change via real-time information systems is thus self-change. The public, ideally, authorizes and warrants social change. Each individual is thus both experimenter and subject in the development of real-time public systems; a new level of participant democracy is needed well beyond anything that has been attempted so far. A socially effective public philosophy correspondingly requires educational changes in the general population that can lead to enhanced participant democracy. The alternative is the eclipse of the public by a new technological aristocracy.

To avoid overconcentrating information power in some new elite, existing democratic procedures must be modified with the aid of new technological capability. In previous chapters, it was urged that mass information utilities be dedicated to online citizen polling for public affairs, and to universal lifelong education. These steps would not only contribute to but would probably accentuate pluralistic checks and balances between competing groups and interests; they would be conducted in the open forum, the time-honored method for preserving a dynamic democratic equilibrium. The design of pluralistic checks and balances for diverse real-time information systems and mass information services would be pouring new real-time wine into old democratic bottles. The electronic potential for public control is so great that we should also be concerned with overcontrol of public officials by a fickle and changeable public, over-control that could lead to a more virulent form of the tyranny of the majority (as de Tocqueville described it more than a century ago). The knife cuts both ways—more power means more work and greater responsibility for the public and its representatives to maintain constructive and equitable equilibrium between shifting majorities and diverse minorities.

The foregoing should make it obvious that the determination of suitable checks and balances between competing groups, competing real-time information systems, between the public and various elites, between majorities and minorities, will require a long and continuing course of competitive social experimentation. Doctrinaire solutions are no match for systematic social experiment and verified empirical demonstration. An essential requirement of the public philosophy, then, is the institutionalization of social experiment in public affairs with a corresponding internalization of experimental values in thought and outlook.

Summing up, what are the key elements of a public philosophy for real-time information systems? The philosophy requires an outlook that links knowledge with action; it needs the support of eclectic real-time sciences concerned with the extension of human mastery over the creation and control of real-world events; it is characterized by diverse democratic means to achieve pluralistic social ends; and it requires an extension of experimental method and experimental ethos to social affairs. Do we have a philosophy that brings these elements together, or do we have to invent a new philosophy for the era of real-time systems in computer-serviced societies?

12.3 THE PROMISE OF AMERICAN PRAGMATISM

The thesis put forth in this section is that we do have the fundamental elements for a public philosophy of real-time information systems in the legacy of American Pragmatism. The following discussion develops the grounds for this position in four steps: a very brief description of the historical development of American pragmatism; pragmatism as a philosophical system founded upon and profoundly influenced by real-time concepts and a real-time outlook; pragmatism as a coherent experimental approach to the democratization of real-time social control; and the extension of pragmatism into systems science and the era of computer-serviced societies.

Do we already have the basic elements of a philosophy of real time in American Pragmatism? This philosophy was constructed over almost a century of hotly contested philosophical labor, as represented by its principal originators, Charles Peirce (1935), William James (1907), John Dewey (1939), and their successors. These three founders portray the three faces of pragmatism—Peirce the mathematical and scientific side, James the psychological side, and Dewey the social side.

"Pragmatism" is derived from a Greek root signifying action. According to James (1907), pragmatism was first introduced into philosophy by Peirce in 1878. For Peirce, the meaning and value of a statement consisted of its conceivable consequences in practice, of its bearing on human understanding and control over future events. Peirce clearly envisioned the union of knowledge with action.

At the heart of Peirce's belief was his conviction of the superiority of experimental method over other methods for gaining and implementing useful human knowledge. For Peirce, scientific method was the best model available to man for understanding and controlling his world. The "truth" of statements is operationally determined by empirical verification of testable consequences achieved by iterative experimental inquiry, as it occurs in scientific progress. Peirce was the first to use the concept of inquiry in this context, a term later adopted and elaborated by Dewey. With Peirce, meaning, truth, and experimental inquiry were cast in a temporal frame, contingent upon and responsive to the cumulative consequences of ongoing human behavior. The long-range, evolutionary advance of science served as the ideal for Peirce's vision of pragmatism which contained the seeds for a philosophy of real-time science.

James was the popularizer of pragmatism and its most eloquent, almost poetic, spokesman. Agreeing with Peirce that the validity of statements is to be continually tested by their consequences, James broadened the domain of pragmatic meaning over the whole of human experience. His earlier preoccupation with the shifting stream of consciousness was expanded into an all-encompassing concept of experience (which he described as radical empiricism) that incorporated subject and object as an undifferentiated unity, a unity consonant with that described by Bertrand Russell (1945) as "neutral monism." For James the temporally conditioned stream of experience, flowing in a "pluriverse," displayed the same strung-along, partially connected, mosaic character as his stream of consciousness. This pluriverse, manifesting a course of creative evolution, was contrasted by James against the "block universe" espoused by idealists of all callings who believed in the Platonic tradition of a fixed, antecedent structure of the universe laid out in some grand, sweeping design. James's philosophical pluralism, more than that of other pragmatists, lays the groundwork for a virtually unlimited multiplicity of real-time sciences and intersciences modeled after the kaleidoscopic configurations of real-time systems.

Dewey was deeply concerned with the accelerating tempo of scientific and technological advance and the need for creative social reconstruction to keep pace with such changes. He seized upon the element of human control in experimental method, developed previously by Peirce, as the method of choice to implement and guide social reconstruction.

In a remarkable anticipation of systems science, Dewey attacked the limited efficacy of archaic notions of true and false and urged, in their place, the adoption of flexible operational measures of effectiveness for human, organizational, and social performance. Social behavior is not true or false—it exists, for better or worse—and our concern, according to Dewey, is to find out how effective it is, and to do it in a manner that will permit us to improve upon it to meet new conditions.

For Dewey, every existence is an event, and all events are potential experiments. Contrary to the prevailing laboratory view of science, Dewey saw the far-reaching prospects of real-world experimentation with real-time events in his doctrine of experimentalism—the extension of experimental method to human affairs. Dewey effectively anticipated a philosophy of real-time science by urging increased human control over social events through scientific method. None of his followers went as far as he did in urging the universal extension of experimental ethos to social affairs.

Dewey's concept of cooperative experimental control over social affairs was consistently qualified as democratic control by an enlightened public. In *The Public and Its Problems* (1927) Dewey put forth his prophetic vision of free social communication and democratized public control in a new machine age—a spiritual specification for mass information utilities (p. 184):

> We have but touched lightly and in passing upon the conditions that must be fulfilled if the Great Society is to become a Great Community; a society in which the ever-expanding and intricately ramifying consequences of associated activities shall be known in the full sense of that word, so that an organized, articulate Public comes into being. The highest and most difficult kind of inquiry and a subtle, delicate, vivid and responsive art of communication must take possession of the physical machinery of transmission and circulation and breathe life into it. When the machine age has thus perfected its machinery it will be a means of life and not its despotic master. Democracy will come into its own, for democracy is a name of free and enriching communion. It had its seer in Walt Whitman. It will have its consummation when free social inquiry is indissolubly wedded to the art of full and moving communication.

The above sketch is only crudely indicative of the philosophies of Peirce, James, and Dewey. It is beyond the scope of this book to set out the distinguishing characteristics, the numerous controversies, and the current diversity of American Pragmatism in any detail. But these brief remarks should suffice to point up the pronounced temporal thrust of American Pragmatism, the continual reconstruction of present belief toward future behavior, with vigilant appraisal of fresh consequences leading to new guidelines for further action. In many respects, pragmatism manifests itself as an evolutionary philosophy of planning. Peirce stressed the self-corrective aspect of the inquiring process; James focused on the human implications of the pluralistic stream of experience; Dewey emphasized instrumental means and experimental control over growing social problems in a precarious world. The flux and pressure of real-time events and adaptive planning are written large in these philosophies, and social mastery over this flux is most apparent and most comprehensively expounded in Dewey's work.

Social control has become a terrifying notion when coupled with computers. It conjures up visions of Orwell's Big Brother (1949) and Wiener's Golem (1964). Dewey, like Walt Whitman, was always a great believer in democracy even though he was acutely aware of its many limitations as he saw them in his time. He also had an abiding faith in the public and the great potential of liberated human intelligence. He felt that if, in some manner, available social knowledge could be made freely accessible to the public, the latent intelligence of the public would be released, and the excellence of democracy would be enhanced.

Is the emergence of public information utilities the instrumentality through which Dewey's dream can be realized? If we design the computer utility to gather and distribute public information on an equitable basis to all, and if we integrate this utility with new, experimentally evolved democratic procedures that will enable the public to use this information wisely, then, to that extent, democracy stands to be the beneficiary of the new concentration of information power.

12.4 THE EXPERIMENTAL SOCIETY

The concept of deliberate, institutionalized, continuing public experiment for public affairs is a new evolutionary force in democratic advance, a challenge that requires new attitudes and revised values. Each individual will have to learn to think for himself as both subject and experimenter, with lifelong responsibility for social planning, selecting and implementing new experiments, evaluating social effectiveness, and applying the results. The realization of this new experimental ethos will require far greater participation and public evaluation of social feedback than has ever occurred before in any democracy, including the personalized democracy of the city-states of ancient Greece. Mass information utilities, linked to the real-time information bases in the public domain, could conceivably provide the leading instrumentality for the public to scan the social scene, identify problems, contribute to social control, and provide continuing corrective feedback on the interplay of pluralistic social experimentation.

The new experimental ethos correspondingly requires an infrastructure of continuing lifelong information and education in real time, the acquisition of new knowledge when it is needed, in time to meet problems as they arise. When education occurs in real time, it is responsively adaptive and becomes indistinguishable from on-the-spot human problem-solving. Real-time education will then articulate with the tumultuous flow of social experience, and education will become an integral part of such experience. The dusty dogma of the academic creed may become a curious relic of the past.

There are those who argue that experimental method is good, true, and beautiful, but only as long as it remains in the domain of natural science, where it originated, and where, they claim, it belongs. As soon as experimental method is taken out of conventional scientific pursuits and is indiscriminately inserted in such fields as democracy and education, or social affairs, then, the critics claim, you enter the never-never land of human values and transcendental metaphysics where statements become meaningless from a scientific point of view. Such is the position, for example, of the logical positivist and most behaviorists.

The pragmatist rejects this view since it would keep scientific method confined within the scientific priesthood and deny it to the public. Experimental method is the most precious legacy of scientific endeavor, and it is too important and too valuable to entrust to any aristocracy, scientific or otherwise. At the heart of the confrontation between science and society is the pivotal belief that values may be formulated as hypotheses, operationally defined, quantitatively measured, and empirically tested, with results subject to further test and evaluation as in any other scientific activity. If values are treated as hypotheses, then democracy and education, social attitudes and social change—when they are operationally defined under empirically verifiable conditions—are correspondingly amenable to social experiment.

The early pragmatists were in a difficult position in defending their stand on the possibility and validity of social experimentation because the means for the universalization of experimental method were not at hand and they could not point to concrete, real-world social experiments. They could defend their position in principle but not in practice—a vulnerable position for one who calls himself a pragmatist. But now conditions have changed dramatically, particularly with the advent of systems science and the proliferation of the high-speed electronic computer. Social experiment is now possible on a scale undreamed of by the early pragmatists.

It is commonplace to point out that computers make it possible to collect, organize, and process vast amounts of data quickly and reliably in real-time experiments that were beyond the ken of the precomputer era. The computer is, in fact, revolutionizing experimental method in the physical, biological, and social sciences, and the end is nowhere in sight. Systematic experimental method is comparatively recent in human history, dating back only to the Western Renaissance (Sarton, 1948). It has changed rapidly since its inception and has received an electronic jolt with the emergence of the general-purpose digital computer since World War II. Social experiments are now possible in a bewildering variety of forms, for a growing number of variables, with real-time collection, reduction, and analysis of data. For many, perhaps most, the question is no longer whether to experiment on a social scale, but how to experiment in the best interests of the public.

The power of systems science in catalyzing and accelerating the extension of experimental method is probably not as well understood as the more obvious impact of computers. The concrete, tangible system, with its specified stages of planning, definition, design, production, installation, and operation, with test and evaluation occurring at all stages, is the organizational vehicle for the breakthrough into real-world experimentation. If a coherent social activity is organized into a formal systems framework, then the system can serve both as subject and object of its own evolutionary series of system experiments, for continuing system test and evaluation. The integrated system is the crucible in which the real-world experiment is forged.

The combination of computers and system science, in a concrete system context, makes possible the universalization of experimental method in an unprecedented manner. The computer complex can and has served as a built-in laboratory for test and evaluation of system performance. This has occurred most notably and dramatically in the earliest large-scale real-time systems, in SAGE air defense and in Mercury-Gemini-Apollo manned spaceflight. In each case there was an attempt to make a great leap forward into new knowledge and new control over uncharted domains. The only way to achieve system goals within planned timetables was to experiment rapidly and boldly with new techniques and new findings.

The system configuration served as its own test bed in measuring and assessing system performance. Simulation, training, testing, and evaluation were indistinguishably intermixed in system development in a new experimental style—in computer-aided, interdisciplinary, mission-oriented, self-experimentation in real time, under common schedules and common system goals. With the advent of other and newer real-time information systems in industry, science, education, medicine, law, and, now, in the mass information utilities, the experimental dance is improvised on new real-time tempos.

In real-time systems the pragmatic criterion of truth is embodied in a coherent systems framework. The true and the false are stripped of absolute implications, and they are replaced not only by the basic pragmatic test of consequences, but by the further test of agreement or disagreement against a specified standard in the operationally defined system context. The pragmatic criterion of truth is thus refined in real-time systems into the extent of agreement between an event and a prescribed standard. The bridge between "truth" and real-time systems is accordingly the theory of correspondence between a specified standard of real-time control and its agreement with a referent event in a temporally contingent system context.

In this context the role of planning is crucial as the plastic design of temporal hypotheses, or potentially realizable standards, operationally specified in the systems context, and continually on trial in the correspondence between standards and associated events. As indicated in the previous chapter, plans can be formalized as the working hypotheses of real-time systems. True and false in real-time systems are ultimately manifested as realized and unrealized plans in system operations, as the cumulative effectiveness of planning hypotheses. And, lest we forget, all plans rest on a motivational base; they are inextricably commingled with the changing fortunes of human hopes and aspirations.

To the extent that a systems approach is deliberately integrated into social organization, and to the extent that such systems are computerized, to that extent will potenial experimental power grow for real-world planning and experimentation. Saying that experimentation is good and noble is not enough; there must be the means and the explicit social configuration—the real-time systems configuration—to make such experimentation feasible. The first step, then, in the evolution of real-world social experiment is the evolution to formalized real-time systems. And the more advanced the computerization of such real-time systems, the more potent are the possibilities for creative social planning supported by ongoing systems experimentation. Social experiment will spread as real-time information systems spread and proliferate into interlocking networks, ultimately into ecological complexes of openly cooperative and competitive real-time information systems.

The form that real-time social control will take will depend on how real-time information systems are implemented. If competitive social experiments are freely conducted in an open forum, if many planning alternatives are explored, if real, not rigged choices are open to the public, if grass roots planning and feedback are built into object systems at the system design stage, if adequate checks and balances and a rational division of labor employed between the public, the managers, the operators, and users of such systems—if these and related conditions are met, then real-time social control may effectively turn out to be of the people, by the people, and for the people, rather than for the old plutocracy or a new technological elite.

When pragmatism was thrust with a "barbaric yawp" into the world of philosophy, mainly through the efforts of William James, a cry arose from many quarters on the crassness and narrowness of this new outgrowth of American materialism. Pragmatism was maligned as opportunistic, self-indulgent, unscientific, anarchistic, and as an ideal comedian's philosophy. The semantic storm over the pragmatic as the narrowly practical was overwhelming; repeated onslaughts from the ideal, the good, true, and beautiful, from the pure and theoretical were launched against this newborn philosophy from all sides.

Peirce, disagreeing with James' exposition of pragmatism, insisted that his theory be called "Pragmaticism." James turned to the more technical concept of radical empiricism to ward off the semantic pitfalls of pragmatism. Dewey lingered longest over pragmatism and somewhat reluctantly turned to instrumentalism and experimentalism to defuse the explosive onslaught from critics.

But the temper of the times has changed and the horrendous connotations of pragmatism have become more respectable in a world that desperately needs intelligent, practical solutions to mounting problems. While pragmaticism, radical empiricism, and instrumentalism remain as distinctive historical hallmarks of their creators, American Pragmatism persists as the designation of their common origin, continued growth, and diversification in contemporary affairs. After being drummed out of court for challenging the established, absolutistic order, American Pragmatism is experiencing a renaissance.

With the emergence of real-time information systems, the pragmatic temper of American science and technology has received a fresh impetus and a powerful new thrust. Peirce's "knowledge of consequences" has become transmuted into the principle of real-time feedback; James's "cash-value" has become cost-effectiveness and system payoff; Dewey's social inquiry has evolved into systems analyses; the early pragmatic focus on future consequences has been transformed into human real-time control. The philosophy of pragmatism has evolved into the philosophy of real time.

12.5 PHILOSOPHICAL RECAPITULATION

In recapitulating the philosophical position put forth in this chapter, six questions may be asked:

- Who needs such a philosophy?
- Why do we need it?
- What are the leading requirements?
- Would such a philosophy have to be built from meager beginnings or is there a relevant philosophical tradition?
- What are the distinctive new features of the proposed philosophy?
- How can such a philosophy be implemented?

First, who needs such a philosophy? Everyone. Barring catastrophic destruction of mankind, computers and information services will spread into growing national and international networks. The accumulated cultural store of human knowledge will be increasingly accessible at online convenience to greater numbers of people. The international information utility may be the first tangible technological embodiment of Teilhard de Chardin's noosphere (1959). The many publics around the world would have an unprecedented opportunity to evolve through a major social mutation—the transition from the historical tradition of passive, impotent spectators to active, constructive participants over an expanding spectrum of social affairs. Hitler's cynical view of the public as stupid, weak, effeminate, cowardly, and manipulable by a strong personality, as he spelled it out in *Mein Kampf,* would be incommensurate with a higher order of effective human intelligence.

Why do we need a public philosophy for the spread of computer services? From the long-range perspective, the computer revolution is fundamentally a revolution in the reconstruction, redistribution, and real-time use of human knowledge. If global civilization is to survive and evolve into a higher order of human life, we must make the necessary arrangements to work toward a higher order of effective public intelligence. To accomplish this, science needs to open its doors wide, and give to humanity its most precious legacy—its method, scientific method. Information by itself does not make intelligence; scientific use of information, following the experimental way, does make for the highest and most successful form of intelligence that man has yet achieved. Not only do we need a philosophy for equitable quantitative distribution of information, but we also need it for enhancing the quality of human intelligence and wisdom in a new experimental ethos.

The third question has many facets. What are the leading requirements of the proposed public philosophy? From the viewpoint of the human species as a closed real-time system on Spaceship Earth (Ward, 1966), such a philosophy should be oriented toward early warning, regulation, and cooperative control of global events to anticipate and meet mounting social problems as they arise. It may become critical to be able to control the rate of social change to prevent homeostatic shock to the social body. The public philosophy should be oriented toward the open-end exploration and development of each individual's potential, toward the public welfare, and toward an expanded democratic ethic. And the proposed philosophy is needed to universalize experimental method in social affairs broadly considered, by public and democratic participation in real-world experimentation to meet changing social conditions.

The next question asks whether we have a substantive philosophical tradition on which to build, or whether the "new" public philosophy will have to be built from scratch. As indicated earlier, the proposed philosophy is eclectic and borrows freely from many traditions, especially from American Pragmatism. This chapter has pointed out the pragmatic parallels of Peirce (1935), James (1907, 1909), and Dewey (1939) toward what might be called a philosophy of real-time social behavior today.

The fifth question inquires into the distinctive features of the proposed philosophy. Culturally, this philosophy calls for the development of a democratic-scientific ethos in which each individual sees himself as an architect of social planning, as an innovative experimenter as well as the object of social experiment in a world of rapid social reconstruction. A corollary feature is the rise of the citizen-scientist, the citizen educated and trained in the values and procedures of experimental method, the citizen who can view our knowledge of the world and of the human condition as a system of competing hypotheses that are continually on trial and continually subject to new test and verification. Another corollary feature is the dedication of public information files and computer networks for pluralistic, diversified experimentation on social affairs in the public forum.

To inculcate the scientific ethos, we need to expose individuals to the rudiments of experimental method at the earliest possible age at home and in our schools, and to cultivate lifelong exposure to experimental inquiry thereafter. The present approach, featuring independent experimentation essentially in exclusive elites at the graduate level, institutionalizes and perpetuates the opposite effect—massive and universal illiteracy in experimental inquiry.

Perhaps the most distinctive feature of this philosophy is the rise of the "real-world" experiment—experimentation conducted on normal, ongoing social affairs with minimal perturbation of social events attributable to the experimental superstructure. Here we have the beginnings of a new experimental paradigm, particularly for the social sciences.

There are various developments pointing toward the real-world experiment, particularly from computer science and technology. The existence and operation of computers in social settings effectively amounts to a built-in laboratory for social experimentation, in principle if not in fact, since the computer can sense, record, and reduce the operations of the embedding system. Powerful computerized techniques, such as regenerative recording (described in Part III of this book) make it possible to reproduce and systematically experiment with any real-time system event. Continuing real-world experimentation can be conducted on object systems if such systems are deliberately designed to conduct such experimentation.

Real-time computing systems represent the appearance of a new type of experimental method in that the results of continuing real-time tests are fed back to the system in time to influence or control ongoing events. The real-time information system is thus the limiting form of a connected series of continuous experiments in which results lead directly to action. The rise of the new experimental paradigm for the social sciences, as charted by Dunn (1969), is characterized by evolving real-world experimentation.

A leading byproduct of the analysis of real-time information systems is a reconceptualization of the idea of the hypothesis. Heretofore, hypotheses have been treated as operationally defined equivalents of abstract propositions in the object scientific area. With real-time systems, the system itself may be represented as a collection of hypotheses concerning its own operation. We have the intriguing notion of the real-world system as its own hypothesis, as operationally defined by organizational goals, plans, system specifications, operating computer programs, and the men and machines that comprise it. The notable difference from classical hypotheses is that system hypotheses are actively and creatively plastic for the system designer and system users, in contrast to the relatively fixed phenomena of the abstract laboratory approach in classical science. There is a radical scientific difference between using the total real-world system as its own model, in contrast to using a simplified laboratory setup with abstract propositions as a hypothetical model. With real-time control, system experimentation becomes real-world redesign and reconstruction based on evolving experimental results. Once we accept the premise of the system, planning and design may be considered as a scientifically regulated art form.

The last question is, "Where do we go from here?" Only the general outlines of the proposed philosophy have been sketched. Far more discussion, debate, and development of this and competing philosophies are needed. Scientists need to ask themselves whether they want to remain aloof from social change or whether they feel that the universalization of an experimental ethos is an improvement over the fixed ideologies, dogmas, and superstitions of the past. The scientific front is not a front for any fixed, scientifically correct set of beliefs, but a hard-hitting appeal to experiment creatively, openly, competitively, and intelligently. The experimental way is our most effective ultimate weapon against the mounting irrationalism we see arising in all quarters. To those irreconcilable groups and factions who hold fast to fixed ideologies, scientists can apply the gentle persuasion of evolutionary social verification toward improved, tested beliefs, perhaps toward new, flexible ideologies that offer mankind more favorable opportunities.

Walt Whitman said "To have great poets, there must be great audiences, too." And great democracies, he felt, must be populated by great people. In *Democratic Vistas,* written in 1871, he predicted "one hundred years ahead" a crisis in vulgar, material, self-seeking individualism, and the emergence of a spiritual, perhaps religious form of democracy. The spiritualized democracy would be scientific, marked by brotherhood, love, and comradeship binding society together while preserving distinctive individuality and "a divine pride of man in himself." If we aspire to social excellence in mass information utilities, let us design them as living testaments to the supreme worth of every individual.

REFERENCES

CHAPTER 1

Durant, Will and Ariel. *The Lessons of History.* New York: Simon & Schuster, Inc., 1968.

CHAPTER 2

Baran, Paul. "The Coming Computer Utility—Laissez-Faire, Licensing or Regulation?" P–3466. Santa Monica, Calif.: The RAND Corporation, April 1967.

Early, Louis B. "Satellite Communications for the Computer Utility." In *Computers and Communications: Toward a Computer Utility,* edited by Fred Gruenberger. Englewood Cliffs, N.J.: Prentice-Hall, Inc., pp. 95-108.

Federal Communications Commission. "Federal Communications Notice of Inquiry." Docket No. 6979. Washington, D.C., November 25, 1966.

Flood, Merrill M. "Commercial Information Processing Networks—Prospects and Problems in Perspective." In *Technology and the American Economy.* Washington, D.C.: U.S. Government Printing Office, February 1966. Appendix, Vol. 1, pp. 233-52.

Gold, Michael M., and Selwyn, Lee L. "Real-Time Computer Communications and the Public Interest." American Federation of Information Processing Societies Conference Proceedings. Washington, D.C.: Thompson Book Company, 198, Vol. 33, pp. 1,473-78.

Hirsch, Phil. "The FCC Utility Inquiry." *Datamation,* April 1968, pp. 32-34.

Hunt, Florine E. *Public Utilities Information Sources.* Detroit, Mich.: Gale Research Company, Book Tower, 1965.

Irwin, Manley. "Time-Shared Information Systems: Market Entry in Search of a Policy." *1967 American Federation of Information Processing Societies Conference Proceedings,* Vol. 31. Washington, D.C.: Thompson Book Company, 1967, pp. 513-20.

Irwin, Manley. "A New Policy for Communications." *Science and Technology,* April 1968, pp. 76-84.

Metcalf, Lee, and Reinemer, Vic. *Overcharge.* New York: David McKay, Inc., 1967.

Minow, Newton M. *Equal Time: The Private Broadcaster and the Public Interest.* New York: Atheneum, 1964.

Pugh, John W. "Message Concentration." *Datamation,* April 1968, pp. 45-48.

Shepherd, William G., and Gies, Thomas G., editors. *Utility Regulation: New Directions in Theory and Policy.* New York: Random House, Inc., 1966.

Stigler, George J., and Friedland, Claire. "What Can Regulators Regulate? The Case of Electricity." In *Utility Regulation: New Directions in Theory and Policy, edited by William G. Shepherd and Thomas G. Gies.* New York: Random House, Inc., 1966.

Troxel, Emery. *Economics of Public Utilities.* New York: Rinehart and Company, 1947.

U.S. Congress, Senate. Senate Subcommittee on Intergovernmental Relations. *State Utility Commissions, Summary and Tabulation of Information Submitted by the Commissions.* 90th Cong., Doc. No. 56, September 11, 1967. Washington, D.C.: U.S. Government Printing Office.

CHAPTER 3

Cordtz, Dan. "The Coming Shake-up in Telecommunications." *Fortune,* April 1970, p. 69.

Goldstine, H. H., and von Neumann, John. "On the Principles of Large-Scale Computing Machines (1946, unpublished). In *John von Neumann Collected Works,* A. H. Taug, general editor. New York: Macmillan, 1963.

Knight, Kenneth E. "Evolving Computer Performance, 1963-1967." *Datamation,* January 1968, pp. 31-35.

Mumford, Lewis. *The Myth of the Machine.* New York: Harcourt, Brace and World, 1967.

Sackman, H. *Computers, System Science and Evolving Society.* New York: John Wiley & Sons, Inc., 1967.

Wiener, Norbert. *The Human Use of Human Beings.* 2nd ed. New York: Doubleday & Company, Inc., 1954.

CHAPTER 4

Anon. "National Standardization." *Business Automation News Report,* July 8, 1968, p. 3.

Anon. "Over 1400 Applications of Electronic Computing and Data Processing Equipment." *Computers and Automation,* June 1968, pp. 124-31.

Association for Computing Machinery. "Classification System for Computing Reviews." *Communications of the ACM.* Bureau of the Budget. *Report to the President on the Management of Automated Data Processing in* the Federal Government, 1965. Washington, D.C.: U.S. Government Printing Office, 1965.

Computer Research Corporation. "Time-Sharing System Scorecard—A Survey of On-Line Multiple User Computer Systems." No. 6, 1968.

Corbató, F. J.; Merwin-Daggett, M.; and Daley, R. C. "An Experimental Time-Sharing System." *Proceedings of the Spring Joint Computer Conference, Spring 1962.* Washington, D.C.: Spartan Books, pp. 335-55.

Emerson, Marvin. "The 'Small' Computer Versus Time-Shared Systems." *Computers and Automation,* September 1965, pp. 18-20.

Ilger, H. J. "A Survey of the Spectrum of Activities of Computer-Based Systems." N–21378/003/00. Santa Monica, Calif.: System Development Corporation, April 4, 1964.

Licklider, J. C. R., and Taylor, Robert W. "The Computer as a Communication Device." *Science & Technology,* April 1968, pp. 21-31.

Lynch, W. C. "Description of a High Capacity, Fast Turnaround University Computer Center." *Proceedings of the 22nd National Conference, Association for Computing Machinery.* Washington, D.C.: Thompson Book Company, 1967, pp. 273-88.

Macdonald, Neil. "A Time-Shared Computer System—The Disadvantages." *Computers and Automation,* September 1965, pp. 21-22.

Pantages, Angeline. "Computing's Early Years." *Datamation,* October 1967, pp. 60-65.

Patrick, R. L. "So You Want to Go On-Line?" *Datamation,* October 1963, pp. 25-27.

Schwartz, Jules I.; Coffman, Edward G.; and Weissman, Clark. "A General Purpose Time-Sharing System." *1964 American Federation of Information Processing Societies Conference Proceedings, Spring Joint Computer Conference,* Vol. 25. Washington, D.C.: Thompson Book Company, 1964.

Shaw, C. J. "The JOSS System." *Datamation,* November 1964, pp. 32-36.

Tuggle, F. D. "The Development of a Computer Program System Classification." TM–3604. Santa Monica, Calif.: System Development Corporation, April 8, 1968.

CHAPTER 5

Anon. "Research & Technology Division Report for 1967." TM–530/011/00. Santa Monica, Calif.: System Development Corporation, January 1968.

Coffman, E. G., Jr., and Wood, R. C. "Interarrival Statistics for TSS." SP–2161. Santa Monica, Calif.: System Development Corporation, August 3, 1965.

Fano, R. M., and Corbató, F. J. "Time-Sharing on Computers." *Scientific American,* September 1966, pp. 128-40.

Feingold, S. L. "PLANIT—A Flexible Language Designed for Computer-Human Interaction." *Proceedings of the 22nd National Conference, Association for Computing Machinery.* Washington, D.C.: Thompson Book Company, 1967, pp. 545-52.

Glauthier, T. James. "Computer Time Sharing: Its Origins and Development." *Computers and Automation,* October 1967, pp. 23-26.

Gonter, Robert H., and Smith, Judith. "Statistical Description of the Time-Sharing Systems—UMASS." Technical Note, No. TN/RCC/006. Amherst, Mass.: University of Massachusetts, Research Computing Center, 1970.

Kemeny, John D., and Kurtz, Thomas E. "Dartmouth Time-Sharing." *Science,* October 11, 1968, pp. 223-28.

McIsaac, Paul V. "Job Descriptions and Scheduling in the SDC Q–32 Time-Sharing System." TM–2996. Santa Monica, Calif.: System Development Corporation, June 10, 1966.

Parkhill, D. F. *The Challenge of the Computer Utility.* Reading, Mass.: Addison-Wesley Publishing Company, 1966.

Scherr, Allan L. "An Analysis of Time-Shared Computer Systems." Research Monograph No. 36. Cambridge, Mass.: The M.I.T. Press, 1967.

Schwartz, Jules I. "Observations on Time-Shared Systems." *Proceedings of the 20th National Conference, Association for Computing Machinery.* Washington, D.C.: Thompson Book Company, 1965, pp. 525-42.

Schwartz, Jules I., and Weissman, Clark. "The SDC Time-Sharing System Revisited." *Proceedings of the 22nd National Conference, Association for Computing Machinery.* Washington, D.C.: Thompson Book Company, 1967, pp. 263-71.

Spierer, Monroe M., and Wills, Robert D. "Applications of a Large-Scale Time-Sharing System." SP–3062. Santa Monica, Calif.: System Development Corporation, 1968.

Theis, D. J., and Hobbs, L. C. "Low-Cost Remote CRT Terminals." *Datamation,* June 1948, pp. 22-34.

CHAPTER 6

Becker, Hal B. "Programming Self-Taught." *Computers and Automation,* October 1967, pp. 30-35.

Kennedy, Phyllis R. "The TINT Users' Guide." TM–1933/000/03. Santa Monica, Calif.: System Development Corporation, July 30, 1965.

Machol, Robert E.; Tanner, Wilson P., Jr.; and Alexander, Samuel N., editors. *System Engineering Handbook.* New York: McGraw-Hill Book Company, 1965.

Sackman, H. "Experimental Investigation of User Performance in Time-Shared Computing Systems." SP–2846. Santa Monica, Calif.: System Development Corporation, May 6, 1967.

Sackman, H., and Gold, Michael M. "Time-Sharing Versus Batch Processing: An Experimental Inquiry into Human Problem-Solving." SP–3110. Santa Monica, Calif.: System Development Corporation, and Pittsburgh, Pa.: Carnegie-Mellon University, June 14, 1968.

CHAPTER 7

Anon. "AFADA Programing Systems Evaluation." Unpublished report by Air Force Assistant for Data Automation, September 11, 1963.

Adams, Jeanne, and Cohen, Leonard. "Time-Sharing vs. Instant Batch Processing." *Computers and Automation,* March 1969, pp. 33-34.

Argyris, Chris. "Some Unintended Consequences of Rigorous Research." *Psychological Bulletin,* Vol. 7, No. 3, 1968, pp. 185-97.

Barmack, Joseph E., and Sinaiko, H. Wallace. "Human Factors Problems in Computer-Generated Graphic Displays." Study S–234. Arlington, Va.: Institute for Defense Analyses, April 1966.

Bitzer, Donald L. "Some Aspects of Design and Economics for a Computer-Based Educational System." *Journal of Educational Data Processing,* Vol. 6, No. 1, 1968, pp. 9-27.

Borko, H., editor. *Computer Applications in the Behavioral Sciences.* Englewood Cliffs, N.J.: Prentice-Hall, Inc., 1962.

Bowles, Edmund A. *Computers in Humanistic Research.* Englewood Cliffs, N.J.: Prentice-Hall, Inc., 1967.

Bryan, G. E. "JOSS: 20,000 Hours at a Console—A Statistical Summary." *1967 American Federation of Information Processing Societies Conference Proceedings, Fall Joint Computer Conference,* Vol. 31. Washington, D.C.: Thompson Book Company, 1967, pp. 769-77.

Campbell, Donald T. "Reforms as Experiments." *American Psychologist,* Vol. 24, No. 4, 1969, pp. 409-29.

Dolotta, T. A. "Functional Specifications for Typewriter-Like Time-Sharing Terminals." *Computing Surveys,* March 1970, pp. 5-29.

Dunlop, R. A. "Some Empirical Observations on the Man-Machine Interface Questions." *Proceedings of the Management Information Systems Symposium.* Pittsburgh, Pa.: Carnegie-Mellon University, Graduate School of Industrial Administration, 1968.

Erikson, W. J. "A Pilot Study of Interactive versus Noninteractive Debugging." TM–3296. Santa Monica, Calif.: System Development Corporation, December 13, 1966.

Fano, R. M., and Corbató, F. J. "Time-Sharing on Computers." *Scientific American,* September 1966, pp. 128-40.

Fitts, Paul M. "Cognitive Factors in Information Processing." University of Michigan, Department of Psychology, Human Performance Center, Memorandum Report No. 1, February 1967.

Frye, Charles H., and Pack, Elbert C. "A Comparison of Three Computer Operating Modes for High School Problem-Solving." TM–4356/001/00. Santa Monica, Calif.: System Development Corporation, August 25, 1969.

Gold, M. M. "Methodology for Evaluating Time-Shared Computer Usage." Unpublished Ph.D. dissertation, 1967, Massachusetts Institute of Technology, Alfred P. Sloan School of Management.

Grant, E. Eugene, and Sackman, H. "An Exploratory Investigation of Programmer Performance Under On-Line and Off-Line Conditions." *IEEE*

Transactions on Human Factors in Electronics. HFE–8, March 1967, pp. 33-48.

Jones, C. H.; Hughes, J. L.; and Engvold, K. J. "A Comparative Study of Computer-Aided Decision Making from Display Typewriter Terminals." IBM Technical Report TR 00.1891. Poughkeepsie, N.Y.: IBM Systems Development Division, June 12, 1969.

Lynch, W. C. "Description of a High Capacity, Fast Turnaround University Computer Center." *Proceedings of the 22nd National Conference, Association for Computing Machinery.* Washington, D.C.: Thompson Book Company, 1967, pp. 273-88.

McCartan, Edward F., editor. *EDUCOM.* Bulletin of the Interuniversity Communications Council, September 1969.

McIsaac, Paul V. "Job Descriptions and Scheduling in the SDC Q–32 Time-Sharing System." TM–2996. Santa Monica, Calif.: System Development Corporation, June 10, 1966.

Miller, Robert B. "Response Time in Man-Computer Conversational Transactions." IBM Technical Report TR 00.1660-1. Poughkeepsie, N.Y.: IBM Systems Development Division, January 29, 1968.

Morrill, Charles S.; Goodwin, Nancy C.; and Smith, Sidney L. "User Input Mode and Computer-Aided Instruction." *Human Factors,* Vol. 10, 1968, pp. 225-32.

Murphy, J. V.; Katter, D.A.; Wattenbarger, G. H.; and Pool, H. M. "An Investigation of a Basic Design Feature in Computerized Systems." TM–732. Santa Monica, Calif.: System Development Corporation, 1962.

NASA. "NASA Authorization for Fiscal Year 1967." Hearings Before the Committee on Aeronautical and Space Sciences, U.S. Senate, S–2909. Washington, D.C.: U.S. Government Printing Office, 1966.

Nickerson, Raymond S.; Elkind, Jerome I.; Carbonell, Jaime R. "Human Factors and the Design of Time-Sharing Computer Systems." *Human Factors,* Vol. 10, 1968, pp. 127-34.

Overhage, Carl F. J., and Harmon, R. Joyce, editors. *INTREX, Report of a Planning Conference on Information Transfer Experiments.* Cambridge, Mass.: The M.I.T. Press, September 1965.

Pollock, William T., and Gildner, Gilbert G. G. "Study of Computer Manual Input Devices." Project 9678, Task 967801, Technical Documentary Report No. ESD–TDR–63–545. Bedford, Mass.: L. G. Hanscom Field, September 1963.

Raynaud, Thierry G. "Operational Analysis of a Computer Center." Technical Report No. 32. Cambridge, Mass.: Massachusetts Institute of Technology, Operations Research Center, July 1967.

Rubey, Raymond J. "A Comparative Evaluation of PL/1." *Datamation,* December 1968, pp. 22-25.

Rubinoff, Morris; Bergman, Samuel; Franks, Winifred; and Rubinoff, Elayne R. "Experimental Evaluation of Information Retrieval Through a Teletypewriter." *Communications of the ACM,* September 1968, pp. 598-604.

Sackman, H. "Regenerative Recording in Man-Machine Digital Systems." In *Proceedings, National Winter Convention on Military Electronics,* Los Angeles, Calif., February 1964, Vol. 3, pp. 16-14/16-19.

Sackman, H. *Computers, System Science and Evolving Society.* New York: John Wiley & Sons, Inc., 1967.

Sackman, H. "Time-Sharing and Self-Tutoring: An Exploratory Case History." *Human Factors,* April 1970, Vol. 12, pp. 203-14.

Sackman, H. *Man-Computer Problem Solving.* Princeton, N.J.: Auerbach Publishers Inc., 1970.

Sackman, H., and Munson, J. "The Investigation of Computer Operating Time and System Capacity for Man-Machine Digital Systems." *Journal of the Association for Computing Machinery,* Vol. 11, October 1964, pp. 450-64.

Schatzoff, M.; Tsao, R.; and Wiig, R. "An Experimental Comparison of Time Sharing and Batch Processing." *Communications of the ACM,* May 1967, pp. 261-65.

Scherr, Allan L. "An Analysis of Time-Shared Computer Systems." Research Monograph No. 36. Cambridge, Mass.: The M.I.T. Press, 1967.

Shaw, J. W. "JOSS: Experience with an Experimental Computing Service for Users at Remote Typewriter Consoles." P–3149. Santa Monica, Calif.: The RAND Corporation, May 1965.

Silberman, Harry F. "The Effect of Educational Research on Classroom Instruction." Paper presented at the 1965 Convention of the American Educational Research Association in Chicago.

Smith, Lyle B. "A Comparison of Batch Processing and Instant Turnaround." *Communications of the ACM,* August 1967, pp. 495-500.

Suchman, Edward A. "Evaluation Research." New York: Russell Sage Foundation, 1967.

Suppes, Pat. "The Uses of Computers in Education." *Scientific American,* September 1966, pp. 206-20.

Swets, John A.; Harris, Judith R.; McElroy, Linda S.; and Rudloe, Harry. "Computer-Aided Instruction in Perceptual Identification." *Behavioral Science,* Vol. 11, 1966, pp. 98-104.

Totschek, Robert A. "An Empirical Investigation into the Behavior of the SDC Time-Sharing System." SP–2191. Santa Monica, Calif.: System Development Corporation, July 6, 1965.

CHAPTER 8

Dunlop, R. A. "Some Empirical Observations on the Man-Machine Interface Questions." In *Proceedings of the Management Information Systems Symposium.* Pittsburgh, Pa.: Carnegie-Mellon University, Graduate School of Industrial Administration, 1968.

Karush, Arnold D. "Regenerative Recording." Unpublished Master's thesis, Department of Computer Science, University of California at Los Angeles, 1970.

Sackman, H. *Computers, System Science and Evolving Society.* New York: John Wiley & Sons, Inc., 1967.
Tocqueville, Alexis de. *Democracy in America.* 1835.
Wallas, G. *The Art of Thought.* New York: Harcourt, Brace and World, 1926.
Woodworth, Robert S., and Schlosberg, Harold. *Experimental Psychology.* New York: Holt, Rinehart & Winston, 1954.

CHAPTER 9

Bengelsdorf, Irving S. "Information Utility and Social Change: A Summary." In *The Information Utility and Social Choice,* edited by H. Sackman and Norman Nie. Montvale, N.J.: AFIPS Press, 1970, pp. 161-81.
Borko, Harold. "Experimental Prototypes for International Information Utilities." In *The Information Utility and Social Choice,* edited by H. Sackman and Norman Nie. Montvale, N.J.: AFIPS Press, 1970, pp. 123-41.
Bradburn, Norman M. "Survey Research in Public Opinion Polling with the Information Utility—Promises and Problems." In *The Information Utility and Social Choice,* edited by H. Sackman and Norman Nie. Montvale, N.J.: AFIPS Press, 1970, pp. 275-86.
Dunlop, Robert A. "The Emerging Technology of Information Utilities." In *The Information Utility and Social Choice,* edited by H. Sackman and Norman Nie. Montvale, N.J.: AFIPS Press, 1970, pp. 25-49.
Dunn, Edgar S., Jr. "The Information Utility and the Idea of the Public Data Bank." In *The Information Utility and Social Choice,* edited by H. Sackman and Norman Nie. Montvale, N.J.: AFIPS Press, 1970, pp. 103-22.
Eulau, Heinz. "Some Potential Effects of the Information Utility on Political Decision-Makers and the Role of the Representative." In *The Information Utility and the Social Choice,* edited by H. Sackman and Norman Nie. Montvale, N.J.: AFIPS Press, 1970, pp. 187-99.
Kestenbaum, Lionel. "The Regulatory Context of Information Utilities: Varieties in Law and Public Policy." In *The Information Utility and Social Choice,* edited by H. Sackman and Norman Nie. Montvale, N.J.: AFIPS Press, 1970, pp. 3-24.
Licklider, J. C. R. "Social Prospects of Information Utilities." In *The Information Utility and Social Choice,* edited by H. Sackman and Norman Nie. Montvale, N.J.: AFIPS Press, 1970, pp. 3-24.
Marvick, Dwaine. "Some Potential Effects of the Information Utility on Citizen Participation." In *The Information Utility and Social Choice,* edited by H. Sackman and Norman Nie. Montvale, N.J.: AFIPS Press, 1970, pp. 249-62.
McRae, Duncan, Jr. "Some Political Choices in the Development of Communications Technology." In *The Information Utility and Social Choice,* edited by H. Sackman and Norman Nie. Montvale, N.J.: AFIPS Press, 1970, pp. 201-16.
Nie, Norman. "Future Developments in Mass Communications and Citizen Participation." In *The Information Utility and Social Choice,* edited by

H. Sackman and Norman Nie. Montvale, N.J.: AFIPS Press, 1970, pp. 217-48.

Parker, Edwin B. "Information Utilities and Mass Communications." In *The Information Utility and Social Choice,* edited by H. Sackman and Norman Nie. Montvale, N.J.: AFIPS Press, 1970, pp. 51-70.

Prewitt, Kenneth. "Information and Politics: Reflections on Reflections." In *The Information Utility and Social Choice,* edited by H. Sackman and Norman Nie. Montvale, N.J.: AFIPS, 1970, pp. 287-99.

White, Stephen. "Toward a Modest Experiment in Cable Television." *Public Interest* (National Affairs, Inc.), Summer 1968, pp. 52-66.

Ziegler, Harmon. "The Communication Revolution and the Future of Interest Groups." In *The Information Utility and Social Choice,* edited by H. Sackman and Norman Nie. Montvale, N.J.: AFIPS Press, 1970, pp. 263-74.

CHAPTER 10

American Association for the Advancement of Science. "Secrecy and Dissemination in Science and Technology." A report by the Committee on Science in the Promotion of Human Welfare, February 21, 1969, pp. 787-90.

Black, Hugo Lafayette. "Faith in the People." *Time,* March 29, 1968, p. 76.

Brandeis, Louis D. "Privacy." In *The Great Quotations.* Compiled by George Seldes. New York: Pocket Books, 1968, p. 780.

De Chardin, Teilhard. *The Phenomenon of Man,* translated by Bernard Wall with an introduction by Julian Huxley. New York: Harper & Row, 1959.

Dewey, John. *Logic: The Theory of Inquiry.* New York: Holt, Rinehart & Winston, 1938.

Dewey, John. *Freedom and Culture.* New York: Capricorn Books, 1939.

Dunn, Edgar S., Jr. "The Information Utility and the Idea of the Public Data Bank." In *The Information Utility and Social Choice,* edited by H. Sackman and Norman Nie. Montvale, N.J.: AFIPS Press, 1970, pp. 103-22.

Gagné, Robert M. "Elementary Science: A New Scheme of Instruction." *Science,* January 7, 1966, pp. 49-53.

Garrett, H. E. "A Developmental Theory of Intelligence." *American Psychologist,* Vol. 1 (1946), pp. 372-78.

Helmer, Olaf. *Social Technology.* New York: Basic Books, Inc., 1966.

Helmholtz, H. L. F. von. *Vorträge und Reden.* 1896.

Hunt, J. McVicker. *Intelligence and Experience.* New York: The Ronald Press Company, 1961.

King, Martin Luther, Jr. "The Role of the Behavioral Scientist in the Civil Rights Movement." Address to the meeting of the Society for the Psychological Study of Social Issues, American Psychological Association, Washington, D. C., September 1967.

Lewis, Wyndham. *Time and Western Man.* New York: Harcourt, Brace, 1928.

Mackworth, Norman H. "Originality." *American Psychologist,* Vol. 20, No. 1, January 1965, pp. 51-66.

Miller, Arthur Selwyn. "Drawing the Indictment." *Saturday Review,* August 3, 1968, pp. 39-42.

Murphy, Gardner. *Personality.* New York: Harper & Brothers, 1947.

Osborn, Alex. *Applied Imagination.* New York: Charles Scribner's Sons, 1957.

Parsons and Williams, *Forecast of 1968-2000 of Computer Developments and Applications,* Copenhagen, Denmark, 1968.

Piaget, Jean. "The Giant of Developmental Psychology and His Collaborator Talk about Children." *Psychology Today,* May 1970.

Rossman, Joseph. *The Psychology of the Inventor.* Washington, D. C.: Inventor's Publishing Company, 1931.

Sackman, H. *Computers, Systems Science and Evolving Society.* New York: John Wiley & Sons, Inc., 1967.

Sackman, H. *Man-Computer Problem Solving.* Princeton, N.J.: Auerbach Publishers Inc., 1970.

Tocqueville, Alexis de. *Democracy in America.* 1835.

United Nations. *Human Rights.* New York, 1967.

Wallas, Graham. *The Art of Thought.* New York: Harcourt, Brace, 1926.

Westin, Alan F. *Privacy and Freedom.* New York: Atheneum, 1967.

Whitman, Walt. *Democratic Vistas.* New York: The Viking Press, 1945.

Young, J. W. *Techniques for Producing Ideas.* Chicago: Advertising Publications, Inc., 1940.

CHAPTER 11

Allport, Gordon W. "The Fruits of Eclecticism—Bitter or Sweet?" *Proceedings of the XVIIth International Congress of Psychology,* August 20-26, 1963, Washington, D. C. Amsterdam: North Holland Publishing Company, 1964.

American Academy of Arts and Sciences. "Toward the Year 2000: Work in Progress." *Daedalus,* Summer 1967.

Ayres, Robert U. *Technological Forecasting and Long-Range Planning.* New York: McGraw-Hill Book Company, 1969.

Barnard, D. J. *Organization and Management.* Cambridge, Mass.: Harvard University Press, 1948.

Bell, Daniel. "Twelve Modes of Prediction—A Preliminary Sorting of Approaches in the Social Sciences." *Daedalus,* Summer 1964, pp. 845-80.

Branch, Melville C. *Planning: Aspects and Applications.* New York: John Wiley & Sons, Inc., 1966.

Bureau of the Budget. "Planning-Programming-Budgeting." Bulletin No. 66-3. Washington, D. C., October 12, 1965.

Clay, Sir Henry. "Planning and Market Economy." *American Economics Review,* Vol. 40 (1950), p. 3.

Dalkey, Norman D. "The Delphi Method: An Experimental Study of Group Opinion." AD–60–498. Santa Monica, Calif.: The RAND Corporation, June 1969.

De Jouvenal, Bertrand. *The Art of Conjecture.* New York: Basic Books, Inc., 1967.

De Jouvenal, Bertrand. "Utopia for Practical Purposes." *Daedalus,* Spring 1965, pp. 437-53.

Emery, James. "The Planning Process and Its Formalization in Computer Models." *Proceedings of the 2nd Congress of Information System Science,* 1964. Mitre Corp., Bedford, Mass. (preprint), pp. 223-40.

Feingold, Samuel L. "PLANIT—A Flexible Language Designed for Computer-Human Interaction." *Proceedings of the Fall Joint Computer Conference,* 1967, pp. 545-52. Washington, D.C.: Thompson Book Company, 1967.

Florence, P. S. *The Logic of British and American Industry.* London: Routledge & Kegan Paul, 1953.

Fromm, Erich. *The Revolution of Hope.* New York: Bantam Books, 1968.

Helmer, Olaf. *Social Technology.* New York: Basic Books, Inc., 1966.

Helmer, Olaf. "Systematic Use of Expert Opinions." P-3721. Santa Monica, Calif.: The RAND Corporation, November 1967.

Jungk, R. "Forecasting as an Instrument of Social and Political Power." Paper given at the Third International Conference on Science and Society, Herceg-Novi, Yugoslavia, 1969.

Kahn, Herman, and Wiener, Anthony J. *The Year 2000.* New York: The Macmillan Company, 1967.

Kelly, G. A. *The Psychology of Personal Constructs.* New York: W. W. Norton & Co., Inc., 1955.

LeBreton, Preston P., and Henning, Dale A. *Planning Theory.* Englewood Cliffs, N. J.: Prentice-Hall, Inc., 1961.

MacCorquodale, K., and Meehl, P. E. "Preliminary Suggestions as to Formalization of Expectancy Theory." *Psychological Review,* Vol. 60, 1953, pp. 55-63.

Mannheim, K. *Man and Society in an Age of Reconstruction.* London: Kegan Paul, Trench, Trubner, 1940.

Mason, Richard O. "A Dialectical Approach to Strategic Planning." *Management Science,* Vol. 15, April 1969, pp. B–403–14.

Mayo, E. *The Human Problems of an Industrial Civilization.* New York: The Macmillan Company, 1933.

Mead, G. H. *Mind, Self and Society.* Chicago: The University of Chicago Press, 1934.

Meyerson, M., and Banfield, E. C. *Politics, Planning and the Public Interest.* Glencoe, Ill.: The Free Press, 1955.

Miller, George A.; Galanter, Eugene; and Pibram, Karl H. *Plans and the Structure of Behavior.* New York: Holt, Rinehart & Winston, Inc., 1960.

Millett, J. *The Process and Organization of Government Planning.* New York: Columbia University Press, 1947.

Mockler, Robert J. "Theory and Practice of Planning." *Harvard Business Review,* March-April 1970, pp. 148-59.

Mowrer, O. H. *Learning Theory and Personality Dynamics.* New York: The Ronald Press Company, 1950.

Nadel, S. F. *Foundations of Social Anthropology*. London: Cohen & West, 1951.

Novick, David, editor. *Program Budgeting*. Cambridge, Mass.: Harvard University Press, 1965.

Platt, John. "What We Must Do." *Science,* Vol. 166, 1969, pp. 1,115-21.

Roethlisberger, F. J., and Dickson, W. J. *Management and the Worker.* Cambridge, Mass.: Harvard University Press, 1941.

Rosove, Perry E. "The Use of Contextual Mapping to Support Long-Range Educational Policy Making." SP–3026. Santa Monica, Calif.: System Development Corporation, December 1967.

Rotter, J. B. *Social Learning and Clinical Psychology*. New York: Prentice-Hall, Inc., 1954.

Sackman, H. *Computers, System Science and Evolving Society*. New York: John Wiley & Sons, Inc., 1967.

Steiner, George A. *Top Management Planning*. London: Macmillan & Company, Ltd., 1969.

Stogdill, Ralph M. *Individual Behavior and Group Achievement*. New York: Oxford University Press, 1959.

Tolman, E. C. *Purposive Behavior in Animals and Men*. New York: Appleton-Century, 1932.

CHAPTER 12

Compton, Karl Taylor. "The Social Implications of Scientific Discovery." An Address to the American Philosophical Society, 1938. In *The Great Quotations,* compiled by George Seldes. New York: Pocket Books, 1968.

De Chardin, Teilhard. *The Phenomenon of Man,* translated by Bernard Wall with an introduction by Julian Huxley. New York: Harper & Row, 1959.

Dewey, John. *The Public and Its Problems*. New York: Henry Holt, 1927.

Dewey, John. *Intelligence in the Modern World,* edited by J. Ratner. New York: Random House, 1939.

Dunn, Edgar S., Jr. "Economic and Social Development: A Process of Social Learning." Unpublished draft, 1969. Washington, D. C.: Resources for the Future, Inc.

Durant, Will and Ariel. *The Lessons of History*. New York: Simon & Schuster, Inc., 1968.

Hitler, Adolph. *Mein Kampf,* translated by John Chamberlain, Sidney B. Fay, et al. New York: Reynal & Hitchcock, 1939.

James, William. *Pragmatism: A New Name for Some Old Ways of Thinking.* New York: Longmans, Green & Company, 1907.

James, William. *A Pluralistic Universe*. New York: Longmans, Green & Company, 1909.

Orwell, George. *1984*. New York: Harcourt, Brace, 1949.

Peirce, Charles S. *The Collected Papers of Charles Sanders Peirce,* edited by

Charles Hartshorne and Paul Weiss. Cambridge, Mass.: The Belknap Press of Harvard University Press, 1935.

Russell, Bertrand. *A History of Western Philosophy*. New York: Simon & Schuster, Inc. 1945.

Sarton, George. *The Life of Science*. Bloomington, Ind.: Indiana University Press, 1948.

Toqueville, Alexis, de. *Democracy in America*. 1835.

Ward, Barbara. *Spaceship Earth*. New York: Columbia University Press, 1966.

Weinberg, Alvin M. "In Defense of Science." *Science,* Vol. 167, 1970, pp. 141-45.

Whitman, Walt. *Democratic Vistas*. New York: The Viking Press, 1945.

Wiener, Norbert. *God and Golem Inc.* Cambridge, Mass.: The M.I.T. Press, 1964.

INDEX